𝕻egasus: The White Man. The Red Horse. The Black Boy.

Eddie J. Washington

Dedication

To Lester E. and Dariel E. Price, father and son, respectively, who were the white proprietors of Price Mobil Service, 922 Wright Avenue, Little Rock, Arkansas. They allowed me the opportunity to work at their Mobilgas Filling Station in the 1950s, which provided the genesis of this book.

To my lovely wife, Mary, who continually encouraged me through the years to write this book. She had the arduous task of proofreading numerous drafts and being my most fervent critic. Although we have been married for over thirty-five years, she learned much she didn't know about my life during this process.

Table Of Contents

Pegasus: The White Man. The Red Horse. The Black Boy.

Acknowledgments

I would like to express my gratitude to Lyn Pilcicki, who proofread this book, offered many constructive comments and assisted in the editing of my early drafts. Lyn, a former coworker, strongly encouraged me to write this book.

I thank Michelle Cheseldine, also a former coworker, who read my draft and offered engaging comments and performed the book's initial formatting.

Above all, I want to thank my wife, Mary, who supported and encouraged me in spite of all the time it took away from us as a family.

Lastly, I thank all of those, especially the Pegasus People, who inspired me to write this book without being aware of their contribution.

Section One: A Kid's Life - Pre-Pegasus Period: 1941 – 1953

Introduction

I always knew I would write this book about my life in Little Rock. It was just a matter of how and when. Only now do I have the time and ability to fully recognize and understand the historical significance of my life during this period in Arkansas' Capital City. Only now do I have the experience and skills necessary to describe my life there in the proper detail and context. The timeline described in this book extends from 1941 to 1962, after which I entered the United States Army. This book is part diary, part autobiography and part history.

From my earliest memories on West Capitol Street, I was always fascinated by transport vehicles, including the trash trucks that drove through our alley emptying garbage cans, the street cars carrying passengers that rolled on the tracks in front of my shack and all the delivery trucks ferrying goods to the State Capitol. But I was captivated by the beehive of activity at two business enterprises located across the street from my shack: The Esso Filling Station just across Cross Street and the Packard Dealer just across West Capitol Street. From that time on, my passion was to drive and maintain cars. The first nine chapters in this book track and describe my journey along the long, narrow and winding virtual road that ultimately led me to a place called Pegasus. Each chapter describes a landmark along this road and how it prepared me to meet all the challenges of Pegasus.

This is my personal story as a Negro kid growing up in the turbulent South, living reality, recognizing the need for change and hoping to help facilitate it. This narrative illustrates the passion, both love and hate, exhibited on both sides of the color line. The color divide was shaped by social mores, discrimination and history. This book describes people, black and white, who touched my life, gave me encouragement, enlightenment and balance, to help me understand the racial status quo. It also describes those who gave me pause, shock and fear.

Some deeds were so significant that I also remember and use the characters' real names; others I only remember the deeds, the characters I can visualize but their names are forgotten. In a few instances, I slightly changed the real names to protect the person's privacy; in others the names are part of history and remain unaltered. Either way, I try not to praise or condemn a deed or discourse, just state the facts as I remember them and interpret them in context.

The book is broken into major chronological sections including: West Capitol Street, which chronicles my life from birth to six years; Philander Smith College, which chronicles my life six to nine years old; the Allan Jones period covers age ten to thirteen years; and finally the Pegasus period, which is the most eventful, covering 13 to 21 years of age. It was during the Pegasus period that I interfaced with, among others, Ferrell Faubus (son of Governor Orval E. Faubus), Daisy Bates, the Negro Nine, Fats Domino and Jimmy Reed. It was also the period of Governor Orval Faubus' integration defiance and federal troops stationed at Central High School.

I gave special attention to the Negro Nine, also known as the Little Rock Nine. They were all my friends. Since 1962, I have only had conversations with Terrence Roberts.

Even though both my mother and father were dead by the time I was nine years old, I realize that I was extremely fortunate otherwise. This was especially true during the Pegasus period, a period of extreme enlightenment. It seemed that each customer imparted to me a little bit of knowledge, wisdom, constructive criticism and confidence with each encounter, which left me incrementally better. Collectively, this diverse group of souls became my surrogate extended family who led and guided me through the transition from adolescence to maturity.

During and before the Pegasus period, I owned two working (although not very well) cameras: a Kodak Brownie Hawkeye and my first 35mm camera, an Argus C-3 Rangefinder. Unfortunately, I did not use them diligently, taking pictures as often as I now wish I had. However, I did take some. If I had the foresight that I have now, I would have recognized the historic value of period photographic documentation and taken more pictures. The images displayed on the Photo Gallery at readpegasus.com, with one exception, were reprinted from my personal documents, slides, negatives and photographs, which were created about fifty years ago. I cleaned many of the negatives and slides and digitally restored some of the photographs to mitigate some fading and discoloration. One really wrinkled, folded and chipped photograph included here shows all of the wear and tear it endured over fifty years, but it, like the others, tells a great story. However, I really regret not having pictures, of Allan Jones or his shack, my 1939 Chevy, 1949 Plymouth or my 1950 Ford.

I have special respect and admiration for Lester E. and Dariel E. Price, father and son, respectively, who were the white proprietors of Price Mobil Service, 922 Wright Avenue, Little Rock, Arkansas. They were my surrogate grandfather and father, with all the rights, privileges and responsibilities thereof, whether or not they knew and fully understood our virtual kinship. The Prices, who were with me seven days a week for years, spent far more face time with me and had more influence on my character than any of my blood relatives. By all measures, we were a happy, productive family.

In this book, I appeared to have lots of experience with sex. Actually, there are many sexual situations but little actual sex. I had no perception of sex between my mother and father; they never even displayed any affection towards each other in my presence. My father died when I was five years-old and my mother never remarried or had a boyfriend. My mother died when I was nine years-old. My parents died without discussing the idiomatic expression about *birds, the bees, the flowers, and the trees*. As a result, I entered puberty as a sexual neophyte, a naïveté for certain, enlightened only by my peers. I was not a voyeur by any means, but any visual display of female sexuality, whether on purpose or not, strongly captured my attention.

I saw prostitutes on West Ninth Street when I was six years-old and burlesque shows by age nine and did not really understand either. At the time, husbands and wives in the movies slept in separate beds, which I considered normal.

By the time I witnessed my uncle's extramarital trysts, along with a continual sexual education by my peers and my research at the library, I had a good understanding of sex. Then puberty kicked in and so did all the associated testosterone. After I entered the Pegasus Period, I reconciled all of my questions and issues concerning sex.

The Black Power and Black Pride movements of the late 1960s and most of the 1970s tempted me to refer to Afro Americans as black. But I remembered one of my conversations with an African college student, Daniel Mboi, at Philander Smith College during the Pegasus period. He said, "Eddie, you are an American Negro; I am a black man, an African. You may have African heritage, but I am full African. I will never be American. You will never be African. You will always be a Negro."

According to my birth certificate, he was right. During the Pegasus period, we were Negroes; black as a check block for race came later. In this book, I use Negro and black interchangeably. One big enigma for me: why Daniel Mboi, dressed in his native African garb, could enter Frankie's Cafeteria in downtown Little Rock, be seated and be served and I could not join him.

While the people, events, incidents and experiences I encountered during the period are indelibly seared into my memory, I did maintain a few handwritten notes. I read these notes periodically, about every ten years, to replay vignettes of this era. Extensive national and international travel and the opportunity to live outside the United States for over ten years provided me with ample time to reminisce and gain a balanced and fresh perspective of this period. Basically, I was just an ordinary Negro kid thrust by circumstance into an extraordinary life. This book is that account, first person, first hand.

Please enhance your Pegasus reading experience by visiting readpegasus.com. There you will find pictures, interesting facts and the opportunity to be a Pegasus Person.

1

West Capitol Street Years – A Tiger Precedes the Horse

West 5th Street, because it led directly to the State Capitol from the center of downtown Little Rock, was also known as West Capitol Street or simply West 5th Street as long as it was west of Main Street.

I was destined at birth to interface with Pegasus. There must have been a toy horse in my cradle. I was born Eddie Joe Washington on April 3, 1941, in Pulaski County, Big Rock Township, in the city of Little Rock, Arkansas. My mother told me I was named after Eddie Joe Powell, although she never explained to me who he was or why. My parents always called me EdJoe. I never really liked my first and middle names, but in time grew accustomed to them. These names, even today, cause people to say I was given two nicknames and should have been named Edward Joseph instead.

I was born at University Hospital, which was a free public health care facility located in the east end of the city. It primarily served the poor, downtrodden and those who had no insurance. My parents had no insurance. According to my mother, I was born by caesarian section; according to the family Bible, I weighed seven pounds at birth. My Certificate of Live Birth states I was born at 8:52 a.m., which was a Thursday.

I can distinctly remember vivid details about my life dating back to age four. I use that as a benchmark because I remember my mother taking me to a portrait photographer on West 7th Street for my fourth birthday. From that point forward, my memory is rich in detail.

My first address was 1103 West 5th Street, Little Rock, Arkansas. This structure was a two-room tar-paper-covered shack with no indoor plumbing or electricity. A freestanding wood cook stove provided heat, and coal oil lamps and candles provided light. There was an icebox, which was supposed to keep food from spoiling, but there usually was no ice. A slop jar or honey pot stored bodily liquids and solids excreted during the night until they could be transported to the nearby outhouse for disposal.

A much smaller nearby structure with a tin roof served as our outhouse. It had all the characteristics of one: a cesspool, a gagging stench, and replete with maggots. I have fond memories of my mother comforting me in our cold, dark outhouse in the winter when I was constipated or had diarrhea. In those instances, she was right there hugging me and assuring me everything would be all right.

A few feet away stood an omnipresent pile of rubble, changing only in design and composition. This heap was not garbage. The pile was mostly construction trash, including scrap wood, old clocks, broken bricks, nails, broken fans and the like. This was *my* rubble pile; it served as my jungle gym and playground. The pile provided the ingredients for many improvised toys, such as a bus, streetcar, motorcar and a mountain. Since real toys were nonexistent, my imagination was often in hyper drive, which helped me design a new play experience every day.

Directly outside the only door to the shack was my mother's wash station. It consisted of a water faucet which extended about three feet out of the ground and a dominant black cast-iron kettle used to boil white clothes clean. The kettle had tall legs, between which a wood fire could be built. There were also three large galvanized tubs, lye soap, washing board, bottle of bluing, supply of wood for a fire and two long wooden sticks to move clothes out of the hot water and to stir them in the wash and rinse water.

The wash station was one my mother's ways to earn extra money. She washed, starched and pressed white dress shirts for several white businessmen on a recurring basis. I witnessed my mother's skillful choreography of sorting, washing, boiling, rinsing, starching and drying these shirts – all outdoors, year round. This was followed by the inside work of ironing the shirts. My mother had four flat irons. Since we had no electricity, each had to be heated on our wood cook stove and then used while hot. My mother had a system of rotating the irons so she always had several at the correct temperature to press the shirts properly. In the summer, the heat around the wood stove was so unbearable that I stayed outdoors. When she finished pressing the shirts, the collars were stiff and the folds were impeccable, which her customers liked.

I have no idea how much she charged for her shirt service. I do remember she was cheaper and better than any of the local cleaners. I watched the customers drive up the alley to our shack to pick up their shirts. My mother would quickly take the money inside and stash it deep inside the mattress on her bed, hiding it from my father.

My parents never really got along. My father was very abusive and often threatened to (and several times did) strike my mother with a stove lifter (really a stove lid lifter) from our wood cook stove. Sometimes, using the stove lifter as a weapon, my father would give my mother ten minutes to produce fifty cents. He knew she had ways to earn money and he demanded it. She always cowered down; I could tell she was afraid. However, most of the time, my mother was clever enough to strategically hide some change she could quickly retrieve in order to avoid a beating. My father never discovered the money in the mattress.

A tall, rusty device stood like a silent sentry, its butt resting on the floor and its barrels leaning into the corner of the kitchen. My mother told me it was a shotgun, which was very dangerous and could kill animals and people. She also told me very sternly not to touch it. I was about four years old (My sister was not born until I was five.) and had no practical concept of how a gun operated or killed people, since I had never seen one in operation. I followed my mother's no touch rule until one day when I saw my father threaten my mother with the stove lifter and realized that soon he would probably really hurt her. My father had to be stopped. I reasoned that I could examine the shotgun and determine how it worked and use it to stop my father.

One day when my mother was away, I decided to investigate the shotgun. I picked it up about six inches, was surprised by its heavy weight, and immediately dropped it back down on its butt. The gun discharged with a very loud noise and blew a small hole in the roof. Scared, I ran outside and hid behind the outhouse, until my mother came home. She saw the shotgun on the floor and the hole in the roof and knew what I had done. I explained as best I could why I did it. She simply hugged me and told me she would clean up the scene so my father would never know what happened. My father never found out what I had done. I never touched that shotgun again.

Both of my parents enjoyed nicotine but used different delivery systems. My mother used Bugler Tobacco, which contained cigarette papers, and rolled her own. My father dipped snuff; I do not know the brand. His lower lip was distorted from being constantly packed with snuff.

During my first six years of life, my world was primarily limited to one specific half-city block. This block was West 5th Street bounded by Ringo Street to the east, Cross Street to the west, and 6th Street to the south. West 5th Street seemed really wide to me. It was about three times as wide as Ringo or Cross Street. A service alley, which connected Ringo and Cross, bisected the block and defined my half-block. A multistory apartment building and its detached garages consumed the entire eastern half of my world. Our shack, outhouse, a small commercial building facing Cross Street and *my* rubble pile filled the western half.

My first and only real toy this entire period was a windup yellow Caterpillar with a dozer blade on the front. I don't remember who gave it to me. I kept restoring it until it was completely worn out. Even so, I still kept it for a number of years.

There was only one kid who lived close by. Sally was a blond girl my age, who lived just across the alley from our shack. Her house, which faced Cross Street, had no front yard, but a large back yard. Sally's yard was not fenced and was adjacent to the alley. When we were outside playing, only a few feet separated us, so we naturally migrated towards each other. However, her parents would not allow us to play together. Whenever her mother discovered such, she had harsh words for me and sent her daughter inside their house.

One day Sally's father came home from work, caught us playing together, and yelled at both Sally and me. I do not remember what he said, but it caused me to cry. He also talked to my mother about this "serious" situation. As a result, each of us was forbidden to be in or cross the alley into each other's yards.

When possible, though, we would stand in our respective yards, talk, and gesture across the alley. Soon her mother also forbade that. A short time later, Sally's family moved away. I never saw or heard from Sally again. I do not know what happened to her; I do know that at the time she was my only playmate, and we always had fun together.

My father, Sam Washington, worked formally as a janitor at the huge apartment building and our shack, or servants' quarters as they were called then, was rent-free and his only benefit. My mother, Berniece Washington, was a freelance maid who worked part-time directly for the residents of the apartment building. Her family, clients, friends and my father always called her Bea. Her sister, my Aunt Babe, called her Sister.

My father was an alcoholic, adulterer and addicted gambler. As a result, he was seldom home or at work. For my mother and me, it meant little or no money, few clothes and little food. He spent most of his time in the company of his lovers, either Teney or Lovey (the only names I knew them by) or both at the same time. They both lived just a few blocks away from us. Sometimes during emergencies, my mother would walk to one of their houses to get him. He was always too drunk to respond. I remember several times he brought both of them to our shack and demanded that my mom prepare meals for the three of them, which she always did.

My father's second hangout was Tucker's, a juke joint two blocks away on West 7th Street, midway between Ringo and Cross Streets. The place had a back bar room entrance for Negro patrons, where they could drink and gamble. My father's favorite game of chance was rolling the bones (shooting dice). I have no idea which alcoholic beverages my father drank, since he never drank at home. I just knew he drank a lot and was always inebriated whenever he did come home.

My mother's clients in the apartment building, including Mrs. Harris and Mrs. Wynn, knew our plight and always tried to help. They gave my mother their old clothes and shoes for her and me. My mother could alter anything to fit me without a sewing machine. My mother's foot was long and narrow and the shoes she was given were often too short. To accommodate her foot, my mother would cut out the toe of the shoe. They also gave us food. When my mother prepared food for her clients, sometimes she could bring something home for the two of us. Other times, residents would drop half-empty cereal boxes and cookies from windows to me, since I was not allowed in the building. I never saw the inside of that building. It was razed years ago.

My mother was very creative while stretching our meager food supply. She prepared an entrée called *Cush,* which had primary ingredients of cornmeal, onions and salt meat grease, which provided the tasty, meaty flavor. It was a staple in our household until she died.

I remember often walking alone to the closest neighborhood store, Ted's Grocery, at Seventh and Victory Streets. Our grocery list was always short, since we had no ice and thus no way to store food. A typical written list read: two eggs, a half-pound of salt meat, ten cents worth of cornmeal and a small box of oatmeal.

Mr. Ted was a very nice Jewish man who provided my mother a very small line of credit. On one occasion, I remember Mr. Ted telling me, "Little Eddie, tell Bea I can't fill her order because her bill is overdue. She owes me a dollar and a quarter." I went home and told my mother. She did not have the money, so she borrowed it from her sister, my Aunt Babe. The next day I returned to Mr. Ted's, paid her bill and returned home with the groceries.

Even though I had no access to a radio, telephone, newspapers or magazines, somehow I knew there was a war going on. I knew certain metals and rubber were rationed and not available to the public. I also knew because of this, certain foodstuffs were only sold in bulk. Occasionally, I saw soldiers in uniform, walking either on West Capitol Street or on the streetcars. In fact, two white soldiers probably saved my life. On a return trip home, my mother and I were exiting the rear door of the streetcar, which ran on tracks in the middle of the street. Somehow, as I stepped off, a passing car with a claw-type rear door handle hooked onto my clothes and slowly started dragging me along the street. The driver was unaware of my situation because I was behind him and below his field of view.

Two soldiers who were exiting the front door of the streetcar saw my plight just as the car dragged me past them. The soldiers ran and unhooked me just before the car started to speed away. They delivered me back to my mother who was in a state of panic. Thanks to these anonymous soldiers, I escaped with torn clothes, some minor scrapes, bruises, and a greater sense of safety when disembarking from a streetcar. That accident reflected my lack of experience with streetcars; it was my first ride. I remember riding the streetcar maybe three more times after that.

Hygiene in my household consisted primarily of a weekly Saturday night bath. Water was warmed in a teakettle on our wood stove and emptied into one of my mother's galvanized tubs, which was placed in front of the stove. I stood up in the tub, bathed, and rinsed in the same water. After drying my body, my mother liberally applied Vaseline to my body to lubricate my skin. Dental hygiene, at least for me, was not a high priority for my mother. I do not remember having a toothbrush until I started school, which was too late: by then I had multiple cavities.

My mother never had a new dress or shoes. I never saw her in makeup or with any hairstyle; she always wore a colorful headscarf, which hid her graying hair. She was tall and thin and had the poise, grace and cheekbones of an African princess. She was my hero. To me, she seemed to be able to do everything. She taught me the alphabet, numbers, colors, basic phonics and elementary reading. I later learned she did not finish high school, and there were limits to what she could teach me.

My first church experience was at First Baptist Church, located at Seventh and Arch Streets, a few blocks from where I lived. It was the only church I knew for the first nine years of my life. My mother took me there regularly on Sundays. As a four year old, I was really impressed by the dynamic speaking ability of the pastor, the Reverend Doctor Roland Smith, and the great gospel singing of the choir. My first Sunday school teacher was Mrs. Maxwell, a dark, petite, gray-haired church elder who was a disciplinarian and demanded that the children, regardless of age, show respect in God's House. She also required us to learn and recite from memory a new verse from the Bible every week. She was a stickler for regular attendance so she could continuously keep the attendance banner for our age group in front of her room.

I was born with chronic allergies and, as a result, had frequent visits to the Allergy Clinic at University Hospital. I was allergic to everything, it seemed, including grasses, trees, dust (still am), mold (still am) and foods such as dairy, wheat/barley/oats/rice products, eggs, citrus fruits, and figs and probably others. Frequently, my entire body was covered with hives and welts, which itched and caused incessant scratching. My Aunt Babe called these itchy-twitchy episodes the St. Vitas Dance. Countermeasures included taking prescription capsules (which were difficult for me to swallow), avoiding problem foods and bathing and washing only with Saymans Soap. Luckily, I outgrew most of the food allergies.

A Packard dealership was located on the northeast corner of West 5th and Ringo Streets. One of my favorite pastimes was watching the activities going on there. The only black face that I saw regularly was a man who detailed the cars on the lot. I watched him move these cars around the display lot and in and out of the service bays. His job seemed incredibly important because he made the cars look brand new. I wanted to grow up and be like him. I always wanted to visit the dealership and especially talk to this man. I never did visit the Packard dealer. *In fact, I never crossed West 5th Street.*

An Esso filling station was located one block west of the Packard dealership at West 5th and Cross Streets. It, too, was a beehive of activity. Attendants were pumping gas, changing tires and servicing cars. I often walked across Cross Street to the filling station but was always told to go back across the street so I would not get hurt. I really wanted to stand under the elevated grease rack so I could see what was on the underside of cars. This filling station was a landmark on the road to my destiny with

Pegasus; I just did not know it. On one occasion, a customer bought me my first Coca-Cola. I was spoiled. I took the bottle with me and added it to my debris pile. It was a long time before I was able to drink another Coca-Cola.

Sam Storks, the apartment building landlord and my father's employer, was very tolerant with him, in part because of my mother and me. My father was not very reliable, punctual or sober most of the time. Usually, he was absent without notice, while gallivanting or gambling. To insure that my father would not lose his job, my mother often performed his tasks. In one instance, she unloaded a truckload of heavy fire extinguishers; in another, she moved furniture to and around the apartment building.

During this period, I had contact with few people other than family. I learned to entertain myself, usually with something improvised from the rubble pile. My growing imagination filled my head with possibilities. That pile became my best friend.

Another great pastime of mine during this era was observing the streetcars that traveled east and west on West 5th Street. Perched high on the rubble pile, I had a great vantage point to study the details of their operation. I built what I considered to be a replica of the operations console, complete with crank. I pretended to be a streetcar motorman and made all the associated sounds of starting, stopping and rolling a streetcar down the track.

The most dominant structure within view of my home was the Arkansas State Capitol. It was just a few blocks away, and I saw it all day every day. Several times, I walked the three blocks down to High Street alone, glanced up at this huge building and was overtaken with awe. There it stood, on the high ground, in all its majesty. I never walked any further by myself. One night during a Christmas season, my mother and I walked to the capitol to view the Nativity scenes up close. We also heard choirs singing Christmas Carols. The capitol, including the dome, was adorned with blinking and sequencing Christmas lights. It was a spectacular and memorable event. But I also remember I was very cold.

On many days, when my mother was performing her duties at the apartment building, I was left home alone. I was supposed to remain in the immediate area and entertain myself. However, since there was no one to really check on me, sometimes I set out on a walking tour of West 5th Street. I would venture one block away and return, then two and ultimately several blocks east to Broadway Street. Broadway was a major thoroughfare and my first encounter with a traffic light.

One day, I followed a small crowd across Broadway Street. I was standing there trying to make sense of all the traffic – both cars and pedestrians. Suddenly, a very strange-looking white man, who was big, burly and bald pulled up, offered me candy and tried to lure me into his car. "Come on, sonny," he said as he opened the passenger door. I was scared, but I remembered what my mother said, "Don't get into anybody's car unless I am with you." I ran into a paint store and stayed for a long time. I looked out the window and saw this man go around the block several times. I assumed he was looking for me. Then he came no more.

I left the store, used the traffic light to get back across Broadway and hurried towards home. I never lost my orientation because I knew all I had to do was look up West 5th Street towards the State Capitol and walk in that direction. I made it home safely and had no more encounters with the stranger in his car. I never mentioned this incident to my mother.

Emboldened by my Broadway escapade, my next solo walking tour took me all the way to West 5th and Main Streets – the center of town. There was a lot of hubbub here, but the real discovery of this adventure was Sterling's Department Store and its Toyland. Here I spent hours composing a very long mental wish list. Here I also developed many ideas for the rubble pile. I sneaked back to this store several more times before we moved away.

My mother had told me for some time that I would soon have a little brother or sister, but I really had no idea what it meant. When she went into labor, I remember my mother and father arguing about how she would get to the hospital. My father insisted that she go by streetcar; my mother said she was in pain and wanted to go by ambulance so she could lie down. My mother's sister, my Aunt Babe, knew neither had any money, so she hailed a cab and accompanied my mother to University Hospital, where I was born. A few days before my fifth birthday, on 30 March 1946, my sister Alice Faye was born. According to my mother, she was named after the actress, Alice Faye.

After my mother and sister came home, my father's antics became more outrageous. He seemed to hang around more and was always sick, agitated and drunk. My mother kept reminding him that the doctors told him to stop drinking if he wanted to live. I noticed he seemed to be much thinner. When my mother asked my father to go to the store to get some Pet Milk and Karo Syrup, the ingredients of my sister's formula, he said he was too weak and continued to lie in bed. Once again, I visited Mr. Ted and picked up the formula.

One day I heard my father say, "Bea, I need to go to the hospital." For once, he sounded humble.

"Sam, I can't leave Alice," replied my mother. My father accepted that without argument.

"I would like for you to hail a cab, but we don't have any money."

"Bea, I got to go," my father said. When my father said he was experiencing difficulty seeing, my mother thought he was deathly ill. He managed to get himself out of bed and dressed. I walked with him very slowly through the alley next to our home towards Ringo Street, then left to the corner of West 5th and Ringo Streets.

There we waited for the streetcar to take him to University Hospital, which seemed to take much longer than usual. My father was very subdued, saying nothing. For the first time in my life, I felt sorry for him. He trembled while supporting himself by holding onto the corner street sign. I wanted to go to the hospital with him, but knew I could not. Finally, when the streetcar came, he walked to the center of West 5th Street, waved goodbye to me and slowly climbed aboard. He never returned home.

I ran back home to be with my mother and baby sister. I think we both knew our lives had forever changed and my father would not be a part of it. My mother knelt to say a silent prayer and told me to do likewise.

A few days later, my Aunt Babe stopped by, gathered my mother, sister and me, hailed a cab and took us to University Hospital to see my father. I do not know where my sister went at the hospital, but she was not with us as we approached my father's ward. I was told to wait in the hallway for a few minutes.

Soon a doctor came out to talk to me. He said they were going to allow me to visit my father on this occasion, even though it was not normally allowed. I was only five years old and did not understand what was going on. I went in and was alone with my father. The room was empty with the exception of the wheeled-gurney, which he was lying on. His hands were at his sides and two wide belts, one around his thighs, another around his arms and chest, strapped him to the gurney. I climbed up on a small stool so I could see his face. He asked me to get his glasses, which were also on the gurney, and place them on his face so he could see me.

I do not know how many words he spoke to me that day. However, these I distinctly remember, "EdJoe, don't be like me. Mind your mother. Be a good boy." It seemed after that he just stopped talking. He remained silent when my mother came to retrieve me. We left the hospital, and I never saw him alive again. Even now, I do not know why my father was strapped to that gurney.

Shortly after that visit, my mother told me my father was dead. I learned later that the cause of death was listed as cerebral hemorrhage. I do not recall much about his funeral. There was a graveside service, which few people attended. My mother, sister, Aunt Babe and her husband, my cousin, Catherine, and I were there. Teney and Lovey did not attend. I never met or heard anything about my father's family. As far as my mother knew, he had none. If he had family, none of them came to his funeral. I watched the workers lower my father's casket into his grave, which was in an obscure overgrown field somewhere in North Little Rock, Arkansas. My father's gravesite location remains a mystery.

2

Shotgun Houses - Indoor Plumbing and Electric Lights

Shortly after my father's death and just after my sixth birthday, my mother, sister and I moved from West 5th Street to 1104 Izard Street. The house was a detached shotgun house that was one room wide, one story tall and four rooms deep with front room, bedroom, bathroom and kitchen, front to back respectively. Some say the shotgun house is so named because it has doors that are lined up, so that one could fire a shotgun through the front door with the shot exiting the back door without ever having touched a wall.

Anyway, this house had innovations that I was not used to: electricity, indoor running water, a heated bathroom, and natural gas stoves for heating and cooking. We still did not have an electric refrigerator or telephone like some of our neighbors. However, it was great to have working windows and a house that looked like everyone else's. There were many Negro neighbors and plenty of Negro kids ready to play. The dominant landmark near this house was the campus of Philander Smith College – a Negro institution of higher learning – that was right across the street from our house.

Our house was directly across the street from the College President's mansion. Shortly after moving there, I was sitting on our steps near the sidewalk when a tall man in a black suit walked up the sidewalk to me. "Hi, son. "Do you live here now?" "Yes, sir," I answered. "My name is Dr. Harris and I'm the President of this college. "What's your name?" he said. I answered, "Eddie." "Ok, Eddie," he said as he shook my hand and walked away.

I talked to him many times while we lived on Izard Street. He always had words of encouragement for me. One day he sat down beside me on our steps. "Eddie, I think you are smarter than some of my college students," he said, making me feel much smarter than I really was. "I'm going to teach you a really big word, Mississippi. Are you ready?" " Yes, sir. I'm ready," I answered. "Pronounce it like this: Miss is sippi," he said as he walked through the syllables. "Now, Eddie, you try it," said Dr. Harris. "Miss is sippi," I said as he walked me through it. "Now that you can say it, let's learn to spell it," he continued. He pulled out a small piece of paper from his pocket and began to write on it.

"Let's break the word down. Notice there are three letter i's, one big letter M, a double set of s's and a set of p's. Notice also how the i's separate and frame the twin s's and twin p's," said Dr. Harris. "Now notice the rhythm, Mi-ss-i-ss-i-pp-i," he said as he spelled it on the piece of paper. Then he put the paper away. "Eddie, now you spell it." "Yes, sir! Mi-ss-i-ss-i-pp-i," I spelled dutifully. "Great! Don't ever forget it," he said. He smiled, shook my hand and walked away. I had learned to spell my first big word. I ran inside and shared the good news with my mother. I never forgot how to spell Mississippi.

One day while going through several open and close cycles on one of our windows, a broken piece of glass somehow dislodged from its frame and fell on my head. Bleeding profusely, I ran screaming to my mother. She quickly and calmly placed a wet towel compress on a gash above my left ear, which stopped the bleeding. My mother, sister and I walked to West 9th Street, hailed a cab and went to University Hospital. I received five stitches and was released. I still bear that scar.

I was six years old when I started first grade at Gibbs Elementary School in September 1947. Gibbs was only eight blocks away, and I walked to and from school every day. Going to school was my first age of discovery. My first teacher was Mrs. Wells, who was a very nice, orderly lady. I learned so much, so fast. I learned to formally read with the *Dick and Jane* series followed by the *Friends and Workers* series. I was reading three grade levels ahead and soon surpassed my mother's reading comprehension level. One major highlight of my first year of school was when my mother visited Gibbs and spent several hours with me in my classes. That was the first and last time she ever did so.

Another first grade highlight was watching my first movie, a special feature at school titled *Pioneers of the Frontiers*, a western starring William Boyd as Hopalong Cassidy. It was shown in the auditorium and the admission was five cents, which I did not have. I was the only student in my class who did not have his money that day. My teacher, Mrs. Wells, paid the fare for me. I saw the movie and was hooked; I wanted to see more. I never forgot that movie.

In terms of learning, first grade was a breeze. However, mingling daily with so many different adults and children clearly showed me the lack of social equality. I quickly saw that I did not possess the variety, style and quantity of clothes that my peers wore. Even then, most kids had money to spend in the stores before and after school. Some parents drove their kids to school in Chevrolets, Fords, Buicks and even Cadillacs. My family was aided by the Welfare Department and I was in the free and reduced lunch program at school. The program was embarrassing to me because I had to pay with tokens, which everyone could see.

To me, the most important person at Gibbs Elementary was Mr. Gaines, the janitor. He had an important job and a huge ring, which held many keys. He controlled everything, all doors, heat and school grounds, including the playground. He could open any door, find anything and fix everything. When a student, teacher, or parent had a facilities issue, Mr. Gaines had the answer. He was a very dark man with a baldhead and a gentle demeanor, and he always answered my questions. In first grade, I wanted to be a janitor like Mr. Gaines when I became a man.

One of the most embarrassing moments of my elementary school experience was the vacation report. Teachers used this to encourage us to show and tell about our most recent vacation, i.e., Christmas and/or summer. Some students went to visit grandparents in Chicago or Los Angeles. Others went to visit uncles on farms in Louisiana and Texas. I had no uncles or grandparents living in large cities or on farms; I never had anything to report, since I never left Little Rock. As a result, I hated the vacation report.

In the summer of 1948, I looked forward to playing with the neighborhood kids. I was also anxious to discuss with Dr. Harris all the things I had learned in first grade and accept his challenge to learn even bigger words. My mother had other plans. She informed me that because of our deteriorating financial condition, we could not keep the big, detached shotgun house on Izard Street. She had secured a smaller duplex shotgun house in the alley directly behind the Izard house.

That summer we moved to 916C West 12th Street, a house much smaller than the Izard house. This cluster of two duplexes, four households, was unusual because the entrances faced an unpaved service alley, similar to the West 5th shack, which provided access to our house. A tall chain link fence separated Izard Street houses from the alley houses and neighbors, including the kids, did not associate with each other. When I lived on Izard Street, I never even walked through the alley. Now, as alley dwellers, we were in a much lower social order than before the move. I never talked to Dr. Harris again. However, I did see him driving his car and we always waved to each other.

Someone from Philander Smith College, which was a Methodist-affiliated school, invited me to attend their summer-vacation Bible school in 1948. This was my first such event and I attended despite the move. It was held on the campus at Wesley Chapel. I met Negro kids from all over the city. I experienced tremendous growth, interacting with the other kids, watching Christian movies, attending classes, performing arts and crafts and eating delicious foods and candies. I liked it so much, that I attended the following year.

The twin shotgun duplexes housed a menagerie of personalities. Mr. and Mrs. James Morton, a childless couple, lived in the first house. He worked for the Post Office and owned a car. Miss Oney, as we called her, was a reclusive, quiet and seldom-seen housewife. I never saw the inside of their house.

In house two was an interesting family: there was Miss Evelyn, who had two kids, Mary Ellen Jones and Ivan Jackson; Miss Evelyn's sister, Mildred, who did not look like her whole sister because she was dark, short and fat while Miss Evelyn was tall, thin and fair-skinned with straight hair. Then there was FJ, no other name known, who was Mildred's husband or boyfriend. He was the only one who appeared to work, but I never knew where. They had no car. I did not understand their social arrangements.

We lived in house three.

A young woman and her two kids lived in the fourth house. She said little to me and I never learned her name. Her younger daughter, however, I knew very well. Her name was Linda Ann Moses and she was my age, very cute and sexually inquisitive. These houses had pier-and-beam foundations, which mean they had crawl spaces under the floors. In the summer, these crawl spaces were cool and private. Linda invited me to accompany her to the crawl space and explore each other's anatomy. "Look, show me yours and I will show you mine," she said, referring to our genitalia. Soon, we were regularly playing show-and-tell. We transitioned to simulated sex, based on what Linda had learned from secretly watching and listening to her mother and boyfriends having sex. I was a willing pupil. Linda moved away before I did, but I never forgot her.

Directly behind the twin duplexes stood a tall wooden privacy fence, which surrounded the backyard of a large white house facing Chester Street, rumored to belong to the son of our landlord. Inside the fence stood a very large fig tree, which dropped many ripened figs in the walkway on our side of the fence and attracted plenty of flies. On one side of this fence was a silver, fabric-covered, single-engine, wingless airplane, which was always locked but piqued my interest in flying. On the other side, was the stripped hulk of an old car. I never learned why either vehicle was there, they were just part of the neighborhood landscape. When I walked the most direct route to Chester Street, I had to pass one or the other of these landmarks.

In the fall of 1948, I returned to Gibbs Elementary and started second grade. Mrs. Anderson was my teacher. Everything was progressing normally when suddenly, for reasons I never understood, I had to transfer to Capitol Hill Elementary School, which was in a different part of town. I quickly got used to the new teachers and students at this school. I also discovered my first love interest – a tall, slender, brown-skinned girl named Martha Jean Williams. I admired her and asked her to be my special friend. She declined and told me why: I did not wear my belt in a loop, hanging from a right belt loop on my pants. It was some kind of fashion trend. I did not even have a belt. Anyway, that love was unrequited, so I had to move on.

At the beginning of second grade, Gibbs passed out student badges, which provided discount public transportation fares and reduced admission to the Gem Theater. It was a round, white pin badge with the word *STUDENT* in red letters printed on it. It did not mean much to me at the time, since I walked to school and had never been to a public movie. However, it looked official, so I kept it. I used it later.

About the same time I entered Capitol Hill, my mother fell ill. I learned a new big word without the help of Dr. Harris: tuberculosis. Somehow, she had contracted this disease and no one had a clue to its origin. No one in our immediate circle had heard of it. Immediately, my mother was committed to a state tuberculosis sanatorium for Negroes, located about a one-hour drive from our house. My sister and I were checked for tuberculosis and were both negative.

With my mother admitted, my sister, who was now two, and I had two possible fates: live with our Aunt Babe or become wards of the state. Luckily, Aunt Babe decided to keep us. The level of comfort I enjoyed with my mother did not exist with my aunt. I am not sure how many months my mother was in the sanatorium, but my sister and I survived. Because we were children, we were not allowed to visit our mother while she was being treated.

My Aunt Babe and my Uncle Albert lived in a very small basement apartment at 1102 West 21st Street, which was located at the corner of 21st and Ringo Streets. The rooms, including a living room, bedroom, kitchen and a bath nook containing only a toilet, were not large enough to accommodate four people, and my sister and I were not comfortable. We never had enough to eat. Since both my aunt and uncle worked, we were farmed out to a babysitter, Mrs. Marie Davis. I found the entire experience cold and alien. My uncle, who drank plenty, reminded me of my dad, except he was generally gentle, though aloof and non-responsive.

I slept on a chair-bed and wet the bed every single night. I simply could not stop wetting the bed. The only way to prevent it was not to go to sleep. My bedwetting angered my aunt and, because of it, I was always in trouble with her. I also could not stop sucking my right thumb. I guess it was another coping mechanism. I just wanted to be back at home with my mother.

During the several months I lived with my aunt and uncle, I met a number of new friends, the most notable of whom was Milton Barnett Smith. He was the landlord's grandson, who lived upstairs, and was the same age as me. I thought of him as a very rich Negro kid. He had his own room with a radio, plenty of toys, clothes and a new J.C. Higgins bicycle. His bicycle was top of the line, with a horn, light, luggage rack, chain guard and white wall tires. Milton always had plenty of food and sweets, like Twinkies, while my sister and I were often hungry and ate salad dressing sandwiches. The previous summer, he had ridden the train to Detroit for a vacation with relatives. He was very kind to me and often invited me upstairs to listen to the radio and play in his room.

I continued to attend Capitol Hill while my mother was in the sanatorium. It was a much longer walk, about 16 blocks compared to the eight blocks before. I developed alternate routes to and from school, which made it scenic and fun.

When my mother was released and rejoined my sister and me at home, she was very different physically. She explained to me, she was not cured. Her tuberculosis was merely arrested. One of her lungs was so ravaged by this disease it had to be collapsed using compressed air, which had to be replenished every two weeks. Essentially, she had only one good lung and it, too, had a spot of TB on it.

I did not know it at the time but my mother was terminally ill. In retrospect, she may have known. I remember her telling me many times, "EdJoe, if I go back into the sanatorium, I will not be coming back." I heard her but I reasoned as long as she continued to get her air treatment, she would not have any reason to be readmitted to the sanatorium.

Tuberculosis is highly contagious, and my mother took measures to protect my sister and me from the disease. Her eating and drinking utensils were separate from ours, and all were washed and boiled before each use. She did likewise with sheets, towels and face cloths. My mother never shared food with us. We were screened for TB every six months until after my mother died. Neither my sister nor I ever tested positive.

I continued to attend First Baptist Church after the move from West 5th Street even though, after my mother's release from the sanatorium, I went alone. I remember the pastor, Reverend Doctor Roland Smith, praying for and asking the congregation to pray for my mother. He also asked for some angels to drive Sister Berniece Washington to her compressed air treatment. One Sunday after church, Brother Buster Young and his wife, Emily, met me and volunteered to drive my mother to receive her treatments. As far as I remember, Brother Young drove her every time.

I also remember an anonymous man who often gave me a nickel after church, I assume to keep me coming or perhaps he knew of my plight. My mother gave a specific route to walk to Sunday school and church, which I initially followed. It took me through the intersection of 9th and Arch Streets. A soda jerk was located on one corner. I went inside and learned that I could get a Coca-Cola or root beer float for that nickel. From then on, if I had money, I drank a float on my way home from church.

My burning desire was to walk the length and breadth of 9th Street, although my mother told me not to do so. One Sunday my curiosity got the best of me, and I walked outside the soda jerk, turned right and headed west up 9th Street. I was amazed by all the Negro businesses I saw, most of which were open. I saw grocery stores, funeral homes, hotels, pawnshops, churches, nightclubs, and a filling station. The most curious place was a Tonsorial Parlor (not open that day), which I did not understand from mere observation. It turned out to be a barbershop. The most important discovery of the day was the all Negro-run Gem Theater. I did not have any money to purchase a ticket to see what went on inside.

One Saturday afternoon, after I had washed Brother Young's car, and with my mother's permission and ten cents in my pocket, I quickly walked the four blocks to the Gem Theater on West 9th Street. I do not remember what was playing but I was very excited. Using my student badge, I paid the five-cent admission and with my remaining nickel bought a box of popcorn at the concession stand. The Saturday matinee had a typical format that I quickly became accustomed to: two one-hour westerns, a serial, cartoon, newsreel and coming attractions, which consumed about three hours. I always saw everything twice so I was in the theater about six hours, from noon to 6 p.m. every Saturday.

My walking tours continued, and I traveled increasingly greater distances and discovered some very interesting landmarks. Close by, I discovered United Friends Hospital, Charmaine Hotel, and the House of Beauty – all owned and staffed by Negroes. There were numerous alleys replete with trash heaps, which dwarfed the one I had on West 5th Street. I found old broken cash registers, radios, and other miscellaneous tools, lumber and wheels. What really amazed me was the number of discarded soft drink bottles. I gathered enough parts and wheels and made a cart, similar to a rickshaw, to transport my sister and parts for my projects.

My sister, Alice, was five years younger than I was and could not help during my treasure hunts. I was very close to Alice at that time and tried to spend as much time with her as possible. I was also my mother's only reliable babysitter. My homemade cart was the ideal solution; it allowed me to simultaneously spend time with my sister, babysit for my mother and retrieve valuable treasures.

I quickly learned that discarded soft drink bottles were cash cows. Some bottles, Barqs, Royal Crown, Pepsi Cola and Coca-Cola could be redeemed for the original two-cents-each deposit at some grocery stores. Likewise, TruAde and Grapette bottles could be redeemed for one cent each. Through tedious trial and error, I learned the correct bottle type and grocery store combinations to generate the most revenue. The two-cent-deposit bottles were the most popular and profitable for me, so I diligently sought those. On a good day, ten bottles (not cracked or broken) earned me twenty cents – enough for me to go to the movie, buy a drink, popcorn and a Baby Ruth candy bar, all for five cents each. Sometimes, however, after delivering popular bottles to a store via my homemade cart, the owner paid me only one cent per bottle and sometimes I had to visit multiple stores to sell all the bottles.

Later, when my bottle business was going well, sometimes I had as much as 30 cents, which meant I had a feast while watching the movie. I bought popcorn, a snow cone, and a couple of candy bars – a Snickers and Baby Ruth. My favorite western stars were Lash LaRue, Whip Wilson, Durango Kid, Roy Rogers and Rocky Lane. My favorite serials or chapter plays were Dick Tracy, Captain Video, Congo Bill, Rocket Man and Captain Marvel. My favorite movie was *White Heat,* starring James Cagney. I was introduced to Mantan Moreland and Pigmeat Markham, two of the first big Negro movie stars to appear on the silver screen.

Brother Young owned a green 1941 Dodge (I asked him.) four-door sedan. He was the first person I knew personally who owned a car. Whenever I was not in school, I rode with my mother, sister and Brother Young to my mother's treatment facility. My mother and sister rode in the back seat, while Brother Young and I rode up front. My attention was equally divided between activities inside and the scenery outside the car. I studied and committed to memory every driving detail from operating the foot starter, clutch, brakes, to shift patterns and steering. I had the perception that I could drive this or any car. I planned to drive my mother to her treatment one day.

Brother Young and Miss Emily, as I addressed them, were black, but both had very fair skin, light eyes and straight hair. This was in stark contrast to my mother and me. We both had very dark skin and eyes and nappy hair. Miss Emily was a housewife and Brother Young worked at Worthen's National Bank of Little Rock, a highly respected financial institution. I was treated like their adopted son; they had no children of their own.

Brother Young and Miss Emily invited me to visit their apartment one Saturday morning. They showed me two of the high tech devices they had: an electric refrigerator that made miniature ice cubes and a console radio/phonograph combination. I was fascinated with both. The first record I ever heard was a 78-RPM version of Frankie Lane's *Mule Train.* Brother Young played the song several times for me during my subsequent visits.

Brother Young knew how much I enjoyed movies. One day he said to me, "Little Eddie, how would you like to help me wash my car every Saturday morning? I will pay you ten cents, which will be enough for movie fare. How about it?" I thought to myself, I would have money for Saturday afternoon movies and be able to wash and learn more about Brother Young's Dodge. "Yes, sir! I really want to do that."

"Ok, we'll start next Saturday," he replied.

I reported dutifully every Saturday morning that I can remember during this period. Brother Young's apartment building had a detached multi-car, open garage (The front was not closed.) so inclement weather was not an issue. Even if we did not wash his car, he would let me look under the hood, check the oil, radiator fluids and hoses. Sometimes I just cleaned the windows of his car; either way, I earned ten cents.

To me, Brother Young and Miss Emily epitomized what a husband and wife should be: friendly, successful, respected and *rich*. Moreover, they had interesting household gadgets, including a wringer-type washing machine.

Although sick, my mother had no choice but to continue to provide summer domestic services for Mrs. Harris and Mrs. Wynn, who by now had moved to Pulaski Heights, an affluent Little Rock subdivision. When she worked, I babysat my sister, Alice, ostensibly with the help of neighbors, if needed. I knew how to feed her and change her cloth diapers. I never had any emergencies and over time, my mother became comfortable with the arrangement.

The Christmas season was always sad at our house. There were no wrapped gifts and no new toys – ever. My sister and I never even had a Christmas tree while my mother was alive. I heard the Santa Claus myth elsewhere, but he never visited my house. My mother simply could not afford it. In contrast to West 5th Street, there were plenty of kids here, and on Christmas Day, they played with their new toys. My sister, Alice, was too young to notice, but I did and it made me very sad not to be able to join the show-and-tell with my new toys. The kids paraded their new skates, Radio Flyer wagons, tricycles, air rifles, cap pistols, dolls and bicycles on the nearby sidewalks on Chester Street.

I did receive some things during Christmas seasons that did make me happy. One year Capitol Hill Elementary School gave each student a fruit bag gift, which contained an apple, orange, Brazil nuts, candy canes, and hard candy. I enjoyed eating all of it. One time a person, who said she was from the Goodwill, stopped by my house to deliver an erector set that was used but in good condition. I had seen the exact set in Sterling's Department Store before we moved. I saw all the possible things you could make pictured on the front of the box. I was very excited, but my mother would not let me open the box until Christmas.

When I opened the box on Christmas Day, I was disappointed to find that a critical, common part, albeit small, was central to every project. Without this part, it was impossible to build any of those things displayed on the front of the box. My happiness quickly turned to sadness. The most enjoyable gift at that time was from next-door neighbor, Ivan Jackson, who was a couple of years older than I was. He gave me his old cap pistol with a broken cocking hammer. Even though it had no holster and did not shoot caps, it was the greatest gift I could have received that Christmas. I repaired the pistol to shoot caps. I finally gave the gun away when I was thirteen – five years later.

During the last Christmas that I spent with my mother, Brother Young surprised me with something that I had always wanted – a bicycle. It was not new. I had seen it at the Goodwill Store at 7th and Cross Streets. I hoped my mother could afford it, since it was much cheaper than a new one, so I told her about it. She perhaps told Brother Young. The bike was basic and bare: It had no light, horn or chain guard. It was not a J.C. Higgins or Schwinn. The handlebars were no longer chrome plated but painted with silver paint. The front frame was straight, not contoured to fit around the front fender. Nevertheless, I loved it.

I finally had real mobility. One of the first practical things I mastered with the bike was to devise a way to retrieve a 25-pound block of ice from the icehouse at 14th and Ringo and deliver it to our icebox. The first time I came home with a block of ice slung from my handlebars, my mother could not believe it. I was very proud of myself. My pressing goal was to drive my mother to her semimonthly treatments at the sanatorium.

Reverend Smith, the pastor of First Baptist Church, came to our house several times to pray for and with my mother. He usually parked his car on 12th Street and walked up the alley to the house. What was distinct about his prayers was the fact that he never went into our house. He prayed with my mother through the bedroom window.

In contrast, Reverend Caldwell, the gospel-singing, praying vegetable man regularly went inside to pray with my mother. Reverend Caldwell drove a vegetable truck, an old Chevrolet, packed with fresh garden wares. Our alley was a regular stop on his circuit. His singing and ringing his bell announced his presence long before he started up our alley. The reverend was an affable man in overalls with a song and a prayer for everyone. He ended every transaction with "God bless you." I was more interested in his showmanship and the mechanical aspects of his truck than his vegetables.

"Amazing grace, how sweet the sound," sang the reverend after he stopped his vegetable truck. Then he rang the bell on the back of his truck several times. A small crowd started to gather. "Sister Washington," he said to my mother, "Everything on the truck is right fresh, got watermelons, too. Praise the Lord! Great day in the morning! Sister Washington, I am coming inside to pray with you. Sister Martin, what can I get for you?"

"God bless you," he said to Sister Anderson, after he sold her a pound of okra. Then he went inside to pray with my mother. Those prayers were always private.

In September 1949, I started third grade at Capitol Hill. My teacher was Mrs. Quick, one of my all-time favorites. She made me feel very comfortable and was like a second mother to me. During one week in third grade, my mother ran out of baby-sitting options when she had a series of medical appointments. So I asked Mrs. Quick if I could bring my four-year-old sister to school with me. Surprisingly, she said yes. That week, my sister and I slowly walked to and from Capitol Hill every day. During class, the students and teacher gave Alice various activities to keep her pacified, and she caused no problems. I am still amazed that I was able to pull that off.

In third grade, I met the second love of my life – Helen Wilson. She was a high yellow, beautiful, well-dressed girl who was always very friendly to me. I wanted to invite her to go to the Gem Theater's Saturday matinee with me. I had plans to sell many bottles so I could treat her to popcorn, candy and a snow cone. However, I never got up enough nerve to ask her for a movie date. She remained very friendly to me until I left Capitol Hill, and I never saw her again.

In the fall of 1949, I contracted a very serious case of mumps and could not attend school for two weeks. A doctor saw me at home several times from the Welfare Department (now called social services). At one point, my mother thought my condition was life threatening. I was very anxious to get back into the routine of walking to school again, interacting with my favorite landmarks along my 11th Street route – the Pulaski Street Truck Route, trolley barn and St. Vincent's Hospital.

Pulaski Street was part of the truck route, which took big trucks safely around the city, rather than through it. Every time I approached Pulaski Street – whether going to or coming from school, I prepared to play a game. The challenge was to identify as many tractors propelling the 18-wheelers as possible, the bigger the better. I was very good at this game. I still remember some of the big rigs traveling Pulaski Street: Macks, Peterbuilts, Kenworths, Whites, Internationals, Reos, GMCs and of course Fords, Chevrolets and Dodges. I waved at the drivers and wanted to drive a big truck one day.

The trolley yard, as I called it, was located at 11th and High Streets.

Electric trolleys, which had replaced the electric streetcars that I knew and loved from West 5th Street, were serviced and parked here. I often stood for long intervals, watching all the activities, always inching closer, until one of the men backed me away for my safety. However, there was one nice man, always in coveralls, who several times allowed me to tour the yard. In fact, one time he gave me a guided tour, including the pit where I could see underneath the trolley bus. This was similar to looking underneath Brother Young's Dodge, only bigger, better and easier.

By the end of second grade, I had experienced two memorable field trips: one to the local Wonder Bakery, maker of Wonder Bread, which "Builds Strong Bodies Eight Ways" and Finkbeiner Meat Packing Company, maker of Capitol Pride Franks.

Just before spring 1950, my mother fell ill with tuberculosis again, this time it was the second lung. The spot had grown, and my mother went to the sanatorium for the second time. At the time, I was not so concerned about my mother's health; she had come back home the first time, and she would come back this time. I was anxious about having to return to live with my aunt and uncle.

My sister and I moved back to the environment we hated so much. I felt sorry for my sister, Alice, who really needed love and got none from my aunt or uncle. I continued at Capitol Hill as I did before. At recess, I discussed my situation with Helen Wilson and she was always sympathetic and gave me hugs.

The first night back at my aunt's place, my bedwetting started again and recurred nightly. One night, my aunt made me drink a combination of her and my urine. I assume this was a desperate attempt by her to break my habit, which was destroying her chair-bed. Her strategy failed and the bedwetting continued until I was nine and a half, when, miraculously, it and the thumb sucking stopped. There was no significant event to cause these dramatic changes; I believe it was a combination of pure grit, determination and final resignation.

The long walk to and from school alone gave me ample time to reflect about the quiet times I had with my mother. I never forgot some of the things she said, "EdJoe, I don't worry about you. You are smart and will make it in this world. Just do not steal. I do worry about your sister; she will always have a problem." Prophetically, my mother was right. My sister has had marital and continual health problems and has been supported by social services for all of her life. The most depressing thing my mother said was, "If I go back to the sanatorium, I won't be coming back." I did not fully understand what that meant when she said it, but I thought about it often after she returned to the sanatorium.

One warm spring day in 1950, after the long walk from school, my aunt was waiting for me in the yard. This was unusual, since she was normally at work this time of the day. She said to me, "EdJoe, Sister (my mother) is dead." At that moment, all I thought about was the last time I saw my mother alive, which was about two weeks earlier. Brother Young had driven my aunt, sister and me to see my mother at the sanatorium. My sister and I could not go inside. My mother came to a first floor window and talked to me through the screen. She never said she would not be coming home, but she looked smaller, weak, and her voice was different. I know she must have said something to me, but I do not remember any of it. That was the last time I saw her alive. I told her bye, but not *goodbye*, formally.

On the first school day after my mother's death, I returned to Capitol Hill. During the walk, I thought about the fact of my mother's death, but I did not accept it. I thought her death was still reversible; that way she would come home again. I also pondered three other death-related events in my life:

1) On a very warm summer night while walking alone to an early evening event at First Baptist Church, I approached another church at 9th and Gaines Streets. There was a woman, who looked about my mother's age, sitting outside the church's open door fanning her face with a fan advertising the services of Dubison Funeral Home. She was chanting continuously as I passed her position, "Lord, bring him back! I need him! Just bring him back for ten minutes. I have to tell him something. I have to tell him something!" I felt her sorrow as I walked away.

2) I recalled something my mother once said to me, "EdJoe, when I die, I expect you to be a good boy. If you are not, I will be standing outside this very window (her bedroom) watching you with bright red eyes. And I will come inside and scratch your eyes out." I did not really believe her, but I was afraid not to.

3) There was a cemetery near the twin shotgun duplexes at 11th and Broadway Streets, which I passed by on many of my walks. I heard all the superstitions regarding ghosts, haints and the walking dead that moved around cemeteries at night. I wanted to walk through that cemetery late one dark night to see for myself. One such night, I found the courage, climbed over the fence on Broadway Street, and started towards the other side of the cemetery. I passed flat grave markers, upright tombstones,

mausoleums and freshly dug graves. I was two-thirds of the way through and had heard and seen nothing, when suddenly someone said, "Son, what are you doing in my cemetery?" I saw no one.

I wanted to run, but I could not move. Slowly, a tall, lanky man walked from behind what appeared to be a large mausoleum. By now, I was really scared. I thought this must be Frankenstein! I just wanted to go home, but I still could not move. The man slowly walked over to me and placed his hand on my shoulder and said, "Son, you are a brave little boy. I am the groundskeeper for this cemetery and over here is where I live. I want you to go home and never try this again." I looked up at his white face and said, "Yes, sir." He walked me to the Arch Street side of the cemetery and let me out through a gate. I ran the few blocks home. On the way, I recalled that this was an *all-white* cemetery. However, I never expected to encounter a living person. I took the groundskeeper's advice – I never tried that again.

My mother's funeral was held at our church, First Baptist, and the Reverend Doctor Roland Smith delivered the eulogy. This was the first time I had seen my mother since her death. Her coffin was on an elevated bier, which required a stool for me to see her face. Looking at her, I remembered some words she had said to me, "When I'm gone, your best friend is gone." I knew this was true and for the first time since her death, I started to cry.

I remember riding in the limousine, provided by Ruffin and Jarrett Funeral Home, to my mother's burial plot in Haven of Rest Cemetery in Little Rock, Arkansas. In contrast to my father, I know exactly where my mother is buried.

After my mother's funeral, I knew my life had forever changed. I had just turned nine years old and both of my parents were dead. I finished the third grade at Capitol Hill with the support of my teacher, Mrs. Quick, and my special friend, Helen Wilson. The last day of school was the last time I saw Helen; I think she moved away.

One of my favorite pastimes after my mother's death was touring Little Rock and North Little Rock by city bus. The problem was I had no money for the fare. Very rarely, I had a nickel, which with my student button, provided my initial fare. After studying the two city transit routes, which crisscrossed at 20th and High Streets, I devised the transfer solution. I noticed that about half the people who boarded a bus or trolley requested a paper transfer. I also noticed that a number of people never used their transfers: they discarded them on the ground at the designated transfer locations.

Transfers were color coded and torn in such a way to indicate the day and time of issue. They had to be used within one hour of that date and time. I simply walked to a transfer location, picked up a discarded unexpired transfer on the ground and boarded a bus. I rode that bus to the end of the line. On the return leg, I disembarked at a different transfer location and started the process all over again. Using this scheme, I could ride all day long, any time I wanted. I did this until I knew from memory all the city transit routes from end to end.

I still remember some of the routes and their end-to-end destinations: Oak Forest – Seventh and Main, West 15th Street – Protho Junction and South Main – Pulaski Heights, and others, just destinations: Levy, Biddle Shop, Granite Mountain and Fort Roots and Cammack Village.

After I boarded a bus, I followed the protocol of the day: Negroes moved immediately to the rearmost seats possible, standing, rather than sitting forward of an unmarked demarcation line. I always went to the rearmost window seat as soon as it was open. I also looked for discarded unexpired transfers on the bus; often I found several.

Neither my aunt nor Mrs. Davis, the day-care provider for my sister and me, ever challenged my daylong absences.

3

Allan Jones Years – Period of Enlightenment

Allan Jones literally walked into my life in the early summer of 1951. I was sitting on the curb near 21st and Ringo Streets with two other kids, Allen Quinn Toggle and Charles Diggs, when he came up to me and said, "Hi, boy. What's your name? Do you want to work?"

I thought for a moment and said, "Eddie. Yes."

He said, "Good! My name is Allan Jones," and he instructed me to meet him the next morning at the corner of 20th and Ringo Streets at 6:30 a.m. While he spoke, I noticed he had several missing teeth, and his dental hygiene was lacking.

I never found out why he chose to ask me to work and not the others. I also never understood why I said yes, since I did not know him or the type of work we would be performing. I was ten years old and somehow I knew it was the right decision.

My first impression of Allan was mostly curiosity and disbelief. He was a very old, dark, hulking figure, over six feet tall. He wore granny glasses, a cowboy hat, overalls and Brogans, all of which were unkempt. He took his hat off to fan himself, which revealed a baldhead. His mustache was completely white, and so was the stubble on his chin. He carried a pocket watch on a chain, which he looked at several times during our short conversation. Finally, in his right rear pocket was a large red handkerchief with black polka dots.

As he walked away, Allen Quinn and I immediately started discussing the merits and demerits of meeting Allan the next morning. What type of work would I be doing? Would I make lots of money? Was Allan a sex pervert or child molester? Was he for real? Would he even show? Our final assessment of this brief episode: weird.

I mentioned nothing about Allan Jones to my aunt or uncle that day. There was no trepidation when I went to bed that night. In fact, I was anxious for the next chapter of this strange tale. I slept very well that night.

I was up the next morning at 6 a.m., donned my clothes and rushed to the meeting location, which was a half block from my house. Allan was right on schedule. He was wearing the exact same clothes he had on when we first met, including the red polka-dot handkerchief.

I had expected to see a truck or some type of work vehicle. There was none. The only thing about him that was different from the previous day was the addition of the mowing implements in his possession. As I surveyed the numerous mowing tools, including two push-reel mowers, two large bushel baskets, two leaf rakes, grass shears, a sling sickle and a hand sickle, all neatly arrayed for transport, I knew the type of work I would be doing.

We quickly exchanged pleasantries. He then explained the plan of the day to me. We would start with Dr. Woods' (a prominent Negro physician) lawn, which was located at the intersection where we were standing. Then we proceeded to Mr. Fontaine's (owner of Fontaine's Tonsorial Parlor on West 9th Street, mentioned earlier) lawn and finally we were scheduled to mow two other lawns in the vicinity for four jobs for the day.

Since neither of us had eaten breakfast, he sent me to Powell's Grocery, which was two blocks away, to get several long johns and several slices of baloney. The tab was on him. I had no money anyway. We quickly ate and by 7 a.m., we started to work.

The first two lawns were huge, probably half an acre, with steep sloping front terraces, which had to be manually cut with a hand sickle. Since I was new, young and agile, I was directed to cut the terrace. Allan demonstrated how it should be done and turned the sickle over to me. I finished the terrace, and Allan had me start the second reel mower in the pattern he specified: start on the outside periphery, square the corners and continuously work inward until done.

We finished the first job around 11 a.m. and, after I made another quick trip to the grocery store, we had more baloney and long johns for lunch. After we drank Barqs sodas, also known as belly washers, we moved the short distance to the second lawn. This lawn was very similar to the first one and it, too, took us about four hours to complete. The last two lawns were a few blocks away and smaller. We finished the last lawn at about 8 p.m. that night.

We prepositioned our equipment at the next job site, which was about a half mile away. Then it was payday. Allan paid me ten dollars for my efforts. I had never had that much money before. I was really tired, but elated about having earned so much money – in one day! Allan told me to meet him where we were standing at 7 a.m. the following day. Allan walked off in one direction, and I in another. I noticed he walked with a slight limp. It took me about 20 minutes to walk home.

The second day, we had only three lawns scheduled and none with terraces. Like the previous day, we dined on long johns, baloney, and Barqs sodas, but this time we added cheese. The pace seemed much faster, but easier as I became used to Allan's routine: do the hard things like terraces first, sling and/or hand sickle areas where it is impractical to use the push mower, trim lawn edges, shape the shrubbery and rake all grass clippings. The bushel baskets were used to gather and transport clippings to trash cans for pickup by sanitation workers (garbage men of the period).

I could see every tool in Allan's arsenal was important and used for a specific purpose. If he did not need or use it, he did not bring it. Allan carried two hand files in his pockets. He used them often, sharpening the reels on the mowers and the blades on the other implements. Sharpness was a virtue.

At the completion of the last job on the second day, Allan informed me we had to transport his tools to his house. I pushed one mower/basket/rake combination and he the other. He could actually transport both mowers simultaneously by himself. He had delivered all the implements, including the two mowers, to 20th and Ringo Streets that morning. As we walked, we talked, and I got to know Allan better. He called me Joe or Boy; I don't remember ever addressing him by name.

"Joe, I guess you notice I walk everywhere," said Allan.

"Yeah, why?"

"I don't trust those buses, cars or trucks. If I can't walk there, I don't need to go. I have never been in one. Gimme a mule and a buggy."

"You've never even been on a bus?"

"No. I don't like that newfangled stuff."

"Do you go to church?" I asked.

"No, but I read the Bible. Listen, boy, I have no family that I know of. I don't know when or where I was born. I know that I am at least 80 years old. I know my mother and father was slaves. I don't know what ever happened to them."

"How do you know that you're 80?"

"Boy, I just know. I can remember about 80 years; I seen a lot of changes."

"What fun things do you do?"

"Only sleep and work. I am too old for much else."

"Ever been sick? My mother died in a sanatorium," I explained.

"Never been to a hospital. Never been sick. It don't matter. The world is coming to the end soon. I just know it in my soul."

"Do you read anything other than the Bible? Listen to the radio? Read the Gazette or Democrat?" I asked Allan.

"None of that," he answered.

By the time we reached his home, I had heard most of his philosophy of life. He did not like socializing with people in his private moments. He spurned all forms of modern medicine and technology. He seemed to be stuck in a 1900 time warp. Allan was diametrically different from Brother Young, who embraced everything modern.

As we approached the intersection of 25th and Park Avenue, I was anxious to see his house. After our conversation, I did not expect much. We crossed 25th Street, which was also known as Roosevelt Road. I saw a huge Esso filling station (That station, called a service center, would have significance about a decade later.) and the Arkansas Livestock Yard, which hosted the annual livestock show, rodeo and carnival, and not much else. A

44

tall chain-link fence separated the livestock yard and the filling station.

"Here it is, my boy," said Allan. What I saw was an inconspicuous makeshift shack adjacent to the fence on the livestock yard side. Structurally, this shack was far more fragile than the one I lived in on West 5th Street. Once inside, though, I was amazed at how utilitarian the place was. The interior was congested; every space had something in it. There was a twin bed in one corner, an icebox in another. A wood stove stood in the middle of the floor; a small stack of wood stood in a third corner. A coat and some winter clothes hung on two walls. The rear wall hosted the only window, providing a view of the filling station through the fence. Every other space seemed to be filled with push lawn mowers, lawn mower parts, sickles, shears and sharpening tools.

The place had no running water or electricity.

"Where's your bathroom?" I inquired.

"I use the one at the filling station when it's open and nobody is watching. Sometimes I use the ones in the stockyard. I know how to get in. And the woods in the back."

Allan gave me the schedule for our next job. He told me to meet him at his place at 6:30 a.m. when we would transport the equipment to a Battery Street job site. Then for the second day in a row, he paid me ten dollars cash. I walked the mile or so back home in financial bliss.

Throughout the summer of 1951, Allan and I had many more jobs and I many more paydays, although not always as lucrative as the first two. We worked together very well and became a well-oiled efficient machine. Allan organized and scheduled his jobs geographically and in clusters. His clientele was both black and white, educated professionals who had large homes in good neighborhoods. The customer base was established before my time, and it did not change during my partnership with Allan. His work ethic still resonates in my head, work hard and smart, always satisfy the customer and he will always come back. And he will pay you well. Those principles guided my actions during the Pegasus years.

One other thing I learned about Allan: he had a morbid distrust of banks. He took no checks and extended no credit. He always demanded, as he described it, "Cash on the barrelhead." I have no idea here he kept his money; I just know he had nothing to do with banks.

Allan and I finished our final two lawns of the season in September 1951. I helped him gather and return all forward-based equipment to his shack.

Over the winter, he said he would clean, repair and maintain the equipment. Allan paid me and gave me a glowing performance appraisal for my summer lawn maintenance internship. Since neither of us had a telephone, Allan said he would walk over to my house to confirm the schedule and other details of our 1952 season. We both were looking forward to extending our successful venture another year. Finally, after much small talk, I left Allan for the last time that season and walked back home.

I still had the bicycle Brother Young gave me, and I rode it to and from downtown, the West End and the South End. However, I never rode it when I worked with Allan Jones. On three occasions, I thought that bike would cause my death. Once, while riding at a high rate of speed, I rear-ended a parked 1950 Buick near the intersection of 15th and Ringo Streets. The force of the impact was so great; it threw me to the ground and bent the front fork of my bike, which I never repaired. On another day, I was riding south on Howard Street, near 22nd Street, when a very vicious dog started to chase me. He continually tugged on my right pant cuff. I was scared and did not dare stop; in fact to escape, I tried to go faster and faster. Finally, after a two-and-a-half-block chase, just half a block from a dead end, the dog turned back.

One time I started down the steep hill on South Main Street, between 24th and West 25th Streets and my right leg pant cuff became entangled between the bike's chain and the large front sprocket so I could not apply the brakes. This went for approximately two-thirds of a block. Finally, for reasons I cannot explain, my cuff untangled, allowing me barely enough time to apply the brakes and lay the bike down just short of the busy intersection of South Main and 25th Streets. After checking for broken bones, I rolled my right pant leg up to my knee and rode away. My bicycle never had a chain guard.

Prior to meeting Allan, I had returned to Gibbs Elementary School and completed fourth grade. I had two great team teachers, Mrs. Ricks and Mrs. Fitzhugh. Because of lack of space, two fourth grade classes were held in the auditorium; sometimes they were combined and sometimes taught separately. The teachers worked well together and had great rapport with the students. Mrs. Ricks coaxed me to perform in my first play. I do not remember the name of the play. I had few lines, but was very nervous.

That school year, Pearlie Lawson, a female fellow student with hair shorter than mine, and I were the top readers in the class. We were both reading far above our grade level. I had become an avid reader. I read everything I could, from the weekly readers given by the school to the old Hollywood gossip magazines I found in trash bins. I also found the library, which

Negroes could use, at 16th and High Streets, which I fully exploited.

Both my aunt and uncle worked for Missouri Pacific Railroad, she a Pullman car cleaner, he an iceman for the Pullman cars. His job was to load the 250-pound blocks of ice into the ice bins beneath the passenger cars to provide the air conditioning. Although blue collar and union, both jobs were considered great for Negroes in the 1950s. These jobs were among the few offering Negroes benefits, including health care. In fact, the railroad had its own hospital near the rail station.

The Missouri Pacific rail station was called Union Station and was located at Markham and Victory Streets. I visited the station as often as possible. It was a beehive of motion with passengers, baggage, freight and mail continually arriving and departing. A typical train had passenger, baggage, freight, mail and sleeper cars. I often stood on the elevated bridge that spanned the tracks, watched, and heard the bell of trains with curious names like the Midnight Special, Sunset Limited and Chicago Express. Most of the trains were diesel powered, but there were some steam trains. I enjoyed them both, the pulsating sound of the steamers and the roar of the diesels.

The waiting rooms and restaurants were segregated. Whites had larger, plush accommodations on one side and Negroes had a smaller, crowded and usually dank with a displeasing odor, on the backside. The Negro side had a jukebox and pinball machines. Sometimes Negro women in questionable dress, who did not appear to be traveling, loitered there.

My uncle sometimes offered bootleg taxi services to well-dressed Negro unaccompanied men. I rode shotgun occasionally when he had a fare. As soon as we started towards a destination, my uncle offered the passenger some other services:

"Sir, do you need a little trim? I can get you a woman real cheap. I also have some rot-gut, still whiskey in the trunk. I can sell you a pint." Pulaski County (Little Rock) was dry at the time. My uncle called these activities his extra hustle.

Because of my uncle's railroad employment, he was able to get free fares on the trains. He provided one for me to take my one-and-only train ride – a 110-mile trip to Dermott, Arkansas to visit my aunt's Uncle Garland. I took careful note of the Negro conductor's actions, especially how he announced the upcoming stops. I have no idea how many stops there were then, but I remember three, Pine Bluff, Gould, McGehee and of course, Dermott. I found the conductor's pronunciation of McGehee amusing:

"Maaaaghee." The visit to my cousins' was boring and forgettable; the train ride to and from was adventuresome and exciting.

During that school year, before and after school, I returned to the home of Mrs. Davis for daycare. She raised chickens in her backyard, harvesting their eggs. She also had a dog called Sonny Boy. I had to help her with the chickens and walk the dog. I fed the chickens and gathered the eggs, which she sold or gave away. Often she sent me to the neighborhood grocery store to purchase twenty-five cents worth of chicken feed. About half the time, I was robbed by the notorious female bully, Gladys Alexander, who terrorized boys and girls equally. The loss was difficult to explain to Mrs. Davis, although she was well aware of Gladys' reputation. A few times, I bought only nineteen cents worth of feed, which enabled me to buy my favorite candy, a Peanut Pattie. The feed, Pattie and tax, came to exactly twenty-five cents.

Mrs. Davis was a woman who could grab a fleeing chicken by its head and fling it round and round above her head until she wrung off the head and the body of the chicken fell to the ground without a lot of blood spatter. It was especially grotesque for me to see the headless chicken running around frantically during its final few seconds. When she needed a chicken to cook, she expected me to slay it the same way. I never garnered enough nerve to do so.

Mrs. Davis must have been a tough old lady. We had many conversations, but two I will never forget. "I am over 80 years old and through with men. I have buried three husbands; there will not be a fourth," she said. In another conversation, she expressed her disdain for whites. Her father was white but never a part of her life. As a result, she was very fair-skinned. In her younger days, she had the so-called *good straight hair*. Still, she said to me, "Don't trust the white man. And don't even look at a white woman. Please don't grow up and think you are one of those smart niggers and take a white woman out of the state and marry her. Somebody will kill your black ass. Hear me? Don't ever forget that."

Powell's Grocery was half a block away from Mrs. Davis' house at the corner of 20th and Pulaski. The store was significant to me because it was the first large Negro grocery store I had ever seen. Mr. and Mrs. Powell were the co-owners and were usually running the store, she as the cashier and he as the butcher. As far as I could see, their clientele was totally Negro. They had a colorful, wisecracking deliveryman named Floyd, who delivered groceries in an old jeep. I dreamed of one day having his job. There were two other important facts about the store: Mrs. Powell drove a new black four-door Kaiser sedan, which she parked in front of the store when she was at work. And amazingly, they did not carry Peanut Patties in their store.

The way to and from Mrs. Davis' house, which was three-and-a-half blocks from my aunt's apartment, took me west along West 20th Street, from Ringo across Cross and Pulaski Streets, where I encountered some memorable Negro families.

First, there was Calvin Scribner, probably the first Negro uniformed police officer in Little Rock. He often showed me his gun and badge on his front porch. Several times, either I saw his wife, Rose, nude, through the window or when she came to the front door while I was sitting on her front porch. He did not drive a squad car. Officer Scribner's beat was a walking patrol along the Negro center of commerce, West 9th Street.

Ms. Frazier, who lived next door to the Scribners, changed dramatically over a two-year period. The retired first grade teacher grew drastically in size, grew a thick mustache and grew increasingly less tolerant with us kids. The hair on her head thinned and she began to wear it in a bob. Her voice became lower and lower, until she sounded like Tennessee Ernie Ford. I thought she was changing into a man. I know now she had probably just gone through menopause.

Across the street from Calvin was Charles Bussey, probably the first Negro deputy sheriff of Pulaski County. He often talked to us at school about fighting crime and passed out badges, making us junior deputies.

Then there was the Martin family. There were 12 children, some of whom I knew well. Dwight, who was my age and in my grade, sometimes took me to his mother's beauty shop near their house. Some of the kids were much older than I was and forgettable, but two had movie star names: Ilga Martin and Yuri Kay Martin. Yuri Kay looked like a young model. Dwight's father was seldom home, always working. Dwight and I never discussed his father's occupation.

Mrs. Quick, my third grade teacher at Capitol Hill, lived with her husband and daughter, Fay Helen, on the corner of 20th and Cross. She

The Fang family was notable because the entire family was considered blue vein, meaning they were high yellow in skin color. There were two beautiful daughters, including Eleanor, who was in my grade. She had little to do with me other than speak; my skin was far too dark. A junk 1938 Plymouth sedan sat in their front yard.

The Morgan family lived across the street from Mrs. Davis. By most accounts, this was just your normal family except for the nicknames assigned to the male siblings. The nicknaming sequence went in descending order from the eldest male: Man, Big Man, Little Man, Toot Man and, finally, Root Man. Man was my age and in my class at school.

The Smith family, Bill and Maytee and their children, lived next door to me during this time. There were at least seven kids in their home. They were like my second family. I often attended their church, Rose of Sharon Baptist Church, at 14th and Cross with them. I especially enjoyed the Sunday night religious movies. The eldest son had been wounded in the Korean War and suffered from shell shock, now called Post Traumatic Stress Disorder. The other son, Ozzie, or O.Z. for short, was handsome and popular with the young ladies.

Mr. Bill was like a father to me. Sometimes I was able to help him repair his car. His wife, Miss Maytee, was a petite yellow woman who wore glasses and spoke very slowly. She was a housewife and mother who cooked very delicious meals. Therefore, I ate there whenever I could.

The Smith's house had a very large crawl space. In fact, it was larger than the basement apartment I lived in. Mr. Bill had lots of stuff stored there. The crawl space was dark, cool and a great location for a summer tête-à-tête. Nancy, my favorite Smith, was one year younger than I was. She was tall, slim and beautiful. We spent many interesting moments in the crawl space. Nancy unilaterally declared herself my girlfriend; I did not protest. As such, we had invitations to play doctor, which we did often. One day, Nancy said, "Let's do what Oridell, my older sister, and her boyfriend do."

"What's that?" I asked.

"You just do what I say, ok?"

"Ok."

Nancy lay on the ground beside some cardboard boxes. She said, "Get on top of me, Ok?"

I did. "Now what," I asked.

"Talk to me."

"Where did you learn this?"

"My sister Amy and I sneaked and watched my sister Oridell and her boyfriend doing this in the back seat of his car."

"In the Buick?" I asked.

"Yes, Then she'd go in the house. You're supposed to move around on me. And talk to me."

"Ok. But I really don't know what to say."

We performed these simulated sex acts many times. I was not sure what I was supposed to experience. However, I enjoyed it a lot. Soon Nancy was kissing me on the lips. I enjoyed that, too. That was as far as it went. These episodes reminded me of my original play doctor partner, Linda Ann Moses, my neighbor at my mother's house on West 12th Street.

In the late summer of 1951, I started fifth grade. My homeroom teacher was Miss Jackson, a music teacher who played the piano. She was also my music teacher. As such, she taught my music class to sing numerous patriotic and traditional songs. Two of my favorite songs were *Home on the Range* and *Little Liza Jane*.

Etta B. Wheeler, a fellow student in my music class, had a beautiful singing voice and played the piano. She was an attractive fifth grader, with brown skin, big bright eyes, pearly white teeth and a shape that made all the boys take notice. Sometimes, Miss Jackson let Etta lead and accompany us in song. I had a crush on her that lasted through high school.

That school year, I was chosen to be one of the two projectionists for Gibbs Elementary School. In this position, I had the opportunity to set up and operate a Bell and Howell 16mm sound projector in classrooms from first through sixth grades. I knew how to thread and splice film, maintain the loop and focus, synchronize the sound, change bulbs and rewind the film. Other students looked up to me. This experience was the highlight of the fifth grade.

In the summer before school started, a very attractive divorcee moved to the apartment building at 20th and Ringo. She had two cute daughters, Janice and Gloria Berry. Janice was in my fifth grade class and Gloria was a grade behind. Since we lived just one block apart, Janice often asked me to carry her books after school to her apartment. During one of these missions, Janice opened one of her books and took out a Dagwood and Blondie eight page. An eight page was a two-inch wide by seven-inch long, short eight-page pornographic comic, usually portraying popular characters. This was the first one I had ever seen, which piqued my interest and amazed Janice. In time, she showed me several more, including the pornographic adventures of Popeye and Olive Oyl, and Tubby and Little

Lulu. She never told me where she got them.

Janice who was one year older than I was and already having sex with guys in their mid-teens. She often demanded that I have sex with her. I was both naïve and scared to have real sex. Because of my reluctance, she called me a little wimp with no balls.

A three-foot-wide drainage ditch bisected the block between Janice's house and mine. One time Janice lured me into the part of the ditch that ran beneath Ringo Street. She showed me her genitalia, which she called the black cat. She then told me to feed the cat. She was so aggressive, I literally froze. She jumped up, shouted some expletives at me, and left in a huff.

Janice told her sister, Gloria, of my reluctance to have sex with her. Gloria told me about that conversation and was sympathetic in my favor. She told me to forget her sister because she was a whore. Gloria also told me that she was in love with me and would have sex with me whenever I was ready. For the rest of the school year, she was my unofficial girlfriend. When school was out, Janice, Gloria and their mother left town. I never saw or heard from any of them again. I really missed Gloria.

The remainder of fifth grade was routine and unremarkable. My sister and I returned to full-time daycare with Mrs. Davis in the summer of 1952. The routine there was essentially the same as before, except I spent a lot of time exploring the nearby large drainage ditch and the branch library at 16th and High Streets.

The large ditch was open from Wright Ave and ran south parallel to High Street for about a mile and a half. The smaller ditch, which was directly behind near my aunt's apartment, was a tributary to a larger ditch three blocks away. Toni Faye, a new girl my age, had just moved across the street from Mrs. Davis. Toni was a cute, brown-skinned young lady who had a blend of moves and personalities to equal those of a burlesque performer, exotic dancer and stripper rolled into one. She was my constant companion, whether I was digging for worms (for sale) or exploring the big ditch. The ditch was her stage and she was the consummate actor. I could appreciate her talents because her amateur performances were better than the professional burlesque queens I had seen illegally at the Gem Theater. Our relationship was very platonic.

The library was my favorite respite. It was the only library in Little Rock that was open to Negro patrons. It was just a short walk or bike ride away for me. I was a prolific reader, so I was there often. The librarians there knew me very well and gave me access to the back storage room where out-of-circulation books and outdated magazines were kept. My favorite magazines were *Boys' Life*, *Popular Science*, *Popular Mechanix* and *Mechanics Illustrated*. In the storage room, I had access to editions dating back to 1940, and I read them all. I read the entire Boy Book series, which included titles like *Boy Magician*, *Boy Salesman*, *Boy Scientist* and others. I read the Inventors series, including books about Thomas Edison and Eli Whitney. I also read books describing how the Erie and Panama canals were built.

My uncle owned three cars during the Allan Jones years: a 1939 Plymouth, a 1947 Hudson and a 1941 Chevrolet. The Plymouth was in poor condition and seldom started. Eventually, its engine just quit. The Hudson, a black four-door sedan was the best car my uncle ever had. It was smooth riding and had a great radio and heater. One night, after driving home drunk, my uncle parked the car on our Ringo Street hill. He failed to turn the front wheels into the curb, leave the car in gear or apply the emergency brake. By the time my uncle staggered to the front door, the Hudson had rolled down the hill, veered across the street, jumped the opposite curb and rolled over down a four-foot embankment into the back yard of the Scribners, nearly a block away. The car was destroyed.

I was a passenger in my uncle's Chevrolet during a family trip to Dermott to visit a great uncle and cousins. It was my second trip; my first was by train. My aunt and uncle rode in the front seat. My sister and I were in the back. The muffler was leaking profusely. As a result, my sister and I suffered severe headaches and nausea from carbon monoxide poisoning. By the time we reached Dermott, 110 miles away, we were zombies. My aunt and uncle did not appear to be affected.

I spent most of my time this trip talking to family, including the patriarch, Uncle Garland, and my many cousins. There was not much for Negroes to do there. There was one black juke joint and a movie theater that allowed Negroes to enter through a side door and sit in the balcony. After exploring Uncle Garland's huge farm, which had everything needed for survival, including a well, outhouse and animals, the next best pastime was eating bountiful meals. My favorite food during this trip was the homemade biscuits made by Uncle Garland's wife. They were huge and weighed a ton, but tasted great with butter and syrup.

During one of these big family-reunion type meals on Sunday after church, Uncle Garland's neighbor and his daughter joined us. The daughter was my age, tall, endowed and beautiful. Her eyes were green, her skin was yellow and her name was Mary Pillar. When our eyes met, they locked in stare. Finally, after our meal, I went over to talk to her. She said she was part Creole. I never saw, and we never talked about, her mother. She told me her dad kept a very short leash on her in public, seldom letting her out of his sight. However, she said things were quite different at home. After I found out where she lived, I understood. She and her dad were Uncle Garland's closest neighbors; they lived two miles due north along a narrow trail, very isolated and protected.

Mary said, "Dad and I will be leaving here to go home soon. I will take off my Sunday clothes and meet you at the wood line in one hour. My father never looks for me at home. If you start walking after we leave, you should be there by then. Are you coming?"

"I think so. I have no idea when my uncle is leaving."

"I've never met a guy from a big city like Little Rock. We can talk and walk in the woods. I know lots of secret places. I'll wait for you. See you later."

Mary and her dad departed for home within minutes of our conversation. Before I could sneak away and start the two-mile trek to Mary's wood line, my uncle told my sister and me to get in the car because we were leaving in 30 minutes. There were no phones, so I told one of my cousins to tell Mary the next time he saw her that I had to leave, that I would see her the next time I came to Dermott. I never returned to Dermott. I never saw Mary Pillar again.

We started back home and drove through McGehee, Gould, Pine Bluff and stopped in Sweet Home. My uncle had taken ill and could no longer drive. He stopped at a filling station, bought some gas and asked to use the bathroom. He was refused. He threw up on the highway. My sister and I were sick again from the leaky muffler, and I assumed my uncle was sick from it, too. My uncle was too sick to drive, and my aunt did not know how. My uncle asked several of the white men there to drive him to a hospital. They all refused.

My uncle managed somehow to drive the Chevy up the highway about a half mile to a country store. A white man there drove all of us, at my uncle's direction, to Missouri Pacific Hospital in Little Rock. Later that evening, my aunt, my sister and I took a cab home. My uncle was not suffering from carbon monoxide poisoning as my sister and I were, but had an ulcerated stomach (called a bleeding ulcer today) which required an operation to save his life. He had a successful operation.

Finally, fifth grade was over. One afternoon during the early summer of 1953, Allan Jones just walked up, as I expected. "You ready to work, Joe?" he asked. "I'm ready to make money," I answered with excitement. "Meet me at 7 a.m. tomorrow at my place," he said. "Ok," I said in reply.

The next morning I walked to Allan's shack and arrived ahead of schedule. Everything looked the same as it did the previous summer when we closed the mowing season. However, all implements had been cleaned, oiled, sharpened and, if necessary, repaired. Allan pre-positioned some equipment near my neighborhood. Again, our first customer was Dr. Woods. The customer circuit was the same as the previous year.

Allan was precisely the same as before. I learned nothing new about him. It was all déjà vu. We learned to work even more efficiently together and were able to complete jobs significantly faster than the previous year. Because of my work with Allan, the summer passed very quickly, and we parted company for the second season. We exchanged our pleasantries, and we simply understood that next year we would do it all over again. I looked forward to the sixth grade, which was the final year of elementary school.

Sixth grade turned out to be the most interesting in elementary school. I was in the homeroom of Mr. Clarence Leonard Horn, my favorite teacher at the time. I knew more about him than any other teacher to date; I knew where he lived, met his wife and knew his kids, Clarence, Jr. and Dana LaJoyce. He drove a black 1938 Chevrolet the entire school year.

I still remember some of the room's layout. Facing Mr. Horn were six columns of desks, five rows deep. I sat on the leftmost column next to the windows. My seat was fourth from the front; in front of mé sat Robert House, Cleo Graggs and Terrence Roberts. We were the smartest in the class and known as the Four Musketeers. Behind me sat Betty O'Connor, a girl even more beautiful than Dorothy Dandridge. Although she was skinny, she had the potential to be a model. She had the attributes that most Negroes coveted at the time: thin lips, very fair skin, naturally straight hair, a sharp thin nose, dimples, light eyes and high cheekbones. All the boys tried to curry favor with Betty, and I was no exception. For some reason, she courted my friendship. It was probably because I always helped her with her schoolwork. Betty was beautiful but not likely to win any scholarships. She knew her limitations.

She usually wore wide skirts supported by many petticoats, probably because it made her look bigger. Her offer to me was to let me "count her petticoats" in our private moments. On two occasions, I tried to create these private moments. One day after school, we planned to go to an abandoned house across the street from Gibbs Elementary. That day, Betty wore a wide black skirt with a pocket, white blouse and bobby socks.

After school, we walked across the street and entered the house. Betty immediately leaned against a wall in submission. Before I started any "counting," I noticed something terribly wrong. I heard the hissing and smelled the pungent odor of escaping natural gas. Betty was completely oblivious. I grabbed her by the arm and pulled her out of the house. "What's wrong? We have time. I don't have to…"

"Don't you smell that gas? This place could blow any minute!" I yelled, as I dragged her outside.

I ran back into the house to grab our books and discovered the source of the leak, a broken pipe. We had no backup plan, so we started walking slowly towards Betty's house, which was only four blocks from school. On the way, we concocted other plans, but nothing seemed viable because Betty was under scrutiny and supervision of her mother, father and older brother, Donald.

I often visited Betty at her home near 15th and Chester. While sitting on her front porch one dark summer night in 1953, we hatched one final plan. When her parents went into the house for the night, she was supposed to sneak away to the rear of the community center a half block away. I left early so there would be no reason for her parents not to go into the house. I waited at the rear of the community center for an hour. There was no sign of Betty. I went back within earshot of her house where I could still hear her parents' voices. After another half hour of waiting, I gave up and walked home. The next day, Betty told me her parents sat on the porch until very late and made her go inside with them.

I do not remember the names of any other students in my sixth grade class. I do remember one of the main tenets of Mr. Horn's philosophy: argue your point of view until you are decisively proven wrong, and then gracefully concede. This was his concept of critical thinking. He introduced his students to the ancient philosophers, such as Plato and Aristotle. He taught us about ancient history, including the civilizations of the Egyptians and Phoenicians and the Seven Wonders of the Old World.

Mr. Horn led us through many experiments in physical science. We had a science kit which let us recreate experiments that were first performed by Volta, Faraday and Telsa. He led us through spirited discussions about the consequences and aftermath of World War II and the Korean War; about the international politics of India and Berlin; and about the local perils of Jim Crow and segregation in Little Rock. In short, he did more to help me develop into an excellent student and prepare me for seventh grade and high school than any other teacher.

There were two occasions when my uncle, Brother Albert, and I spent the entire day together sharing personal time. The first was my one-and-only fishing trip with him. Early in the morning, we gathered two cane fishing poles, some line, and several hooks and dug enough worms and moist soil to fill a quart canning jar. My uncle had no car at the time so we caught the Oak Forest city bus and disembarked near the end of the line on Fair Park Boulevard. We walked about a mile to a small lake, where we spent the day talking and fishing. At the end of the day, I had caught one small fish; my uncle caught none. My fish was so small that it should have been thrown back into the lake, but since it was my first catch, I brought it home anyway. Just before dark, we caught the bus back home. The next day I threw the fish away. It was simply too small.

The other was my only experience as a cotton picker. My uncle wanted to teach me how to earn money picking cotton. Most Negroes of the era were experienced cotton pickers and choppers. To my uncle, learning to pick was a rite of passage that all young men should experience and I was no exception. We met the bus that would take us to the cotton fields at a local church. My uncle and I, along with about 30 others, boarded an old school bus and rode across the bridge through North Little Rock to a small rural town call Cotton Plant, Arkansas. There, I surveyed the endless rows of cotton that dotted the landscape. My uncle gave me some interesting statistics: An experienced, motivated male cotton picker could pick as much as 300 pounds a day under ideal conditions; he could routinely pick between 150 and 200 pounds daily. I could expect to pick as much as 100 pounds my first time out.

Some of the men moved at breakneck speed, snatching the cotton from the stalk and stuffing it in a single motion into a long burlap sack that they dragged along the ground. I wondered how long these men could continue to work like machines in the withering, shadeless summer heat. Some did so for the full 12 hours we were there, taking time only to drink water and relieve themselves without leaving the cotton rows. At the end of the day, several men had picked 300 pounds; most were between 150 and 200 pounds. Everyone, including several ladies and one kid, a couple of years older than me, picked at least 100 pounds. My all day effort tipped the scales at a disappointing 38 pounds. I do not remember how much we were paid, but I think we earned ten cents a pound.

On the trip back, the bus wreaked of human sweat. A few people were sleeping, but most were in a festive mood singing spirituals. A few said they would be on the bus again the next day. I knew I would not be. I learned from these two experiences that neither fishing nor picking cotton would be my vocation. I knew I had to learn other skills that offered greater financial potential.

I looked forward to continuing my joint venture with Allan Jones; I counted the money in advance, twenty to forty dollars a week. When he had not made preliminary contact with me by the first week of June 1953, I became concerned. I rode my bike out to his shack. To my chagrin, the entire shack and Allan's mowing implements were gone without a trace. The station attendants at the Esso Filling Station said the shack had been gone for some time, but no one knew what happened to Allan. I assumed he had died and the city cremated his body. He told me he had no relatives. Even today, I wish I could have told him goodbye.

I thought about trying to service Allan's customers. But the reality was I had no equipment or help. I simply could not do it alone. As a result, the summer of 1953 was a complete bust for me. I was able to earn little money. Nothing was the same after Allan. Furthermore, I never got those private moments with Betty O'Connor. She and her family moved to Chicago that summer; so did Robert House. I never saw or heard from them again. Then Milton Barnett Smith went to Detroit for the summer. Dispirited, I was left to contemplate starting seventh grade in September at Dunbar High School.

Without Allan, I had lots of time to look at my life up to now and the lives of those around me. I realized for the first time that my uncle, Brother Albert to me, was addicted to alcohol. In a very short time, I witnessed it ruin his life. His job with Missouri Pacific Railroad was one of the best a Negro man could expect in the 1940s and 1950s. He eventually lost this job due to the effects of alcoholism, including tardiness, absenteeism and safety violations at work. Even the powerful union could not save his job. Then I remembered several other incidents that foretold his demise. On numerous occasions, someone would stop by our house and tell my aunt that my uncle was lying prostrate in the street outside a watering hole at 15th and Pulaski Streets. My aunt always hailed a cab and retrieved him.

One night someone stopped by to tell my aunt that my uncle was drunk and had walked into the street near the intersection at Wright Avenue and High Street and been hit by a car. He was still on the side of the road when my aunt arrived. My uncle's left leg was broken and was not set properly, leaving his leg severely bowed. He walked with a limp the rest of his life. By the time we moved from the basement apartment at 21st and Ringo in the summer of 1953, my uncle had been relegated to a shoeshine boy in a white barber shop.

When I thought about my uncle's shoeshine stand in the barbershop (which he did not own), I thought about my first experience with a real barbershop after I came to live with my aunt. Prior to that, my mother cut my hair with old manual clippers or I patronized the Barber and Beauty School on West 9th Street. My first journeyman barber was an old gentleman named Mr. Black, who was hearing impaired and walked with a severe limp. He ran a one-man barbershop located at Wright Avenue and High Streets. His shop had a shoeshine stand that was never manned. My first haircut was on a Saturday morning and cost twenty-five cents. In time, I started going to Woods Barber and Beauty Shop at 16th and High Streets. This shop was much bigger, newer and classier, but did not have a shoeshine stand. A cut here initially cost thirty-five cents, then fifty cents and finally, seventy-five cents. The shops had a few things in common: old men sitting around playing checkers, cards and dominoes, exchanging salacious gossip and solving local political problems.

That summer, I also had time to reminisce about Milton, who lived upstairs in the big house with his mother, Miss Hazel; his aunt, Juanita (Aunt Nee-nee to him); and his grandmother, Mrs. Josie. His mother sang in her church choir. Sometimes she rehearsed gospel songs on their front porch or in the car while Milton and I listened. My favorite song she sang was *Satisfied*. The family always had a very nice car, usually a top-of-the-line Chrysler.

Milton often felt sorry for me, especially when he saw me eating one of my staple foods, salad dressing sandwiches seasoned with black pepper. He often invited me upstairs to his room, where he had his own radio. We would listen to the top radio shows of the day, including *The Shadow, Lone Ranger, Crime Busters* and one of my favorites, *Straight Arrow*, sponsored by Nabisco. I cannot forget this commercial, which aired as a voice-over with thundering Indian drums in the background:

N-a-b-i-s-c-o

Nabisco is the name to know.

For a breakfast, you should eat

Nabisco Shredded Wheat!

Many times Milton took me with him to his Aunt Juanita's (Aunt Nee-Nee to him) College Grill, located at 15th and High Streets, directly across the street from Arkansas Baptist College. There, I ate all the hamburgers, cheeseburgers and chips I could and drank all the soda I wanted. Those were the good times. Now Milton was in Detroit on summer vacation.

While he was gone, we moved to a detached house at 1005 Wright Avenue, just three and one-half blocks away. However, the impact was the same as if it were three and one-half miles away. Milton never invited me to his house again, and he never came to mine. The Allan Jones years were gone forever.

4

Dunbar High School Years – Bridge to Pegasus

The distance between main entranceways was no more than one hundred yards. However, the activities inside Gibbs Elementary School and Dunbar High School seemed worlds apart. It was 1953, and I had graduated from sixth grade at Gibbs in the spring and just started seventh grade the fall semester at Dunbar. There were no kindergarten or middle schools at the time, so grade levels ran from one through six at Gibbs and seven through twelve at Dunbar.

Although I had walked and played around Dunbar, I was still astounded by the sheer size of the school once inside. Then there were the things I did not have at Gibbs, including the thousands of student lockers, a huge cafeteria, health room, a dedicated library, auditorium and gymnasium, hundreds of teachers and two deans, one each for boys and girls.

Dunbar had a robust industrial arts and trade curriculum where students learned numerous skills, including short courses in woodworking, electricity, metalworking and plumbing. There were formal courses in 1) automotive mechanics, supported by a complete automotive repair shop; 2) trade printing, supported by a complete print shop, which printed the school newspaper; 3) trade laundry, supported by a complete commercial laundry facility; 4) bricklaying, supported by a complete bricklaying shop;

and 5) carpentry, which was supported by a framing shop.

In addition to great teachers, the school had a marching band and competitive basketball, football, and track teams. I was proud to be a student at Paul Lawrence Dunbar High School, by all accounts the best Negro high school in Arkansas.

One of my immediate aspirations was to be a member of the marching band. I wanted to be one of the snare drummers, who helped the band march in perfect cadence. I imagined myself proudly strutting to the beat in the purple and gold uniform with the reversible breastplate, one side purple and the other gold. I saw myself participating in the amazing band festivals that Dunbar hosted and traveling with the football team and performing at out-of-town football games. I dreamed of performing at local games, parades up Main Street and down West 9th Street and other events, drawing admiration from the girls. However, all of that was just my imagination in hyper drive, and soon reality prevailed. I could not afford to rent or buy a snare drum; in fact, I could not afford to purchase drumsticks or a drum pad to practice. I did not even have the money to buy a flutophone, the primer for all beginning music students.

However, not all was lost; I settled for a music course, which was music appreciation, especially classical music. The course was dull at the start, until Mr. Ransom, who became one of my favorite teachers at Dunbar, found a way to get my attention. He explained that numerous television shows and movies had classical music as themes. One day in class, he went to the piano, played the Lone Ranger's theme song (from radio, TV and the movies), and looked straight at me. Of course, he knew the *Lone Ranger* was one of my favorite shows. He said, "The *Lone Ranger* theme is only a small portion of the *William Tell Overture*, which is the overture to the opera *William Tell* composed by Rossini." Another day, he played the theme to Dragnet. I was hooked. I made an A in the course.

Industrial arts was a mandatory program for boys, which was one school year in duration. Each subject, such as woodworking or metalworking, was one six-week marking period long. My favorite among those subjects was electricity. Mr. Arthur Fox, who was two years from retirement, was the instructor, and he quickly became my favorite industrial arts teacher. He had an unusual way of teaching us the principles of resistance and grounds. He preceded his demonstration with this warning, "Please don't ever attempt this. It can kill you!" Next, he plugged a pig-tailed extension cord into a live room receptacle. He asked a student to measure the voltage at the receptacle, which measured 110 volts. Then, he attached the pigtails to the binding post of a light bulb we used for experiments. The bulb illuminated. We knew the extension cord was live. Then he really startled us. He grabbed the pigtails barehanded, one in each hand. With 110 volts flowing through his body, he should have been dead.

He knew he had our attention, so he began to explain, "I've done this many times. I know the resistance of my body. My palms and fingers are dry. My feet are in rubber-soled shoes, insulating me from ground. Therefore, my body offers very high resistance, and I can do this safely. If you provide a circuit to ground because of wet hands, body, or feet, you are dead!" Because of his demonstration, I have never forgotten the practical concepts of voltage, resistance and grounds, which was a primer on Ohms Law. Mr. Fox was the inspiration for me to excel in the principles of electricity and electronics. He gave me an electricity book from his library that I kept for over forty years. I visited him at home several times after he retired; he was still the teacher, and I his inquisitive student.

I had been working at the station since the summer, when I began my second year at Dunbar. Finally, I had a steady source of income. I could now purchase or rent that coveted snare drum or anything else, it seemed. Now that I had to work every day after school, I could not attend band practice, even if I made the band. In addition, I had missed that all-important first year of band preparation. I had a new goal; I enrolled in Trade Automotive Mechanics. Participating in that program in parallel with my filling station job could make me a master mechanic by the time I graduated from high school, I reasoned.

Mr. Cullens, a Billy Eckstine look-alike, wore designer-style suits during lectures and neat blue coveralls during demonstrations and practical exercises. The huge auto repair facility, located in the back of the school, rivaled any of the local commercial auto repair shops in Little Rock. After a year in the program, we could bring in personal repair jobs, but cars could dwell in a bay for no longer than one week, and we had to generate an approved diagnosis and repair plan before any work began. Mr. Cullens was a stickler for cleanliness and orderliness. He expected repairs to be done in accordance with the relevant *Chilton's Repair Manual* and within the time schedule set forth in *The Flat Rate Manual*.

I really excelled and thrived in this informal work-study program and expected to receive my certificate of completion after four years in the program. However, Mr. Cullens received a lucrative offer to teach students in Africa. He accepted the offer and resigned at the end of my ninth grade school year. The Pulaski County Board of Education did not replace Mr. Cullens and the automotive repair training facility at Dunbar was closed. The BOE did not reinstate the program during my tenure at Dunbar.

However, I still had the job at the filling station.

The high school caste system at Dunbar was obvious, even to new seventh graders, like me. Respect, influence and privilege rose with grade and floor level. For example, seventh grade homerooms were on the first floor and the higher grades (eight through twelve) homerooms were dispersed throughout the upper floors, second through fourth. Social skills at the school ranged from immature seventh graders, who acted like sixth graders or lower, all the way to some twelfth graders who were twenty-one-year-old adults, legal in all aspects. I also noticed that some students, regardless of grade (well-dressed, handsome young men and beautiful young ladies) were granted accolades, toleration and acceptance from teachers, staff and students, which eluded most of us.

The majorettes and homecoming queens were unconditionally beautiful and treated like royalty. The majorettes were a bevy of sexy, baton-twirling, strutting young ladies, who performed in front of the marching band. However, the real first student young lady and Queen of Dunbar, by all accounts, was Millicent Clayborne, a bishop's daughter. She was a fair-skinned beauty with the stride, strut and head-turning quotient of a movie star, like Dorothy Dandridge then or Halle Berry now. What set Millicent apart from other girls was that she projected class. Most of us did not understand class, but we knew she had it.

In addition, there was her prince, Pellester Hollingsworth, who was similar in appeal to Harry Belafonte then or Terrence Howard now. They strolled the corridors and campus, hand-in-hand and cheek-to-cheek, drawing favorable comments from teachers and students. They were the royal couple of Dunbar living a fairy-tale life. I fantasized how great it would be if I could switch places with Pellester just for a day. I imagined how sweet life could be now if Betty O'Connor had not left town and we were a power couple like Millicent and Pellester. Then quickly the fantasy faded; I did not have the wherewithal to support such a dream.

Mrs. Dozier, a pert, pretty, sexy, well-dressed lady in her thirties, was my first homeroom teacher at Dunbar. I was elected homeroom president for both seventh and eighth grades, and Carolyn Porter was elected homeroom vice-president for both grades. The president's duties included taking attendance and leading the class through the Pledge of Allegiance. Both duties required me to stand in front of the class, which I hated. The clothes I wore were not in vogue; they were awful. They had some unique feature that was characteristic only to that piece of clothing.

For example, the only pair of blue jeans I owned had an external patch grafted to the right inner pant leg to cover a jagged hole; another pair of pants was far too short. I had two shirts that had repaired rips, which were highly visible. My fellow students quickly recognized the extent of my meager wardrobe. I often wished I had just one pair of new jeans. That way, if I wore jeans for three weeks straight, students would not know whether I had just one pair or multiple pairs of the same jeans. I was embarrassed, but I soldiered on with my morning duties. I knew soon my cash flow would improve. I had the job at the filling station.

Mrs. Alice Seville Bush, who lived in a huge box house at 16th and Ringo Streets, was my English Literature teacher. She introduced me to literature appreciation. I was overwhelmed initially by the breadth and scope of her required reading list for the school year. Everything we read, books, poems, novels and short stories, required a mandatory in-class discussion and debate, plus a detailed book report according to her instructions. After a short while, my interest peaked, and I became a prolific reader of great literature. Even today, over half a century later, I still remember the great tragedies of Shakespeare: *Hamlet, Julius Caesar* and *Romeo and Juliet*; Sophocles' *Antigone*; *Evangeline* by Henry Wadsworth Longfellow; Phoebe Cary's great poem, *The Leak in the Dyke* and short stories by Washington Irving, including *Rip Van Winkle* and *The Legend of Sleepy Hollow*. I took a very interesting senior level literature course in college, but it was no match for the one Mrs. Bush taught. She was simply the best, one of my all-time favorites.

At Dunbar, I made some new and interesting friends. The remaining Four Musketeers, Terrence Roberts, Cleo Graggs and I moved from Gibbs to Dunbar together, each of us assigned to a different homeroom. Robert House left town after sixth grade. In homeroom, I met Mae Helen Coakley, who became my long-term, up and down, on and off, pseudo girlfriend for the next five years. She gave me my first wet passionate kiss, and she was the first girl to run her fingers through my hair. I also met Samuel Tenpenny, Herman Jones and Wayman Barnes, who became my enduring friends. LaVerne Lyles was a pretty young schoolmate, who lived on Howard Street just a few blocks from Terrence and Cleo. She quickly became buried in my psyche.

From the first through sixth grade, I was on what is now called the free and reduced lunch program. I brought a bag lunch from home, which was always ample until my mother died and I moved in with my aunt. At my aunt's, I never had enough to eat, especially for lunch at school. Often for lunch, I had peanut butter and jelly, mustard or salad dressing sandwiches. Social Services issued me a little red token, which I could redeem daily at lunchtime for two half pints of milk. Both my mother and aunt made me take them to school, so I could drink nutritious milk; it was good for my bones. I never did like milk and, besides, I was too embarrassed to let other students see me use these tokens, which signified I was poor. Therefore, I either gave or threw the tokens away.

In seventh grade, I was introduced to an informal work-for-lunch program in the school cafeteria. I was one of the students selected to work as a garbage man during one of the lunch shifts. My duties consisted of receiving students' dirty trays at the end of their meals and sorting the food discards into one garbage can. Paper products and milk cartons went into another. We placed silverware into a soaking tray, trays were stacked into a tray rack and glasses and cups were placed in custom racks, all of which were sent to the automated dishwashing machine. To facilitate a rapid recovery, renewal and re-issue of these compartmented metal trays, two students operated multiple receiving lines.

My teammate was usually Willis White, an affable but short student. Since I was tall and skinny, we were often called Mutt and Jeff, after the famous comic book characters. Other times, students just called us garbage men in a derogatory way. For my efforts, I earned a free all-I-could-eat school lunch replete with my favorite cornbread muffins and desserts. This program allowed me to eat my first institutional meal. For the first time, I ate all I wanted for lunch.

I was introduced to and inducted into the National Junior Honor Society at Dunbar and my peers in seventh grade elected me Student of the Month. My biggest accomplishment, however, was finishing second in a school-wide speech contest. My challenge was to research and write three three-minute speeches on my favorite actors.

One speech, chosen by drawing one of three numbers blindly from a cup, just seconds before speaking, was delivered in front of a live school auditorium audience (students, faculty, family and friends) and was judged on content, delivery and language, by the English Department. The speech, which was drawn for me, was number three, My Favorite Actor – Jack Webb, and was my worst. The other two were far better. Nonetheless, I delivered that speech with all the forcefulness I could muster. When the scores were tallied, I finished second overall behind Henrietta Yancy, a senior who earned an academic scholarship to Howard University. That was my first and last speech contest.

Dunbar was framed by two great student hangouts, Harris' Grocery Store, which was just across the street at the corner of Ringo Street and Wright Avenue and Bamboo Inn just seconds away on 18th Street. The grocery store was short on groceries, but it carried the products we wanted: soft drinks, candy, chips, gum, ice cream, pastries, cold sandwiches and cigarettes. More importantly, the store had two nickel-pinball machines and a nickel jukebox, which allowed us to play racy tunes like *Work with Me Annie*, *Annie Had a Baby* and *Sexy Ways*. These songs and their lyrics would be kindergarten fodder in today's Hip-Hop world. However, during my seventh, eighth and ninth grades, these songs were so risqué that they were not licensed for radio broadcast and were sold from under the counter.

Bamboo Inn was a tarpaper shack no more than 10 by 14 feet with no bathroom or wash facilities. After partitioning off a portion for a very small kitchen, there was room for only three very small tables. Therefore, it functioned primarily as a carryout. There was no jukebox and no soft drinks. The menu was extremely limited: a cup or bowl of beans, barbecue pork sandwiches and fried apple or peach pies. The food was the best in the world! The proprietor was a diminutive man who walked slowly with a very small shuffle. He got up at 3 a.m. on school days in order to have food ready for the morning crowd. He usually ran out of food shortly after noon and then shut down for the day. Although I loved the food, I knew the place was very unsanitary. I often saw roaches and rat droppings inside the establishment. I thought the Health Department would shut the place down because it was a health hazard. It never did.

As soon as I had twenty-five dollars for the security deposit, I went to Southwestern Bell, the local phone company, to apply for a home telephone. My aunt and uncle were socialized so long to existing without a home telephone that the status quo would never have changed without my intervention. I was always embarrassed when the guys talked about calling girls at night coordinating dates. When they looked at me, I had nothing to discuss. The guys did not know that I did not have a phone; they just thought I was stupid or did not like girls. The phone company approved my application and, within a week, I had a telephone and a telephone number: FRanklin 6-2245, or when dialing, FR 6-2245. And best of all, it was in my name. None of the other students, guys or gals, could make that boast. While the phone changed the way my aunt and uncle viewed the wired world, it produced no advantages for me during my remaining tenure at Dunbar.

The most dramatic encounter of my Dunbar years was my near fatal experience with spinal meningitis. The entire episode is described in detail in an upcoming chapter of this book.

During this time, I developed a strong interest in baseball, as a fan and potential player. As soon as I had access to a radio, I began listening to game broadcasts of the St. Louis Cardinals, the closest major league team to Little Rock. Harry Caray, the primary sportscaster, before he moved to the Chicago Cubs, captivated listeners the way he brought the aura of the game to our living rooms. In his distinctive style, he started one game with: "Hello, sport fans and welcome to beautiful Busch Stadium in St. Louis. It is a great night for baseball. This is Harry Caray, along with Joe Garagiola and Jack Buck, bringing you all the play-by-play action on the field. The lead-off hitter for the home team will be The Ripper, followed by The Redhead, The Man and The Moon," nicknames for Rip Repulski, Red Schoendienst, Stan Musial and Wally Moon, respectively.

Harry became my favorite sportscaster. I loved the way he dramatized the action when a Cardinal player hit a home run, "Swung on! That ball was well hit, it's going deep. Way back. It might be! It could be! It is a home run." I was disappointed when I saw a professional player hit a home run and how little time it took. The ball would be in the stands before Harry could finish his dialog.

The Cardinals became my favorite team because of proximity, but I also really liked the New York Giants and the Brooklyn Dodgers. Willie Mays, of the Giants, was my favorite player. I read his comic Books, which featured his feats as a power hitter at the plate and a patrolman in centerfield at the Polo Grounds. He was called Willie the Wonder and Amazing Mays. In the field, he always lost his hat, but always found and caught the fly ball. I liked Jackie Robinson, who often stole home, Pee Wee Reese and Duke Snider, who often climbed the centerfield wall at *Ebbets Field* chasing fly balls, of the Brooklyn Dodgers.

At the library, I spent hours reading and studying the hitting techniques of Mickey Mantle, Stan Musial and Ted Williams. I learned all aspects of the game because this was my game. I spent hours shadow rehearsing because I did not have a ball, bat or glove. I practiced stickball with a stick and a jack ball like Willie Mays. He became a great baseball player and I could, too, I reasoned. I just needed practice and perseverance.

I attended two professional ball games in Little Rock at Travelers Field, home of the Arkansas Travelers, a minor league team, Roy Campanella (catcher for the Brooklyn Dodgers) and the Touring Negro All-Stars and the Kansas City Monarchs (a Negro League Team), featuring Ernie Banks before he joined the Chicago Cubs. Ernie hit a home run. I saw in person how the game was played. Interestingly, both the All-Stars and the Monarchs travelled with their competing teams.

Meanwhile, I knew from memory, the managers, starting lineup and stadium names of all 16 major league teams. I could recite the field dimensions, seating capacities and owners of all the teams. I understood the Infield Fly Rule and the definition of a *Texas leaguer*, knew the purpose of a drag bunt and the provisions of the Ground Rule Double. I knew enough baseball rules, history and trivia to fill an encyclopedia. I learned plenty about major league baseball and its players from reading hundreds of articles written by my favorite sportswriter, Joe Reichler, and by watching the sports newsreels on *Movietone News at the movies*. When I was not working or reading about baseball, I headed to the sandlot. The closest one was a few blocks away, directly behind Saint Peter's Rock Church. I was ready to play ball.

I tried out for Little League. Since I had no money for fees or uniforms, I could not officially join a team. I also had no baseball equipment. However, those were the least of my problems. The real truth was I had no talent. The coaches gave me a glove and let me chase some fly balls in the outfield. I could not catch a fly ball, period. Those basket catches made famous by Willie Mays looked stupid when I attempted them. The coaches let me take batting practice, too. The results were the same. I simply could not hit a baseball. Light bat, heavy bat, fast ball, curve ball, junk ball, it was no hit, no cigar. After a dozen or so practices with sandlot and Little League teams, I recognized that I would never have the skills to be a baseball player. In time, I learned that I was not an athlete and lacked talent in any sport. I tried football, basketball, tennis, golf and swimming. I was not even coordinated enough to learn to dance.

By the end of my ninth grade school year, the Pulaski County Board of Education had built a new high school for Negro students and relegated Dunbar to a junior high school. In the fall of 1956, with considerable excitement, I started 10th grade at the new Horace Mann High School, which was located at McAlmont Street and Roosevelt Road.

5

St. Peter's Rock Baptist Church – Fire and Brimstone

Luke 16:10 – "Whoever can be trusted with very little can also be trusted with much, and whoever is dishonest with very little will also be dishonest with much."

From an unforgettable sermon at St. Peter's Rock Baptist Church. Under the shadow of Pegasus, I recalled this Bible verse whenever peers, coworkers or customers tried to persuade me to engage in petty theft of oil, gasoline, services or money while performing my duties at the filling station.

After the death of my mother in 1950, I attended First Missionary Baptist Church several more times, but eventually transitioned to my aunt's congregation at St. Peter's Rock Baptist Church, which had more influence on my life than any other religious institution. St. Peter's was located in a residential neighborhood in the middle of the block on West 18th Street. Although I never became a member, I attended regularly from 1950 to 1954, and sporadically after that, until I left Little Rock in 1962. This church provided an enduring template of what I expect a church to be, both architecturally and organizationally. The all-brick building had three levels from top to bottom: a balcony, sanctuary and fellowship hall. There was no parking lot, so cars parked on both sides of 18th for the entire block between Pulaski and High Streets. Directly behind the church was an unimproved baseball field that led to Wright Avenue, a block away.

St. Peter's Rock was a small Baptist Church with approximately 300 members. Usually about half of the members attended every Sunday except Easter Sunday, when more attended. Every adult member seemed to be an assistant pastor, choir member, usher, Sunday school teacher, elder, sexton, administrator, musician, prayer partner or trustee.

St. Peter's Rock differed from First Baptist in several ways: the secretary, Mrs. Nichols, read the minutes of the various church boards, budget targets and balances, and announcements each Sunday during the worship service. This church also had an organist, who was the pastor's wife, and a pianist, who was the wife of a church deacon. They simultaneously accompanied the choir, which was more lively and colorful to me than the one at my former church. The pastor, Reverend Doctor F.T. Evans, was more mobile and used every square foot of the pulpit while preaching, unlike Reverend Doctor Roland Smith of First Baptist, who was animated but more formal.

Reverend Evans always delivered an interesting and moving sermon, and even we kids in the balcony were spellbound. His sermons were entertaining but engaging and included singing, shouting, moaning, humming and yodeling. His volume, intensity and inflection varied wildly. A chorus of yeses, amens and alrights were sporadically uttered among the congregants. The torrid passages in his sermons often caused some people to shout. Ushers, who wore white gloves, black dresses and suits trimmed in white, carried the shouters, who were kicking and shaking or stiff as a board, from the sanctuary. I never witnessed shouting like that at my former church.

Near the end of his sermon, Reverend Evans would retreat to his study, which was to his right, just a few feet from the pulpit, where a deacon helped him into an overcoat and scarf, regardless of season. He always returned to finish his sermon. I never understood this ritual.

Tithing was another interesting point in the service. Deacons were in charge of collecting, counting and depositing tithes and other funds. Collecting tithes was routine; church patrons at the ushers' behest marched in front of the pews and dropped their tithing envelopes in a basket on a table manned by deacons. Collecting other funds was done in a less formal manner. There were many funds, such as the building fund, missionary fund, pastor's anniversary fund, and the Arkansas Baptist College fund. Often more than one fund had to be replenished on a given Sunday. The deacons were like carnival barkers, using many emotions to solicit funds until targets were met. Deacon Williams would say, for instance, "The building fund was scheduled to have $8000 on this Sunday. It's underfunded by $200.00. I'll start by placing $5.00 in the basket."

Other deacons, not to be outdone, would march up and match Deacon Williams' gift. Soon other members and visitors, as directed by the ushers, would march up to the front and place money in the basket. As soon as the target goal was met or exceeded, the deacons moved to the next fund. If the goal was not met, Deacon Williams would put additional money in the basket and start the process all over again. The posturing, cajoling and praying by the deacons went on until all the budget targets for that Sunday were fully funded.

Part of the closing portion of his sermon was an invitation to join the church. "The doors of the church are open," Reverend Evans would say. Deacons would place one, two or three chairs in front of the pulpit facing the congregation. "Is there someone who needs a church home? Please come now while the blood still flows warmly in your body." If one came, the pastor would solicit another. "Is there one more?" Meanwhile the choir was singing reverent hymns in the background. The pastor's eyes scanned the people in the congregation, pausing briefly on non-members, extending a nonverbal invitation to join. These invitations were sometimes quite lengthy. On one Sunday, four people became members.

After a person joined and gave testimony, he or she was turned over to the elders, who sat in a special part of the church. With the new member by their side, the elders sang, hummed, chanted and prayed. New members started receiving their church orientation and training immediately. They were recruited on the spot to be members of one or more church organizations.

During the Sunday sermon, the elders often sang, in the background, old spirituals and gospel songs a cappella, without cue. Usually, the rest of the congregation chimed in. Sometimes, depending on the mood of the church, the organist or the pianist or both accompanied the joyous noises.

After one sermon, I witnessed my first baptism, a Christian sacrament signifying spiritual rebirth and symbolized by immersion in water. There was a pool hidden under the pulpit floor where Reverend Evans and an associate pastor performed the baptismal ceremony. The candidate was offered prayers before and after being leaned backwards until submerged and quickly recovered. What amazed me the first time I saw it was how quickly the pool disappeared and the pulpit floor was reconstituted.

Although I never sang, I really enjoyed the adult choir. It was outstanding. My favorite choir member was Deacon Bryles, who sang bass. You always heard his voice no matter how loudly the choir sang. His voice was as deep and smooth as that of Chuck Barksdale, bass singer of the rhythm and blues group, the Dells. My favorite gospel song was "Yield Not to Temptation." The lyrics, in public domain, I still remember:

> Yield not to temptation, for yielding is sin;
> Each vict'ry will help you some other to win;
> Fight manfully onward, dark passions subdue;
> Look ever to Jesus, He'll carry you through.

> Shun evil companions, bad language disdain,
> God's name hold in rev'rence, nor take it in vain;
> Be thoughtful and earnest, kindhearted and true;
> Look ever to Jesus, He'll carry you through.

> To him that o'ercometh, God giveth a crown,
> Through faith we will conquer, though often cast down;
> He who is our Savior, our strength will renew;
> Look ever to Jesus, He'll carry you through.

> Refrain:

> Ask the Savior to help you,
> Comfort, strengthen, and keep you;
> He is willing to aid you,
> He will carry you through.

Deacon Bryles usually sang the refrain as a solo.

The sea of hand fans, used by the congregation below to keep cool, created an indelible image from the church balcony, where I usually sat. These fans, provided free of charge by funeral homes, were widely used in summer months before churches were air-conditioned. There was a religious picture on one side of the fan and the funeral home's advertising on the other. They were as ubiquitous as pew Bibles. The aerial view of abstract, undulating rhythmic patterns generated by fanning parishioners was a remarkable sight.

I never forgot Reverend Evans' short but memorable benediction.

"Having done our best we come down to the close of these services. We go back out into the world to battle the many problems there. May the Holy Spirit, grace of God, rest, rule and abide with us now, then and forever. Amen."

The church had two ordained associate pastors who assisted the pastor with services and performed in his absence as required: Reverend Scribner and Reverend Sams. Reverend Scribner's sermons were routine and forgettable. Some of Reverend Sams' sermons I still remember today, especially those based on the Apostle John's letters (Bible books John and Revelations) to Christians while he was exiled on the Isle of Patmos.

Reverend Evans' brother, who lived in Los Angeles, was also a preacher. He came to Little Rock to visit his brother and preach at St. Peter's once or twice a year. It was always a great event. He, too, was dynamic but different. I enjoyed his West Coast style, which included many throaty incantations during his sermons. Reverend Evans' brother, like all guest ministers who delivered sermons, received a love offering.

Reverend Evans and his family epitomized what I thought a church first family should be: elegant. I knew all of Reverend Evans' children: Timothy, Pratt, Paul, Lawrence, Robert and a daughter, Marilyn. They all played various roles in the church. Paul was my favorite. He had juvenile arthritis and, because of constant pain, developed a grotesque gait that was the envy of young males. We thought he was performing a cool bop and tried, mostly unsuccessfully, to emulate him. The reverend's wife was prim and proper, but affable to the congregation. She played the piano and the organ fluently.

The congregation bought the reverend a new car every three years. The first one I remember was a 1953 Oldsmobile 98, then a 1956 Cadillac, followed by new Cadillacs from then on. There was always a cross on a high visibility placard placed inside the windshield or attached to the license plate frame with the word CLERGY printed on the horizontal element, which allowed the reverend to park in specially designated clergy parking spaces. It also allowed him to double park or park in no-parking zones with impunity. Paul, one of Reverend Evans' sons, told me the cross also enabled his dad to bless his way out of several speeding tickets.

Going to church on Sunday was an all-day commitment if you attended all the services as shown. I still remember the schedule:

Sunday Morning Bible Study - 9 a.m.

Sunday School - 10 a.m.
Sunday Morning Worship Services - 11 a.m.

BYPU or Baptist Young People's Union - 5 p.m.
Sunday Youth Ministry - 5:00 p.m.

Sunday Evening Service - 6:00 p.m.

The morning service often lasted until 2 p.m. when we went downstairs to the fellowship hall for dinner. A youth minister concurrently conducted a children's church in the fellowship hall at 11 a.m. The church's program also included a mid-week Bible study, Tuesday night usher board meetings and Wednesday night choir meetings and rehearsals.

I regularly attended Sunday school, too. My class was held in the balcony of the sanctuary, and my teacher was Mrs. Washington, who was no kin to me. The most striking thing about her was her shiny gold tooth. She was not a disciplinarian like Mrs. Maxwell, my Sunday school teacher at First Baptist. She also did not require me to memorize Bible verses. Her husband was a church deacon and sexton who had sleepy turtle-like eyes. They had no children and lived only a block from the church. Their commute vehicle was an old black one-ton truck with a stake bed and dual rear tires, which Deacon Washington drove to church every Sunday.

There were some very interesting kids, including some of the pastor's children in my Sunday school class, but my favorite fellow student was Opal Jane Robinson, who was a nubile young woman. She was older and wiser than I was by a few years and tried to be a mother to me, but was really more like a sister. Before and after class, she shared some of her mature activities, including erotic exploits, with us. The stories she told made the rest of the class feel jealous and immature. Opal was well endowed and a little bigger than the rest of us and probably should have been in the young adult class. One of her statements, I never forgot:

"When my nature comes down on me, I am going to give it to somebody," she said. I was not sure exactly what she meant then. In time, though, I fully understood.

There were several things, even as a young teenager, which I did not like about St. Peter's Rock. Every Mother's Day, it was mandatory that I wear a white rose, which symbolized that my mother was no longer living. All the other kids (My sister only attended when my aunt did, which was not very often.) wore red roses; their mothers were living. I was embarrassed to be singled out. However, it was the rule: no exceptions.

Then we were constantly reminded of the wonderful status of race relations. Reverend Evans explained to us how far we had come and how good Negroes had life now. His message was to maintain the status quo, don't make waves, The Lord will make a way in his time. He reminded us of the dire consequences if we got out of our place. Then in August 1955, the Emmett Till story broke. A fourteen-year-old Negro boy wolf whistled at a white woman in a grocery store in Money, Mississippi. Till, a teen from Chicago, did not understand that he had broken the unwritten law of the Jim Crow South until three days later, when two white men dragged him from his bed in the dead of night, beat him brutally, then shot him in the head and threw his body into a river. The warnings from the pulpit became more intense: "Stop talking about trying to integrate lunch counters and for God's sake (Why his sake?) don't look at white girls or women. Please, keep your eyes on the ground and your hands and thoughts to yourself."

Why did all of this scare me? *I was the same age as Emmett Till.* I was progressive, as Mr. Horn, my sixth grade teacher taught me to be, but I was also pragmatic and realistic, as life taught me to be.

Then I noticed things that I did not expect to see in a church. Other young teens noticed them, too, because we discussed them. Christians were held to much higher standards than normal citizens. Churches, after all, are supposed to be perfect. However, St. Peter's Rock was like all churches: imperfect. I was disappointed to see factionalism and contentious, self-seeking groups within the church congregation; cronyism and partiality to long-standing friends, who were appointed to church positions of authority, regardless of their qualifications.

What I learned was that church bodies suffer the same frailties and sins of society in general; I just had the opportunity to learn that fact early in life. Still, St. Peter's Rock was my first real church home, and it will always be my standard of comparison for churches.

In retrospect, I realize that I was ordained to interface with Pegasus. St. Peter's Rock Church was a significant landmark on my way there. The church was my rock, literally, because it helped me establish my foundation of business ethics, integrity and honesty.

6

Mystery Illness – Spinal Meningitis

One spring morning in 1954, I woke up with an excruciating headache and loss of balance. I had no symptoms the previous night and, as usual planned to attend Sunday School and services at St. Peter's Rock Baptist Church. By early evening, I could not sit up in bed, let alone get out of it. The headache got worse and my sight was fading, too. Finally, my Aunt Babe took me by cab to a familiar place for diagnosis: University Hospital.

Once there, I was quickly admitted. By now, I had no visual acuity. I could only see bright yellow when my eyes were open and dark yellow when they were shut. The next morning several doctors surrounded my bed. They kept trying to get me to sit up in the bed. I could not do so. Even when aided, I still could not maintain my sitting balance.

Throughout the morning, I heard the doctors testing possible diagnoses, including polio or infantile paralysis. I was awake and aware, but the only sense that appeared intact was that of hearing. I could hear everything, but could respond to nothing. I could not move. I was aware that my aunt and uncle had visited me, then I lost track of the next three days. When I became lucid again, the white head physician, Doctor Brown, had a diagnosis for me - spinal meningitis.

I had never heard of this disease. "What is it and how did I get it?" I wondered. As days passed, I learned that the disease was extremely contagious and my room was quarantined. This explained why I had a private room and no visitors other than my aunt and uncle.

During my two-week hospital stay, I did not have a clock or watch, but I had an uncommon method of tracking time: my medication. Once I synchronized my medication with the noon meal, I had my equivalent clock. My medication consisted of four nickel-sized pills (I had no clue what they were.) and a penicillin shot every four hours around the clock. As a result, when the nurses came to administer my medication, I knew the approximate time. If I lost track of time, I resynchronized at the following noon meal.

The nurses, like Doctor Brown, were very friendly and reassuring. They quickly recognized that I was petrified at the thought of swallowing four huge pills. They crushed the pills into a glass of orange juice, stirred the solution, and coached me through the swallowing process. The nurses also helped me with the penicillin shots. Six times a day, I received a 10cc shot in my buttocks. They were nice enough to alternate cheeks and brought me crushed ice to help mitigate the pain and swelling from so many shots.

Over time, I continued to get better and stronger. I had many informative talks with Doctor Brown. He did not know how or where I contracted spinal meningitis. There was not another reported case of it anywhere in Arkansas.

Two weeks into my hospitalization, my vision had almost returned to normal. I had good depth perception, acuity and resolution. I had 20/20 vision in my left eye and about 20/60 in the right eye. Doctor Brown informed me that as soon as I could touch my chin to my chest and my spinal fluid was completely clear, I could go home.

Doctor Brown was very personable and informative. I learned from him that he had summoned my aunt and uncle to my bedside on two consecutive nights because I was not expected to live through the night on either occasion. My teachers and fellow students at Dunbar High School had been told that I was in a coma and would never be seen alive again. These events occurred during my lost or comatose days. Doctor Brown told me I had been in very critical condition and that he had fully expected me to die.

That explained why my teachers and fellow students sent me a huge three by four foot hand-made card. I was surprised by its size, but I was even more surprised by its huge inside heading, which in very large red letters read, not *Get Well Soon*, but *In Memoriam of Eddie J. Washington*. The card was very perplexing to me until I talked to Doctor Brown, then I understood. It was signed by over 300 people.

Touching my chest with my chin was easy at this point. However, this was the first time I had heard anything about spinal fluid. I did not know there was such fluid. The next day Doctor Brown repeated a procedure on me that he had performed numerous times during my hospitalization. He gave me a shot in the arm and after a few minutes had me bow my back until it was tight. Doctor Brown always told me he had his index finger pressing in the small of my back. He further instructed me to remain perfectly still and specifically warned me not to look back. In the past neither was a problem, because I did not have the strength or dexterity to move.

This procedure always felt like someone was sticking a very cold stainless steel knife into my back. It did not hurt, but it felt very cold and unusual. This time, however, I was much stronger and, of course, curious. My curiosity got the best of me. I looked back. What I saw left me frozen in fear. Doctor Brown had in his hand a hypodermic needle big enough to inoculate a rhinoceros. Fortunately, he had just completed the procedure.

Doctor Brown put this huge needle away and told me that he had performed another spinal tap and that I had to endure only one or two more before I would be released. My spinal fluid was virtually clear. The next day Doctor Brown performed the procedure again. This time he cautioned me to follow the rules. I did. I knew the sequence: local shot to numb the spinal tap, bow back, remain still, and don't look back. Doctor Brown drew the fluid once more. I survived. I knew why I had not looked back before: my neck did not have the rotational dexterity to do so. As things turned out, I had one more tap and I was released from the hospital.

After missing four weeks of the six-week grading period, I returned to resume eighth grade at Dunbar High. I was extremely glad to get back. One of the first girls I encountered, Adell White, looked at me, turned pale, and passed out. She had to be taken to the health room to recover. Quickly, I found out why. Since no students or teachers could visit me during my hospitalization, rumors became virtual facts. One rampant rumor had me dead. Some students heard my blood had turned to sugar; others heard my head had drawn backwards and locked against my spine.

After a few hours, everyone accepted the *miracle* of my return. In the two remaining weeks in the grading period, I made up all my tests and assignments and finished the six-week period with all Bs, which was enough to remain in the honor society.

Six weeks after my release, without warning, I started shedding my skin. Just like a snake, within two weeks, I shed my entire outer layer of skin, which was replaced by a new layer underneath the old one. My skin never shed again.

During my three-month check-up, I asked Doctor Brown about my skin. He had no explanation. He did tell me how close I came to dying and how lucky I was to be alive. He reminded me that in addition to the pills and shots that I also had IVs 24 hours a day, 7 days a week, one in each leg. Doctor Brown went on to explain that anything in my head, including my brain and eyes, that had made contact with my contaminated spinal fluid was destroyed. This may explain why my right eye never got better than 20/40. It has a star-shaped scar on the retina, which precluded normal vision. Everything else returned to normal. I weighed 103 pounds when I went into the hospital and 108 when I was released. I had one more check-up with Doctor Brown. After that, I never saw or heard from him again. That was also the last time I was ever in University Hospital.

7

West 9th Street – Commerce of Color

During the Pegasus period, West 9th Street was the largest cluster of Negro businesses in Little Rock. It was sometimes called Little Rock's Harlem. It was to Little Rock what Beale Street was to Memphis; what Bourbon Street was to New Orleans; and what South Central Avenue was to Los Angeles. It was two strip malls, seven blocks long, facing each other, separated by Ninth Street. Both sides of the street were lined with businesses, including physicians, lawyers, nightclubs, hotels, funeral homes, restaurants, liquor stores, pawnshops, churches, a theater, cab company, barber and beauty shops, a drug store, a newspaper, pool halls and others.

Ninth Street, framed by Perry's Night Club at its west end and the West 9th Street Cab Company at its east end, rode a wave of prosperity serving hungry airmen from the nearby air force base, entertainers, businessmen, and citizenry. Electric trolleys, which were part of the city's public transportation system, provided convenient access for patrons without cars.

West 9th Street Cab Company was the street's most visible export. The colorful cabs, with all-Negro drivers, crisscrossed the city. In fact, the entire visible management, including dispatchers and drivers, was Negro. Burl Mack, a driver for the company, was one of the station's long-time customers. The cab company also received attention because it was reminiscent of the Fresh Air Taxi Company portrayed on the Amos 'n' Andy show, the first television series with an all-Negro cast. The Amos Jones character, played by Alvin Childress, always maintained an impeccable uniform, neat and tidy office and professional conduct. I was transported in a West 9th Street cab twice to University Hospital, once with my mother when I received treatment for a large cut behind my ear and another time with my aunt when I received inpatient treatment for spinal meningitis. The Flamingo Club and Hotel was here. I was an underage teen when I sneaked in the club to witness an Ike and Tina Turner Revue. The Miller Hotel was here and accommodated many of the early rock and blues legends when they played this strip or at the Robinson Auditorium.

Fontaine's Tonsorial Parlor was here. He rode his Cushman motor scooter to work and parked it in the alley next to his shop. His wife drove a Cadillac, which I later serviced at the filling station. Allan Jones and I cut his home lawn regularly for two years. Professor Brasswell's grocery store was here. He also taught at Arkansas Baptist College, a Negro religious college. He lived on Chester Street, a half block from the filling station and was a regular customer. He always had a shoebox full of cash in the front seat when he came in for service. I never understood the box full of money, and I never asked.

L.C. Bates and his wife, Daisy, publishers of the local newspaper *Arkansas State Press,* had an office on Ninth Street. They were important figures in the Little Rock integration crisis in 1957. Daisy advised the Little Rock Nine when they enrolled in Central High School. They were regular customers at the filling station. I had long talks with both of them and learned a lot about prevailing social issues. Dr. Robinson, a family practitioner, a neighbor and customer, had an office here.

For a number of years, during the Philander Smith College period, I patronized the Barber and Beauty School at Ninth and Izard Streets for haircuts. The price ranged from fifteen to twenty-five cents.

I ate my first Mexican food here. It came from a tiny tamale stand that operated only during summer months. Tamales sold for two for a nickel. The soda jerk at Ninth and Gaines introduced me to Coca-Cola and root beer floats, which I still enjoy today. The floats sold for five cents each.

United Friends Hospital had an all-Negro staff but did not have a Ninth Street address. It was actually located on Tenth Street, a block away, but still in what I call the West 9th Street corridor. It was sometimes compared to the Howard University Hospital in Washington, DC. Because of its proximity, this hospital served middle and upper class Negroes with Ninth Street connections and the staff at Philander Smith College. Since this was not a free or public hospital, I never had the opportunity to be treated there. Like other poor Negroes and those on public assistance, I was relegated to University Hospital for medical care.

Of all the prosperous enterprises here, my favorite, by far, was the Gem Theater, which was the first movie theater I attended. Like other businesses, the visible staff was all Negro, including concession workers, projectionists and ushers. It was the only movie theater in town where Negroes watched movies (usually second-run white movies) with complete dignity. We had full access to all seating, water fountains, concession stand and bathrooms. I watched some of the all-time classics here, such as *The Day the Earth Stood Still*, *Imitation of Life*, *Samson and Delilah*, *The Ten Commandments* and *Gone with the Wind*; and I saw the great race comedies of Mantan Moreland and Pigmeat Markham.

As a kid, I also watched several late-night black burlesque shows here that included strip tease acts, which captured my full attention. The frontal nudity was full but brief; some of the strippers wore masks. Other times spotlights were turned off during full nude scenes. I was very nervous from fear of being caught during these shows because I was far too young to be there. With the help of a friendly usher, I sneaked in through an alley-side exit door. I have not seen a burlesque show since then.

I had my first car accident one summer night on Ninth Street. While driving my uncle's car west, just a few yards past the Gem Theater, I heard a slight unexplained noise. Nothing big it seemed, so I drove on. The next morning, my uncle noticed a small dent in the passenger-side rear fender. He drove drunk so often, he assumed he had an accident and drove off. I was not so sure. Therefore, I conducted a secret investigation. A quick inspection of the dent on my uncle's car revealed that the other car was white. Most of the cars parked on the street around the Gem seemed to always be there. I walked down to the Gem and found a white car parked approximately where I thought I heard a noise. The car's left rear fender had streaks of maroon paint – the same color as my uncle's 1946 Dodge. It was true. I had sideswiped a parked car and left the scene. If anyone noticed, they never reported it. I was fourteen years old and scared. I did not report it either! I did tell my uncle the truth. Two weeks later, he obliterated that fender in an accident with a tree.

One thing I learned from my activities on Ninth Street: When you mix the right portions of money, liquor and sex in close quarters, you create a concoction called crime. I saw many derelicts, winos and public drunks wandering up and down Ninth Street and loitering in the connecting side and back alleys. Some very visible drinkers tried to be inconspicuous by concealing their intoxicating beverages in brown paper bags.

Prostitutes serviced their johns standing in the shadows and in parked cars. The most famous hooker in the area was Good Love (clean version) Mary. She was normally very inebriated, in various stages of undress, and either lying or sitting in the alley next to the Gem Theater. I often heard her say, "Leave me alone! Somebody bring me some whiskey. Just bring whiskey." I saw men use and abuse her, violating her person in every way, including sodomy. I never saw her sober. I assumed at some point that she was sober enough to ply her trade and earn money. When I first met her, I saw what an attractive woman she could be if she cleaned herself up. However, over time, probably seven years, I noticed that some of her teeth were missing and her health was failing. Nevertheless, men continued to abuse her. I do not know what eventually happened to her.

Gambling was pervasive here, and there were no restrictions – kids just walked right into the middle of this wretchedness. Betting parlors were everywhere, in grocery stores, pawnshops, pool halls and even bathrooms. You could play the numbers, roll the bones (craps) or play poker. You could bet on baseball, usually the St. Louis Cardinals or the Brooklyn Dodgers. You could place off-track bets on the horses at the Hot Springs Racetrack and on the dogs at the West Memphis Track. Moreover, of course, you could play pool or checkers for wagers.

Although crime was rampant here, I personally was never a victim. I first visited Ninth Street during daylight hours when I was six years old. My destinations then were the soda jerk at Ninth and Gaines and the Gem Theater. I was always a little scared, so I was fully aware of my surroundings and ever vigilant, something I learned from James Cagney crime movies. The area was generally not patrolled by white cops, but by Negro cops walking the beat. I knew one of those police officers, Calvin Scribner. He was a neighbor of mine when I lived with my aunt on 21st Street. He was also the son of one of the associate pastors, Reverend Scribner, at St. Peter's Rock Baptist Church.

I learned a great lesson from observing the diverse group of blacks pursuing legal and illegal commerce here. First, I did not ever want to drink, gamble, smoke cigarettes or do drugs. And I never did. Secondly, if I ever had the opportunity to pursue a commercial venture, I would operate it not only profitably, but legally, ethically and morally. Later there would be two notable exceptions: I advanced my age by three years to obtain my driver's license and I received appropriated hot hubcaps after mine were stolen. Finally, despite all the heartrending, illegal and immoral scenes I witnessed, I learned that West 9th Street was a place where possibilities could become realities and dreams could come true. Dozens of successful businesses along this street, including the Tonsorial Parlor and movie theater, demonstrated what was possible and they all started with someone's dream.

8

Driver's License 1954 – Driving Illegally

One spring day in 1954, my uncle drove me to the Little Rock Office of the Department of Motor Vehicles so I could test for my driver's license. At the time, he owned a 1946 Dodge custom sedan with Fluid Drive, which would also be the vehicle used for my road test. We arrived early and I immediately sat for the written portion of the test.

I was completely familiar with the Driver's License Study Booklet, so I quickly finished the written part of the test. I turned it in to the test proctor, who was an Arkansas state trooper, went to the back of the waiting room, and sat down. He returned with my results in about ten minutes. I had answered every question correctly. He sent me outside to queue up for the road test, which was administered by a second state trooper who was an imposing, barrel-chested, huge man who seemed more suited for wrestling than police work

"Next," he said. Suddenly, it was my turn to deal with this man. We walked over to my uncle's Dodge and got in. I positioned myself as the driver and he as the passenger. He raised his clipboard and my heart skipped a beat.

"Are you ready for this, boy?" the trooper asked.

"I think so," I said nervously.

"What did you say, boy?" he asked, as if prompting for a different response.

I thought he wanted me to speak more affirmatively, so I said: "Yes, I am ready."

"Boy, here are the rules: "Don't look at me or say anything to me, unless I ask for a response. Just follow my instructions. Follow all the rules and procedures of the road. Leave this parking lot, go out to the highway, turn left, go to the front gate of the livestock yards, and stop there. You understand, boy?"

"Yes." I started the car, engaged the clutch and simultaneously released the emergency brake, and drove down the hill to the highway stop sign. I pulled the turn signal to indicate a left turn, as well as using hand signals. I made the left turn, merged into traffic and headed towards the first destination, driving directly past where Allan Jones' shack once stood. When I reached the main livestock yards entrance, I applied the emergency brake, turned off the ignition, and secured the vehicle.

The trooper then directed me to drive through a nearby neighborhood across the street along Howard Street, which I performed nervously, but flawlessly. "Ok, boy," the trooper said, there are just two things left: a short drive along Wright Avenue (a major thoroughfare) and a parallel parking exercise." I performed both perfectly.

"Now, boy, drive back to DMV. Remember, you're still being tested," the trooper reminded me.

"Ok." I was filled with anticipation on the way back. I could feel that driver's license in my hands. My uncle was standing outside waiting as the trooper and I drove up to the DMV. I secured the vehicle, relieved the test was over. "Do you think you passed, boy?" the trooper asked.

"Yes, I do," I said enthusiastically.

"What's that again, boy?"

"Yes, I sure do," I said, speaking with confidence like Mr. Horn, my sixth grade teacher taught me. My uncle kept trying to signal something to me. I saw his gestures, but I was so engrossed in the moment that I did not comprehend their meaning.

"Boy, I'm going to ask you one more time, do you think you passed?"

My uncle continued to gesture. I wondered why the trooper continued to ask me the same question, since it was so obvious to me that I had passed. "Yes, I think I passed," I said as my enthusiasm began to wane.

"Ok, boy, let's go inside," the trooper said as he made what appeared to be a final entry on the clipboard.

"Ok."

We walked inside and the trooper said, "Boy, you failed the test! You'll not get a license today." Those comments left me speechless. I could not believe what he said. He quickly walked away from me to test another applicant. I did not have an opportunity to see the results. Dejected, I walked outside to tell my uncle the results. "How could I have failed?" I asked myself aloud. I had never failed any test before.

As soon as I told my uncle, he said, "Joe, I knew it. I tried to signal you. You never said *sir*. You always say yes sir or no sir to the white man, *always!* How did you forget that?"

"I guess I was excited. I'll never forget again."
This was definitely a low point for me. As soon as possible, I wanted to retake this test. Next time I would be successful; I would suffix each phrase with sir.

A few weeks later, I was ready to retake the test. Since the first test, my uncle had wrecked his Dodge, crushing the grille and the right front fender. Although the car was drivable, my uncle and I concluded its wrecked condition would be a distraction and perhaps a reason to fail me again. My uncle's friend, Mr. Lindsey Johnson, knew my plight and was gracious enough to let me borrow his new blue 1954 Chevrolet to perform the road test. It was a stick shift without Fluid Drive, so I had to operate the clutch with enough precision to prevent the car from making jerky starts. Mr. Johnson allowed me to have a practice session to get the feel of his car, and I quickly mastered smooth clutch engagements, gently putting the car in motion.

Once again, on a Saturday morning, I showed up at the Office of the Department of Motor Vehicles. I was prepared to retake the driver's test. After someone looked up the results of my first test, I was informed that I only had to retake the road test portion. This time, like the first time, I was sent outside to wait for an available state trooper.

A young, tall blond trooper walked over to me and said, "Good morning, Eddie."

"Sir, good morning, sir," I said firmly.

"I see you answered all the questions on the written test correctly. That's excellent."

"Sir, yes sir."

"I can't tell by looking at your road test results, what parts did you fail?"

"Sir, I don't know sir."

"Well, we're going to take care of you this time. Let's go to the car," the trooper said.

"Sir, yes sir."

"See those cars in a line next to the fence on the other side of the parking lot. Drive over there and park in the empty space in that line of cars."

"Sir, yes sir."

I started the car and drove over to the other side of the parking lot, being extra careful to execute every procedure properly. Then, I parallel parked the car seamlessly into that line of cars next to the fence. I turned off the engine and waited for the next instruction.

"Start the car and go back to the space you just left," the trooper said.

"Sir, yes sir."

My heart was racing. I had no idea what to think. I did not want to ask the trooper any questions. He seemed friendly, but after my first test experience, I was gun shy. Maybe once back in the original space, he would give me further instructions. As I drove back into the original space, I saw my uncle standing nearby looking perplexed. I turned off the engine and sat motionless.

The trooper wrote something on his clipboard. This took a long time. Finally, he said, "Congratulations, you have passed your test. Let's go inside where you can finish the paperwork."

"Sir, yes sir," I said with great enthusiasm.

During the short walk inside the building, I pondered a lot. Why did this trooper pass me so quickly? Did the first trooper cheat me on my initial driver's test? Did the fact that I did not say sir to the first trooper and did with the second trooper really matter? Why did the second trooper appear to have difficulty interpreting the results of my first road test? I told myself to stop trying to rationalize the results of my two road tests. I told myself to rejoice in the fact that I had finally passed.

Once inside, I went straight to the waiting room to wait for my new driver's license. Soon a woman came to the waiting room and called my name. I followed her to her work counter. She opened her two-ply manifold set of sequentially numbered driver's license templates and asked me to verify personal information that I had submitted, including my age. My submitted age was sixteen, the minimum legal age to hold an Arkansas driver's license. My true age was thirteen. My submitted age was never challenged; no birth certificate was required. Ironically, the license template was filled in by hand and in pencil.

Amazingly, this facilitated eventual age reconciliation when my true age reached seventeen and my yearly incremented driver's license age read nineteen (would have read twenty at renewal). Prior to renewal, I simply changed the age from 19, which was still written in pencil, to 16. At renewal, the clerk changed the age to 17, which was correct, for my 1958 driver's license.

When I left the Arkansas DMV that Saturday, I was as proud as a 13-year-old could be. My uncle and I drove the short distance back to Mr. Johnson's house where I proudly showed him my new driver's license. I promised him that I would wash his car to show my appreciation for borrowing it. For some reason, I never did. However, I never ever again forgot to say sir.

9

Robinson Auditorium – Negro Showcase

Music played a major role in the psyche of black Little Rock. In the mid-fifties, radio stations, like KOKY, helped Negro recording stars reach white audiences. Instead of listening to white cover records, they heard the real McCoy – R&B records by the original artists. This helped Negro artists crossover and become mainstream on Top 40 radio stations. Now, both blacks and whites demanded more – they wanted to see and hear the R&B stars in person, with their own orchestras and bands. In Little Rock, this location was the Robinson Auditorium at Markham and Broadway Streets. I sneaked into the Flamingo Club on West 9th Street to see Ike and Tina Turner and likewise into the Gem Theater to see burlesque, but the main events were held at the Robinson.

Segregation was the rule, so there were two shows – a concert upstairs for white audiences and a show, review and dance for Negro audiences in a hall below the auditorium. The concerts started at 7 p.m. and were over by 9 p.m. The concerts were orderly and quiet, with maybe some clapping and toe tapping. The audience stayed in their seats, and the performers remained on stage.

Things at the show, review and dance were markedly different. These events started at 10 p.m. and ran "until," meaning the show ended when all the musicians were either too drunk or too tired to play any longer or until every patron had lost every bit of his groove and left to continue the party elsewhere. Sensuous ladies were performing shake dances in every corner. Alcohol was served (yes, even the artists drank), and the artists interacted physically with the audience. You viewed the performers from stadium-like seats around the walls or stood directly in front of the stage. For additional money, you could buy a table (four or more people to a table) where you placed alcoholic beverages, cigarettes and food, usually fried chicken.

These events were raucous and smoky. The thick smoke always gave me a headache, but I continued to attend as often as possible. Each show was a unique opportunity to see my favorite R&B performers close up.

I remember my first show, review and dance. The headliner was Little Richard and the opening act was B.B. King. I walked to the Robinson and arrived about 9 p.m., just in time to see the white audience leaving.

I enjoyed B.B. King, but I could hardly wait to see my favorite recording artist, Little Richard. He was the most colorful person I had ever seen. In today's world, Richard was Liberace, Prince and Michael Jackson rolled into one. He had a pompadour that made women envious and wore make-up that made men cringe. His bright green suit would have made Robin Hood throw away his tights.

Little Richard floated through his hits, *Tutti Frutti, Slippin' and Slidin'* and *Long Tall Sally*. I was impressed by the way Richard sang and played the piano. He sometimes played with his back to the keyboard, other times with one leg on top of his grand piano. I liked the sound of his band, especially the trio of saxophones.

I was impressed by the number of women who threw their underwear at Little Richard and how he continued to perform unabatedly. I was further impressed by my close proximity to the elevated stage. I could literally touch Richard's fancy green shoes. I will never forget the number of women who climbed on top of tables and danced erotic come-ons to Richard or the men who sought cheap thrills by peeking under their dresses.

Finally, before Richard left the stage for good, he made an announcement. "If anyone wants to see me after the show, I will be at the Charmaine Hotel, room 18. The party will go on." I left the Robinson at 2:30 a.m. and started walking home. The Charmaine Hotel was on the route I took home, so I stopped there to see Little Richard again. There were so many people (all adults) in and around Richard's room, that I gave up and went home.

I saw Richard perform two more times before I left Little Rock, but that first time was the most exciting. Interspersed among his other performances, I had opportunities to see many other R&B stars at the Robinson. Some shows had as many as 15 group and single R&B acts. For instance, I saw Lloyd Price, Little Willie John, Sam Cooke, Laverne Baker and the Crests. LaVerne and the Crests were on the same program and lodged at the Miller Hotel on West 9th Street. The Miller, like the Charmaine, was Negro owned. One afternoon, I saw LaVerne and Johnny Maestro, white lead singer of the Crests, walking east on West 9th Street towards the Gem Theater. This was an unusual sight in the 1950s: a couple of R&B stars, LaVerne, a Negro woman who sang *Jim Dandy*, and a white man, Johnny, who sang "Sixteen Candles," frolicking up the street together.

Another memorable event at the Robinson involved one of R&B's first sex symbols: Clyde McPhatter. Clyde's good looks and smooth operatic voice drew the overt affection of his female fans. During one show, a group of eager ladies, after bombarding Clyde with multiple volleys of their underwear, jumped on the stage and literally tore off his clothes. As more of his clothes came off, more and more ladies came on the stage. Surprisingly, he was down to his shorts and socks before security intervened. It appeared that everyone, including Clyde, initially thought the fans were joking – until he was overwhelmed and almost naked. Even his shoes were gone. Finally, security rescued Clyde and removed the fans from the stage. He returned shortly in different clothes. This time security kept fans away from the stage.

During the Robinson's R&B heyday, I saw many command performances from such doo-wop groups as the Five Satins and The Elegants and singles such as Bo Diddley and Chuck Berry. I only remember one act that did not live up to expectations. Frankie Lymon, without The Teenagers, missed two program calls before he finally appeared on stage. He could barely stand unsupported but tried to sing his recording of "Goody, Goody" and failed. In less than a minute, he was escorted from the stage. Speculation from patrons around me was that Frankie was stoned from alcohol and drugs. I never saw him in person again.

I paid $1.25 to see my first show, review and dance at the Robinson and $1.75 for my last. By that time, artists like Fats Domino refused to do separate shows and insisted on performing only in front of integrated audiences. They had the clout – record sales and popularity – to force it to happen. Segregated R&B shows at the Robinson slowly ended. The new venue was the amphitheater on the livestock grounds on Roosevelt Road. The audiences there were indeed integrated, but Negroes and whites did not mingle. Blacks sat on one side of the aisle and whites on the other.

However, there was only *one* show. I saw Fats Domino and Chubby Checker headline a show that performed in front of such an audience.

I was able to sneak into musicals and burlesque shows at the Gem Theater. I saw numerous acts at local night clubs on the local chitlin' circuit. The chitlin' circuit was the collective name given to a string of small Negro-owned night clubs, theaters and honky tonks that welcomed Negro musicians, comedians, and other entertainers during the age of racial segregation in the United States. However, to me, the Robinson was in a class of its own. No other venue in Little Rock matched the magic, excitement and raw entertainment generated at the Robinson in its heyday during a show, review and dance.

10

KOKY 1440 on the AM Dial – Black Voices in the Ether

Until 1956, there were no local radio stations that played all-Negro music in Little Rock. Prior to that time, I remember two Negro DJs who had one- or two-hour programs on local white stations. Al Allen had an hour show called *Al's Jive 'til Five*, which played Negro music. Choo-Choo Johnson also had such a show. Neither DJ played the hard-core, low-down rhythm and blues also known then as race music. There was lots of Negro recorded music available; it just was promoted primarily by word-of-mouth and on jukeboxes, not on local radio stations. Visitors and relatives, respectively, brought and sent these records from Detroit, Chicago and Los Angeles to friends in Little Rock.

In addition, during Dunbar High School talent shows, several students sang and played electric guitars emulating the popular blues singer B.B. King and his famous guitar, Lucille, which introduced young Negro students to rhythm 'n' blues. For a nickel per play, B.B. could be heard on jukeboxes everywhere, from nightclubs and juke joints to black teenage hangouts such as Harris' Grocery Store located across the street from Dunbar. Blacks fortunate enough to have a phonograph in their homes ordered 78-RPM records from mail order houses.

All the electronic media, (radio, TV and movies, in Little Rock in the early fifties, were white owned and controlled. Negro-oriented programming was non-existent. Therefore, I listened to Little Jimmy Dickens before I listened to Little Junior Parker; I listened to Hank Williams before I listened to Hank Ballard; and I listened to Patsy Cline before I listened to Big Maybelle or Billie Holiday. This was a great experience for me. I learned to appreciate all genres of music at a young age.

We got our first television set in 1954, a 21-inch black and white Admiral. I was so fascinated with this device that I watched everything I could, including such musical programs as Eddie Fisher's *Coke Time*, *The Perry Como Show*, *The Spike Jones Show* and *Your Hit Parade*, starring Snooky Lanson, Russell Arms, Dorothy Collins and Gisele MacKenzie – all white shows. About the same time, CBS released the *Amos 'n' Andy Show* in syndication, as reruns. The show was a colored situation comedy, which portrayed Negroes as buffoons, stereotypic caricatures as portrayed by American culture. However, it had an all-Negro cast, featuring some of the finest actors to ever appear on TV, including my favorite character Lightnin', played by Horace Stewart (aka, Nick O'Demus). I watched it every Sunday night at 7 p.m.

In the mid-fifties, white teenagers discarded cover versions of Negro records like Georgia Gibbs' version of *Dance with Me, Henry* for the original by Etta James. Black teenagers knew that song evolved from a song written by Henry (Hank) Ballard called *Work with Me Annie*, which was considered sexually suggestive. Hank Ballard, lead singer of a group called Hank Ballard and the Midnighters, cleaned up the lyrics and used his name (Henry) in the title. Thanks to a clear channel 50,000-watt radio station in Nashville, Tennessee, whites as well as Negroes of all ages throughout the South enjoyed rhythm and blues songs.

However, patience, optimal weather conditions and sensitive radios were required to receive these broadcasts. The rhythm and blues program commenced at 10 p.m., which was late for some school age listeners. If the weather was cooperative and the console, car or transistor radio sensitive enough, wonderful sounds soon emanated.

We sat back and enjoyed the great sounds of Little Richard, Fats Domino, Chuck Berry, Jimmy Reed, Lowell Fulson, Bobby "Blue" Bland, Lightning Hopkins, Muddy Waters, Little Junior Parker, The Spaniels, Sonny Boy Williamson, Howling Wolf, and Etta James.

The first radio station in Little Rock to offer all-Negro programming was K-O-K-Y, which made its debut in October 1956. Finally, we heard the complete repertoire of most rhythm and blues artists. We heard other genres, too, including gospel, emerging rock 'n' roll and jazz. Finally, we heard all Negro programming, "urban" in today's parlance, for about 12 hours a day. Ironically, I first heard Elvis Presley singing "Heartbreak Hotel" on K-O-K-Y and thought he was Negro.

Most of us did not have phones, so we often gathered at KOKY studios, before and after school, to personally request our favorite songs. There, we watched the DJs through a large soundproof window.

KOKY did have two major limitations. First, it ran down at sundown. Programming ran from 6 a.m. to 6 p.m., seven days a week. Secondly, it transmitted only 1000 watts at 1440 on the AM dial. The listening area did not cover all of Greater Little Rock, which included North Little Rock. Nonetheless, we greatly enjoyed the opportunity to hear black programming 12 hours every day.

My favorite trio of KOKY secular personalities included King Porter, Joy Boy Jackson and Al Bell. My favorite religious personality was Brother Al Weaver.

King Porter was an unusual DJ. He integrated a piano routine into his on-air persona. He said a few words, then played a few bars, then said a few more words, followed by a few more bars. Sometimes he broke into a full New Orleans boogie-woogie. He was probably the best dresser of the three and like most Negro personalities of the time, wore his hair in a process or conk, which was an attempt by black men to straighten their hair to make it look like that of white men. Singer Nat King Cole sported a process, which was completed by enduring a truly painstaking process of "relaxing" the hair with a solution containing lye. Do-rags, similar to the ones worn to cover the hair today, kept the humidity from causing the hair to return to its natural state. Porter often sang a duet with the recorded artist he was playing. He often did live commercials, which he ended in his signature closing, "You know it is OKY (pronounced oakie), when you hear it on KOKY (pronounced cokie). This is K-O-K-Y coming to you live from 1440 on your AM dial."

Then there was Joy Boy. He was the most handsome, the ladies' man of the trio. He had curly locks and was the most dynamic radio personality. Joy Boy's antics included dancing and hamming it up for the camera or fans while spinning records. The women, young and old, sighed just looking at him.

Finally, my overall favorite was Al Bell, nee Advertise Isabell. Al was tall, young and lanky. I knew him personally. I took a communication class with him at Philander Smith College. I still remember his theme song: *Walking with Mr. Lee*, an instrumental by Lee Allen out of New Orleans. He went on to become the head of Stax Records in Memphis and later co-wrote such hits as *I'll Take You There* and *I Know a Place*, which were sung by the Staple Singers.

King Porter, Joy Boy Jackson and Al Bell played R&B like we had never heard before. KOKY had a program called the West 9th Street Blues Association, where listeners could call in to elect its officers. During one election, B.B. King was chosen President and Bluesman Jimmy Reed was elected Vice-President.

Brother Al Weaver was the gospel DJ. His show came on after Al Bell's. He introduced us to many of the great gospel-recording artists from around the country. Before Al Weaver and KOKY, we only heard these groups when they came to Negro churches in Little Rock and performed for love offerings, board, and a chance to promote and sell their records. However, the big gospel groups, like the Soul Stirrers only played the bigger churches and venues in the larger cities. Now we heard these groups, too.

Brother Weaver introduced us to recorded Sunday church services, especially the sermons and songs of Reverend C.L. Franklin, pastor of New Bethel Baptist Church in Detroit. On his show, I first heard a very young pianist and singer named Aretha Franklin singing gospel songs in her father's church.

To this day, the Soul Stirrers, featuring the young silky voices of Sam Cooke and Johnnie Taylor in the lead, are my all-time favorite gospel group. They sang such memorable hits as *Peace in the Valley*, *Be with Me Jesus*, *Out on a Hill*, *There Is Not a Friend Like Jesus* and many others. Sam Cooke, Johnnie Taylor, and Aretha Franklin later became renowned R&B recording artists.

All Negro recording artists, when in the area, stopped by KOKY studios for live interviews, a chance to spin their own records, and meet fans. I saw Ray Charles, Lloyd Price and Jesse Belvin there. KOKY became a beacon in the entire community, beaming blues, news and pews to Greater Little Rock.

Section Two: The Pegasus Period: 1954 – 1962; Great Googa Mooga! Shorts, Hammers and Cribs

11

The Dawn of Pegasus

My aunt, uncle, sister and I moved to a small-detached rent house with a porch at 1005 Wright Avenue in the spring of 1954. I was thirteen years old. The house was located next to an alley and had a detached garage with an alleyway entrance. For the first time in my life, I was able to bathe without standing in a number 10 washtub; this house had a metal stand-up shower. I no longer had to sleep on a chair bed; I slept in a double bed, but often had to share it with my uncle's son by a previous marriage, James, better known as Sonny, who was a couple of years older than I was.

The new house was only three-and-one-half blocks up Ringo Street, but seemed like a world away. There were four neighborhood stores on Wright Avenue within a block of our new house: Harris' Grocery, Warren's Grocery, Byrd's Grocery and Kerr's Grocery and Meat Market. When I stood on the corner of Wright Avenue and Ringo, I could see all four stores at once. Harris' Grocery was Negro owned and offered a jukebox, pinball machine, and mostly convenience items; Warren's (later became Hedley's) and Byrd's were across the street from each other and had small meat departments in the rear of the stores. Kerr's was by far the largest, and Byrd's offered delivery services via bicycle.

The Dunbar Campus included Gibbs Elementary, Dunbar High School, Dunbar Junior College and the Dunbar Gymnasium, which was shared by all the schools and used for public events, too. These campuses completely filled one square block and were located just one-half block from our new house.

Our immediate black neighbors included the Crumps: Trubedeu and Golena, and children Vendia Ray, Zandria and Trubedeu, Jr. Trubedeu, Sr. worked for the railroad like my uncle, but performed well and kept his job. I saw my first TV program at their house in 1954. It was a championship boxing match. I do not remember the combatants. I do remember the TV set, which the Crumps were proud to own. It had a flip-up top that housed a mirror, which displayed a circular picture reflected from a vertically-oriented picture tube. I was awed by the experience.

The Holdens lived next door, across the alley. They never had a car or children. They mostly stayed to themselves. Mr. Holden was a union official and in public smoked Camels and spoke mostly union speak. Mrs. Holden was reclusive and usually spoke to neighbors through a window. One day, Mr. Holden did something I will always remember. He walked the half-block to the filling station, like he had done numerous times, to purchase a pack of Camels from our cigarette machine. We exchanged obligatory small talk, and he walked away. I can still picture his fair complexion, gold tooth, light eyes and brown ivy cap. For some reason, I had to run home. I was just in time to hear Mrs. Holden scream. I quickly ran across the alley to her house. She just said to me, "He's dead, I found him dead."

Mr. Holden was lying on the living room rug, dressed exactly as I had seen him minutes earlier. His eyes were open, and there was a medium-sized kitchen knife shoved handle-deep into his middle chest. This was the first suicide I had ever seen. Mrs. Holden later told me he had been embezzling union funds and was under investigation.

The Millers lived next to the Holdens. He was a minister, and she was a homemaker. They lived in an all-brick corner house. They were remarkable primarily because they always kept the latest and biggest Hudson in their garage. Their complexions and lifestyle reminded me of the Youngs.

Mr. Henry, his wife and a passel of kids, lived on the other side of our house. His eyes were always red, which made you think he had been drinking. He worked for the city as a sanitation worker. He worked the back of a garbage truck, emptying trashcans at each stop. Negroes were not allowed to be drivers. He fascinated me with the variety and utility of the items he recovered during his routes.

Construction on a filling station on a one-quarter square block parcel located at Wright Avenue and Chester was in progress when we moved into our new house. It was completed, stocked and open for business by early summer. One hot night during the grand opening ceremony, I was captivated by the single beam searchlight (now called outdoor promotion advertising lighting) oscillating across the dark sky. I had never seen one of these lights close up, so I walked up to the filling station to investigate. I toured the new service facility, met the proprietors, took a couple of promotional items, scrutinized the searchlight and returned home.

The following day, I returned to the filling station for a closer, more-detailed inspection. As I walked up, I noticed the proprietors' names above the front door: Lester E. and Dariel E. Price. I learned they were father and son. Banners suspended in the west and north office windows read *Price Mobil Service*. Price Mobil Service was a full-service Mobilgas filling station (a term used in 1954) located at Wright Avenue and Chester Streets. It was a sister station of the Mobilgas located directly across the street from Central High School at 16th and Park Streets.

I hung out at the station so frequently that I expected to be told not to come so often and stay so long; instead, the son, Dariel, commonly known as Bud, offered me a conditional job. If I washed the tires and hubcaps on cars designated for a car wash, I would earn twenty-five cents per car. A car wash cost one dollar. I enthusiastically accepted the offer. One Saturday I washed 21 cars and earned five dollars and twenty-five cents.

Soon, I was cleaning car windows and interiors in addition to the tires and hubcaps. Bud made me a new offer. Wash the entire car and earn fifty-cents per car. I accepted. Some Saturdays or Sundays I earned as much as $12.50, some Fridays, half that. Robert, an old Negro man with a gold tooth and baldhead had worked at a filling station for over three decades. He taught me to be a car wash perfectionist. I was proud of my clean *invisible* windows, shiny hubcaps and glistening white sidewalls. The numerous tips I received seemed to validate the quality of my work.

Friday, Saturday and Sunday were the high volume days for car washes. Other weekdays I volunteered for other tasks like mounting tires, repairing flats and adjusting brakes. With Bud's training and watchful eye, I soon mastered these tasks, too. Surprisingly, near summer's end but before school started, Lester, the father, routinely known to us as *the Old Man*, offered me a salaried job of twelve dollars a week during the school year. The work terms were seven days a week, twelve hours a day on non-school days, 4 p.m. until closing on school days. I received three clean uniforms with the Mobilgas logo and my name embroidered on the shirts, but no benefits. I accepted, of course, and felt like a full partner.

While twelve dollars per week was less than I could earn on a high-volume car wash Saturday, it was a salary – guaranteed. The conditional car wash tasks, performed on an as-needed basis, were rife with uncertainty. The volume was driven primarily by season and fair weather. For example, sunny, summer holiday weekends usually produced high volume; other conditions produced less.

During the 1954-55 school year, my duties and opportunities continued to expand. I was 14 years old, performing full service at the gas pumps, which included tire inflation and fluid checks, window cleaning and pumping gas. I performed brake and lubrication services. I also performed remote automotive service calls.

Both proprietors knew my age, but they also knew I had a driver's license and had no problems, allowing me to drive the service truck on these calls. The truck was a 1941 Ford half-ton pickup, the same red color as the Mobilgas Flying Red Horse. It had a wooden front bumper for pushing cars without damaging the finish on the disabled vehicle. During service calls, I provided a full range of services, including jump-starts, flat tire and out-of-gas service. I learned service call craft well. I knew the solution to numerous other common car problems that stranded drivers: vapor lock, stuck automatic chokes and defective starters on cars with automatic transmissions. On the latter, I usually pushed the vehicles with the truck's wooden bumper and, when we reached the proper engine start speed, I blew the horn to signal the driver to shift the transmission from neutral to the engine start gear. After the engine started, the car was driven back to the filling station for repair.

I remember the very first time I drove the truck. I was sent on an errand to pick up parts for a repair job. I had never driven a vehicle with the shift lever on the floor; this would be my first attempt. I quickly rehearsed the shift pattern before I put the truck in motion. I wanted to be sure that I did not grind the gears while shifting within earshot of my bosses. Once underway, I quietly shifted the full range of gears and successfully completed my errand.

Getting to work and school was easy. Dunbar High School and the filling station were one block apart on Wright Avenue. I lived in the middle, exactly one-half block from each.

During this time, I also became better acquainted with the Old Man, who was in his late fifties and had previously worked at a plant in the East End. He chewed tobacco and liked country music. His favorite artist was Patsy Cline, and his favorite song was Patsy's *I Fall to Pieces*. He was married and had two grown children, Bud and his sister, Emonelle. Bud, who was in his late twenties, was married and had a preschool age son, Ricky. He previously worked for the Rock Island Railroad Line and now was a member of the Arkansas National Guard. Bud had a history of allergies and hay fever worse than mine and was on a regimen of weekly allergy shots. He took auto mechanics as a trade while in high school and was the mechanic on duty at the filling station. During this period, Bud moved to a small duplex directly across the street from the filling station.

My job as a filling station attendant provided me with technical knowledge that serves me well today. My association with the patrons, an eclectic group, helped me to gain wisdom and poise beyond my young years.

Most Negro teenagers of my era, if they had jobs at all, were relegated to performing as short-order cooks, dishwashers, busboys, waiters, elevator operators or cotton pickers/choppers. I had a job that provided trust, training and responsibility. Moreover, I was very proud of it.

One of my collateral duties was to mow the Old Man's home lawn. His home was located in the east side of town, which was a moderate distance away, and another opportunity for me to drive the service truck. I felt proud when my peers saw me in the truck. I thought they looked envious.

One summer, when I was 14, I was dispatched on one of my regular lawn duties at the Old Man's house. This time, however, two things were different: I had a new gas-powered rotary lawn mower, which I was eager to use on a big lawn. I had done a test run on the grass patch behind the filling station. When I got to the jobsite, I unloaded the lawn mower and started mowing in my favorite pattern: ever-decreasing concentric rectangles. This scheme worked well for his very flat rectangular, probably three-quarter acre lot. I had just begun the first leg when the second different thing started to unfold.

The Old Man's neighbor drove up and quickly pulled into her carport. She appeared to be in a hurry, walked around to the passenger side of her car, retrieved a small package and quickly entered her house. Since I was on the closest lawn leg to her house, I could see her well. She wore a loose dress, high heels, and eyeglasses and sported a high bouffant hairdo. In less than a minute, her husband pulled up in his Ford pickup truck. He was dressed in overalls and a denim cap and looked like a railroad engineer. He, too, moved briskly into the house. It only took another circuit around the lawn to realize the neighbors had come home for an early afternoon amative rendezvous. I was instantly distracted by the volume of the amorous feminine sounds emanating from the window, which was not drowned out by the lawnmower's engine. I was spellbound by the synchronized motions of two people joined at the groin and the way the woman's legs were splayed. I was only fourteen and had never seen live and in person, white people engaged in raw sex.

The view left little to the imagination and was filtered only by the window screen. I did not want to be discovered so I completed another circuit, quickly returning to the optimum vantage point. The activities were still ongoing. I wondered why the couple had not sought more privacy, at least closing the curtains. I concluded the window and curtains had to be open because it was a very hot summer day and the house was not air-conditioned. The sun shone obliquely in their window, which probably obscured their view of me. And perhaps they thought the operating lawn mower masked any sounds they made. After another few circuits, the couple was gone from the window. A few minutes later, the man left. Then the woman pranced out, same dress, hair, glasses and high heels intact and drove away. I cut the grass for many more years and never witnessed an encore. I never told the Old Man or Bud what I saw that day. During a casual conversation with the Old Man, he told me that couple was in their sixties and had kids and grandkids.

12

Pegasus 1955

By the summer of 1955, I considered myself a fully qualified filling station attendant and light mechanic. I had learned a lot about our customers and their cars. I knew and understood the profiles and preferences of our regular customers, including their personality idiosyncrasies and the quirks of their cars. I knew all the lubrication points and crankcase capacities on virtually every American car on the road. I was selling, repairing, balancing, rotating and changing tires and adjusting and rebuilding car and truck brake systems.

I had the opportunity to learn tires literally from the tread up. First, there were only a few major tire companies, including Goodyear, Goodrich, Firestone and U.S. Royal (now Uniroyal). Mobil Tires were made by Kelly-Springfield, a subsidiary of Goodyear. There were two types of tires, tube and tubeless, the second of which was less likely to blow out. There were two types of cord in tires: rayon and nylon. I remember the first time I explained the difference. A customer, a white gentleman, came in and inquired about buying a set of tires. I recommended nylon-corded tires for his car and driving conditions because they stretch rather than breaking like rayon-corded tires. I explained, although they cost more, they were safer because they were less prone to blowouts. I expected to sell him two tires – he bought five 7.10 x 15, 4-ply nylon wide whitewalls, including the spare. Now, I had to remove the old tires and mount the new ones on his car.

The station had just purchased a red human-powered, self-standing tire changer. I had used it to mount one or two tires at a time; now, I had to mount an entire set – with the customer watching, a first. I had the five tires, Mobil Double Eagles, mounted, back on the car, with the bluing removed from the white sidewalls, in under 30 minutes. I pulled his car in the wash bay to balance the tires. I was taught to balance tires on the car and under road conditions. I hooked up all the equipment, including the bright strobe light that made the spinning tire appear to stand still so the heavy, out-of-balance location (because of gravity) was straight down at 6 o'clock. The more out of balance or out of round, the more the tire vibrated. By inspection, I learned to estimate the amount of counter-weight to be placed at the opposite location on the tire or at 12 o'clock. When the counter-weight neutralized the out of balance, the tire spun true – without shake or vibration. I had perfectly balanced the tire, the right front, to run true at 70 miles per hour.

Then Bud walked up. I proudly showed him the great job I had done. He said, "Joe, not so fast. Even though the state speed limit is 60 mph, always balance tires to 100 mph. That way the tire is guaranteed not to shake." I spun the tire up to 105 mph, and there was a slight shake. We moved the weights I had already placed on the rim to the right about an eighth of an inch, and we had perfection – smooth and balanced like a jeweled Swiss movement at over 100 mph! I learned something that day. Then we balanced the other four tires to the same degree.

The most dangerous procedure I learned that summer was split-rim or, as they were better known, suicide rim tire repairs. Split-rims often resulted in serious injury or death to tire mounters and repairers employed in filling stations and tire stores, which explains why they were referred to as suicide rims. Unlike a car tire rim, truck tire rims were split into two pieces: the rim and the locking ring. Removing the locking ring facilitated mounting and dismounting stiff, inflexible truck tires. The problem was the locking ring was held in its seat by tire pressure, in my case up to 110 pounds. The ring had to be installed correctly and seated perfectly or it could blow apart with tremendous force, destroying everything in its wake, including humans. The danger hit home when two filling station attendants, one of whom we all knew, were killed in the same week. By that time, I was fourteen years old and had successfully repaired six light truck tires with suicide rims. Bud and the Old Man made a command decision: we would no longer repair tires mounted on suicide rims. I never did another one.

In addition to selling new tires, I learned the proper way to repair tubeless tires. Bud taught me a method to stuff the hole with raw virgin rubber and secure a special patch on top of it with a vulcanizing C-clamp. The clamp was removed when cool; the patch was virtually welded into the tire, never to leak again. I also developed a tire service life extension procedure. This was for customers who were unable to afford new tires. I used a family of two-ply boots, small, medium and large, to repair broken cords, which extended the life of tires by 1000 to 3000 miles, that otherwise would be thrown away.

One of the fun things we performed at the gas pumps was finding the gas tank filler caps. On some cars, it stood right out – behind a flap on either rear fender or in the center behind the license plate. Others were more camouflaged. Often the customers had no idea where it was located. Some, unbelievably, were located inside the trunk (probably formerly belonged to a ridge runner, running moonshine); one, a Volkswagen Bug, was located under the hood; another, a Cadillac, was under the taillight, which was hinged up to permit access.

I read the Chilton's Repair Manual and enjoyed it like a novel. By sight, I picked the correct box or open-end wrench for the target nut or bolt 100 percent of the time. I was enrolled in Automotive Mechanics at Dunbar High School. I had the best of both worlds: Auto Mechanics Theory and Practice, with emphasis on theory at school; and Auto Mechanics Theory and Practice, with emphasis on practice at the filling station. Things simply could not be better.

I always toured the Snap-on Tools truck during its weekly stop at the station. There was a tool, gadget or device designed to make every repair job a snap. If the sales representative did not have what you needed on the truck, you were assured it would be the next week. I was like a kid in a toy store; as long as the truck was there, I looked, examined and learned tools. Of course, the truck was not there because of me; it was there because Bud usually bought something. I was allowed to be his shadow, right in his footsteps.

By now, Bud and the Old Man had assigned me other administrative and business collateral duties, and they all provided an opportunity to learn more. I was already cleaning the restrooms and restocking the newly purchased Coke and Dr. Pepper machines. There was an interesting aspect to the restrooms: Mexicans were allowed to use them and Negroes were not. The restrooms were kept locked, and I was not allowed to give blacks the key, a situation that rankled me. The itinerant Mexicans, then referred to as gypsies, usually traveled in convoys while seeking seasonal jobs. Therefore, they bought a lot of gas when they came in the station. My instructions were to give them the keys to both restrooms and be vigilant – in other words, watch them. I was told they were accomplished thieves. As far as I know, the Mexicans never stole anything substantial, but they did take a toll on the restrooms. They used them to shave, wash-up, and brush their teeth. Usually they left the restrooms trashed – filthy and void of liquid soap, toilet paper and paper towels. However, they did have the opportunity to use our restrooms!

Another business-minded collateral duty of the day for me was gasoline management. I was taught how to stick the tanks, inspect the gas delivery trucks and read the pumps. Two identical ten-thousand-gallon gasoline tanks, one each for Mobilgas (regular) and Mobilgas Special (premium or high octane) were buried behind the filling station structure. They contained no gas gauges, the levels were monitored manually with long graduated wooden sticks. They were inserted at the filler neck and allowed to drop to the bottom of the tank and removed. The stick was read similarly to an oil dipstick to determine the amount of fuel remaining in the tank. The object was to sell lots of gas but never run out. The lead-time to order gasoline from the refineries in southern Arkansas, usually El Dorado or Texarkana, was at least three days. In emergencies, we got up to twelve hundred gallons from the bulk plant in the East End in a matter of hours.

When the gasoline tankers arrived, I inspected each compartment to ensure it was filled to the proper level and again when all the gas was off-loaded to ensure the entire load was delivered. Reading the pumps was the third part of the gasoline management process. The number of gallons sold was recorded in a tabular format in a lined composition book; each of the four pumps had its own column. Each pump had two meters, which worked and looked like a car's odometer: one measured cumulative sales in gallons and the other cumulative sales in dollars. To compute the day's sales, I simply subtracted the previous reading from the present one. This management system was low in technology but high in efficiency. On a very slow day, we sold as little as 150 gallons and on a very good day, usually a Friday, Saturday or the day before a holiday, 3000 gallons. Some stations in good locations with high traffic count sold up to 10,000 gallons daily.

Walk-ups doing this period were interesting, too. A walk-up was a person who entered the station's premises without the aid of wheels of any kind. Terrence James Roberts, one of my best friends and later a member of the Little Rock Nine, was a walk-up. We often had philosophical discussions between customers. However, perhaps the most interesting character was a young kid name Sinclair Goins. He went by the name of Saint, which certainly did not describe his personality or character. Saint, who was a couple of years younger than me, was a seasoned petty thief. He often came up to buy a Coke or a pack of cigarettes from our machine. He usually carried a large grocery bag containing watches, (usually Bulova and Elgin, and numerous rings that he was trying to sell on the cheap. The bag's contents were so hot you saw virtual smoke. Saint took orders for merchandise like hubcaps; just tell him where you saw them. Within 24 hours, they were in his possession, ready for sale. He once offered me a moped, which I did not buy. I bought my only transistor radio, a WebCor (Webster Corporation), from him for five dollars.

Miss Young, my algebra teacher, was another one of my regular customers. She was a fiery redheaded blue vein who constantly chided me to do better academically. I always earned As and B+s in her class, but that was never good enough for her. "Mr. Washington," she always called me, "You can do better! You are not working up to your potential! Do better! Do better! Got to do better."

She was complimentary whenever I serviced her car at the pump or in the bay. "You do a great job at this place, but it is not your life's work," she said in her high-pitched animated voice. I always thought she talked through her nose. Then she switched up on me and said, "Are you still in the Honor Society?"

"Yes, ma'am."

"Do better, young man!" she demanded.

"Yes, ma'am."

I suffered Miss Young's wrath even when someone else waited on her. She found me in the bay and continued her tirade. "How are you doing in school, Mr. Washington?" she asked.

"Great!"

"You can and you have to do better," she preached. "Got to do better," she said, her voice trailing as she walked back to her car. As she walked away, I noticed again what a large woman she was. Everything on her body jiggled, her calves, butt, back, everything. Although I hated to see her drive in, one thing was certain: She was right. I could have and should have done better.

Bud and I were servicing a 1954 light blue DeSoto sedan at the west gas pump island. The driver was a young, beautiful and flirtatious twenty-something brunette with great legs. She had been in the station often with her husband and young daughter and during those times, she was far more reserved in demeanor and dress, which was usually shorts or peddle pushers. This time she wore a very short black skirt, essentially a bedroom skirt (one too short to wear outside the bedroom), black patent leather high heels and a white sleeveless blouse that exposed cleavage.

She and Bud were engaged in what appeared to be trivial conversation, and I was relegated to doing all the servicing, which included pumping the gas, cleaning the windows and checking under the hood. After pumping her gas, I cleaned the rear window first, and then I cleaned the front one. I was very surprised by the eye candy displayed on the other side of the windshield: I had a clear view of her thighs from her knees to her underwear and a great view of her ample chest. I overheard part of their conversation and did not understand something I heard her say, "Do you ever trifle around?" I do not remember Bud's answer but I know I expanded my carnal knowledge that day.

Later I asked Bud what trifle around meant. He explained that it meant running around on your husband or wife, having an affair, or cheating on your spouse. I fully understood now; trifle around described what my dad and uncle did to my mother and aunt respectively. I learned a new word.

I know Mrs. DeSoto had at least one affair because I was her accomplice. Her husband was an insurance salesman and spent numerous days traveling outside Little Rock, so she had many opportunities to trifle around. On two occasions, she paid me to disconnect her speedometer cable so she could visit an out-of-town paramour (my best guess) without accruing suspicious mileage on the odometer. In both cases, when she returned the next day, I reconnected the speedometer cable. I never knew anything about the other party or her destination. She threatened me with serious consequences if I spoke to anybody about her activities. Until now, I never did.

Mrs. DeSoto was a regular customer for many years. She had two personalities: risqué and flirtatious when she drove in alone and demure mother and wife when she came in with her husband and child. Her solo antics were well known and there was a stampede of attendants rushing out to service her car when she needed gas. She obviously enjoyed the attention and always fed us a lot of eye candy. Only when everyone else was busy with customers and could not get away, did I have an opportunity to service her car. She never asked me about trifling around. I was just her speedometer person when needed.

A man, or boy in my case, can see and learn a lot looking backward through the windshield of a patron's car at the pumps. I saw customers openly drinking beer and hard liquor. I witnessed gambling and even domestic disputes. Once, four guys appeared to be planning a robbery. A mature statuesque white Amazon-like queen, a Wonder Woman look-alike, was another interesting person whom I found memorable. She always practiced show-and-tell with her body at the pumps. She remarked to me with a wry smile, "Feast your eyeballs, kid. I'm all show and no action. I'm just messing with you. Know what, I'm just a coquette. Know what that means?"

"Nope."

"Good. Look it up. That is your homework. See you, hon," she said before departing. No one around the station knew what a coquette was, but I was determined to be ready for the teacher when she returned for gas. I went to the library, first, to determine how to spell the word and then to define it. I found it was a French word which meant a woman who makes teasing sexual or romantic overtures. In other words, a tease or flirt. Once again, something learned. Later, one of my favorite singers, Fats Domino, sang a song, "Little Coquette." An excerpt of the lyrics includes:

Hear me why you keep foolin'

Little Coquette

Makin' fun of the ones who love you

I never forgot the meaning of coquette.

Another interesting man was Mr. Cross who drove a gray 1952 Lincoln four-door sedan. He was a large, elderly, soft-spoken Negro man who worked as a door attendant at an upscale hotel located at West Capitol and Arch Streets, across from the main post office. He impressed me with the regal fashion in which he wore his formal uniform. He normally stopped in after his shift at work and flashed a wad of cash he said he earned from tips. Although he was married, he was allegedly a gay prostitute who serviced guests at the hotel and elsewhere. His strong effeminate characteristics were very evident – even to me. Still, he made you like him.

Meanwhile, there was also excitement at school, especially with the girls. Study hall was in the school's auditorium where Willis White, my study partner, and I conspired with the girls to hook up for sex. Mostly we struck out, but it was not for lack of trying. Willis was far more aggressive than I was, so I learned a lot from him. My favorite student was a tall bronze lass named Rosemary Sanders, was the same age and in the same grade as me. She wore a sleeveless blue gingham dress that was not too loose or tight; it just touched her body at all the right places. She often sat next to me (study hall rules required students to maintain an empty seat between them) and performed the universal sex gesture – moving the extended index finger of the right hand in and out of a circle formed by the thumb and index finger of the left hand while panting rapidly like a dog. I tried many times to get her to cut study hall and sneak home with me, since I only lived a half block away.

"Rosemary, come go home with me. We'll be back before the study period is over. We won't be missed. We'll sneak out the side door and down the fire escape. We'll be at my house in three minutes. Come on, baby."

She said, "Eddie, my love," after the song by the same name, "You have to borrow a car and drive out to where I live and, honey, I will give you some side, then a popular term among teens for sex. Come out after school or on the weekend and bring some rubbers (condoms)." Conversations and antics like those caused my hormones to rage like a wildfire out of control. She did not believe that I was sex savvy; in fact, she accused me of being a virgin. She said I needed a teacher like her to show me the ropes. At the time, she was right on both counts.

There also was Barbara Reeves, who invited me to come see her. She and Rosemary lived in the same general neighborhood, a few miles from each other. They both rode school buses to and from school, which meant they lived in the outer limits of Pulaski County. The rest of us walked or took cars or city buses to and from school. Barbara was a couple of years older than I was and did not make my hormones boil, but made me an offer similar to Rosemary's. Her chest was certainly adult-sized, and I thought she was matronly and more sexually experienced, which made her interesting. Were they the real deal? Coquettes? I did not have a car of my own and by summer, Rosemary and Barbara were just fantasies.

Before school was out for the year, Willis convinced one of our classmates, Edna Siller, to cut study hall and accompany us to my house. I was cut in on the deal only because I had the place, and she was only willing if he insured her she would not be caught. She wore a wide green skirt with petticoats. We went in my house and straight to my bed. Edna reclined on my bed in an accommodating position but was so nervous she would not take her books off her chest. Willis kissed her lips, soothed her nerves, and removed her books and some of her clothes. He took care of nature, and I took the role of spectator. When my turn came, I was too nervous to participate. Edna tried to wait for me, but we had to get back to study hall, so she put on her clothes, and we went back to school. Back at study hall, she promised me a rain check, but with just the two of us. When the opportunity came again, Edna was remorseful and got cold feet. The rain check was never honored.

Izola, a fellow classmate, and I were wrestling or "petting the lamb" (canoodling in today's parlance) on the ground behind St. Peter's Rock Baptist Church just before the fall of night when an unusual event occurred. I experienced an unexpected twilight emission. I was startled to the extent that I jumped up, left her on the ground and ran home to take a shower. Convinced that I had contracted a sexually transmitted disease, I could not determine whether I had just experienced pain or pleasure. Had Izola just given me gonorrhea or, as it was commonly called, clap? Worse yet its most virulent strain, bullheaded clap?

About midday the next day Dr. Robinson, a prominent well-known Negro medical doctor and regular customer, drove up to the gas pumps. He always offered to answer any medical questions for me. Today, I certainly had one. I ran out to wait on him. "Fill it up, son," he said.

"Dr. Robinson, can you treat me for clap?" I asked.

"Have you been fooling around with these young girls?" he inquired.

"Yes, sir!"

"Ok, just come on down to the office and show me a cheek of ass, and I will give you a shot of penicillin," he offered.

I thought about how painful those shots were when I had spinal meningitis. Nevertheless, no matter, this was very important.

Then the doctor asked me, "Any pain or pus?"

"No."

"Then how do you know you have the clap?" he questioned. "When was the last time you had sex? And the time before that?" he continued.

I told him last night was the first and only time.

"Did you have a full penetration?

"No, none."

"By the way, who is this lovely lady?"

"Izola."

After I told him, I recalled that she lived on Pulaski Street, a half block from his house.

115

Dr. Robinson laughed at me and said, "Eddie, my boy, sounds to me like you just popped your nuts. Wait a week. If you experience any pain or pus, come see me. Meanwhile go back and finish the job."

A week went by. There was no pain, pus or clap. Nothing. I did not go back to Izola to finish the job. I had nothing more to do with her. I also never told anyone else of my naiveté or my stupidity.

Another very interesting and supportive customer was Reverend Ogden. His parsonage was directly adjacent to the filling station, and his church was close by at 20th and Arch Streets, so I saw him often. He always offered me a very warm reception and a blessing whenever we met. We had several white ministers as customers, but Reverend Ogden was the only one to demonstrate interest in my personal roles, responsibilities and education at and beyond the filling station. He was the only white minister to invite me to visit his church, which he did numerous times.

At the pumps, we always discussed a wide range of social issues, including race relations. He was a pastor at the pumps, but he did not proselytize there. He told me about racial sensitivity classes that were taught at his church. The reverend was always complimentary and inspirational and said things like; "I am glad Mr. Price allows you to grow and take on new tasks. You perform better at this job than most adults. I am very proud of you. Have a blessed day."

One day, the reverend's 1954 Chevrolet had a problem with a sticking hydraulic valve lifter, which was clicking very loudly. He drove over and asked me specifically to investigate the noise. When Bud also started to walk over to his car, the reverend waved him away. He wanted me to solve the problem. I raised the hood and immediately, based on watching Bud, recognized the problem and solution. I pulled the air cleaner and slowly poured some top oil into the carburetor. His car emitted thick dark smoke for a few minutes and then the clicking stopped and the smoke cleared.

"Well, that should take care of it, Reverend Ogden," I told him.

"How much do I owe you, Eddie?" he asked.

"Not a thing."

He responded by reciting one of Beatitudes: "Blessed are the meek, for they shall inherit the earth. Come visit my church next Sunday, you are always welcome."

"Maybe one day," I told him. I really appreciated the offer, but I knew being the only Negro in the congregation would attract far too much attention. He said he would introduce me to the church members, which usually meant you, had to speak publicly. My real excuse was I had to work on Sundays. Nevertheless, he knew the Old Man would let me off for church if I asked. He continued to invite me anyway.

My first solo, complete brake job was performed on Reverend Ogden's car. He was concerned about his car's low brake pedal. Once again, he wanted me to diagnose the problem, which I did. I pulled one front and rear wheel; he needed new brake shoes on all four wheels. I recommended new wheel cylinder kits, too.

The reverend said, "Thanks, Eddie. When can I get the job done?"

"You have to check with the Old Man for cost and scheduling information," I told him.

"Ok, I'll talk to Mr. Price. I'm also going to tell him that I want you to do all the work. I'll tell him I trust you unconditionally," he said.

"Ok, thanks." I had rebuilt wheel cylinders, replaced front brake shoes, rear brake shoes and rebuilt one master cylinder, but I had never done a complete brake job alone on a single car. Bud and the Old Man acquiesced to the reverend's wishes. I ordered the brake shoes, wheel and master cylinder (The master cylinder had to be rebuilt, too.), kits, and completed the task in half a day. I double-checked everything; I wanted to make sure this car was safe. Bleeding the brakes was a two-man job and the Old Man helped me for the ten minutes it required.

When the reverend picked up his car and drove the very short distance to his driveway, I took a moment to reflect on what had just occurred: a white man had enough compassion, confidence and trust in me, a 14-year-old skinny black kid, to place his life and the lives of his wife and family in my hands. That was remarkable. It made me want to learn and do even more.

Except for an adult son, I never saw much of Reverend Ogden's family. I almost never saw his wife. The son was not as affable as his dad was. He was polite, but seemed aloof. One day shortly before the reverend moved away, I read in the newspaper, the Arkansas Gazette, that his son had committed suicide. He shot himself in the head while sitting in his parked car near 21st and Chester Streets, just a few blocks from the filling station.

The following day when I saw the reverend, the man who always gave me encouragement to grow and be the best, I did not know what to say. He must have felt the same way; we mutually reached to hug each other right beside the pumps. I simply said, "I'm sorry." He was lost for words and wept. That was the first white man I had ever hugged.

When it came to cars, Bud had the uncanny ability to see the possible and make it reality. For instance, he retrofitted his vanilla 1954 Ford Custom Coupe with an automatic transmission and power steering. He found the parts, measured the risk, charted the best solution and did it. He rebuilt the engine after 50,000 miles. It was Ford's first overhead valve V-8 and not ready for prime time. He rebuilt a 1952 Ford, including retrofitting a factory A/C unit, for his dad. Through all of these, I was watching, learning and helping, mostly by washing parts. However, the key thing I learned from him was not to be afraid to challenge the impossible. All things were once impossible. Somebody took the risk, found a solution and now the once impossible is routine.

A few weeks later, when I saw Dr. Robinson at the pumps, I wanted to debunk a myth. At least, I believed it was a myth. My uncle, Brother Albert, told me assuredly that ladies, young or old, got pregnant only: 1) during intercourse and 2) when both parties climaxed simultaneously. Any other conditions, you are just firing blanks. If that is the case, it seemed almost impossible to get a girl pregnant. Yet a number of my female classmates had gotten pregnant. I had just figured out what a male climax was. I did not have a clue about a female climax. Although I witnessed the entire sex act between Edna and Willis, I had no idea whether she reached a climax. I greeted him with, "Hello, Dr. Robinson. I have another question for you."

"Fill it up with high test and go with your question," the doctor said.

I posed my uncle's statement to the doctor, and it drew this response: "Absolutely and totally false. Eddie, you don't even need a full penetration. Rubbers are your best baby preventers. Three for ten cents in the drug store. How is your clap? You doing ok?"

"Doctor, I'm fine! Thanks for answering my question."

The good doctor paid and drove away. It was great to service professionals at the pumps. Now, I knew the real deal. I bought some rubbers just in case.

The next day, I observed my first customer, who was not wearing underclothes. Most cars did not have air conditioning, so it was common in the summer for women to pull their dresses and skirts up to the upper parts of their thighs to help cool their legs. Numerous ladies did not pull their clothes down when they came in for gas, so we attendants saw a lot of leg. But Genovese Bryant, who was a fiery freckled-faced, redhead, perhaps in her mid-thirties, was the first to display her body in such a way that there was no doubt she was not wearing underwear. It was in natural sunlight, high resolution, 3-D and in living color. She seemed to be an expensive dresser, who always wore sunglasses, so I never saw her eyes. Genovese had well-toned thighs and calves. I never saw her outside of her car, so I do not know whether she had a great figure. In the several years she was a customer, I never saw her wearing undies. She was the first white woman to show me her private parts.

Another redhead, Paul "Red" Speirling was one of Bud's high school friends and an expert car upholsterer, designing and making fabric and nylon convertible tops, headliners, door panels and custom seat covers. I did not have his talents, but I learned a lot from him. One day, he stopped in the station, like he often did, on his way to and from work. I was in the battery room in the back of the station office, when I heard Red ask Bud, "Where's your nigger?" I do not recall how Bud answered, but I do know that was the first time I heard someone refer to me in slave terms, your nigger. I heard him say it many times after that day, especially when he thought I was out of sight or he thought I was in school. Other customers used similar terms like, "Where is that nigger kid of yours?" However, I heard Red Speirling use the slave term more than all the others.

Bud knew I was anxious to get my own car. He knew a free 1934 Ford that he could get for me. It needed some work, but the price was right – free. However, there were problems with the title, and it never materialized. By midsummer 1956, Bud headed to Fort Sill, Oklahoma, for his two weeks of active duty with the Arkansas National Guard. He told me to wait until he got back and we would explore other car options for me.

Impatience and imprudence got the best of me. I had a down payment of a hundred dollars, a budget of two hundred dollars and two weeks without Bud to filter my decision. Most used car dealers would not even talk to a kid, but I found one who would – J.C. Whitley and Sons, located downtown at 7th and Center Streets. I dealt directly with Mr. J.C. himself, a grandfatherly, Walter Brennan type. He said, "Boy, let me show you a car with your name on it."

He walked me to the very back of the lot and showed me a shiny black 1939 Chevrolet Master Deluxe Coupe. I sat in the car, started the engine, turned on the radio and windshield wipers. I stroked the plush velour interior and drove the car in the alley behind the lot. Mr. Whitley told me the terms of sale: "The special sales price this week is $175.00. $100.00

down and $7.50 a week for ten weeks." I tried to pretend that I was not in a hurry, so I said, "I may be interested, but I have to think about it. I will come back tomorrow or the next day. Thanks, bye."

Mr. J.C. said, "Remember the price goes up next week."

I said, "Ok," and left.

Walking home, I had things to ponder: Is this the right car for me? What would Bud say? Did I inspect the car closely enough to know whether it is a good value? Why did he not let me drive the car off the lot for a test drive? Did he take me seriously? The more I walked, the more I wanted this car. I talked myself into going back the next day for a more-detailed inspection. I checked everything: tires, engine, transmission and shock absorbers for excessive bounce. Everything passed, except the steering wheel had excessive play, which I thought I could adjust out. I especially liked the Town and Country radio, which pulled in distant weak stations as well as the strong local ones. Again, I left with another big issue to ponder: how to catch my uncle sober and lucid enough to present him to the used car dealer to sign over the title and again at the Department of Motor Vehicles to obtain license plates. I was a minor, too young to sign a contract or register a car, so I needed my uncle.

Bud had been gone one day short of a week when I caught my uncle in a rare state of sobriety. I knew I could get him to sign everything, especially if I promised him some money for a nip of whiskey afterward. I also knew he would want to borrow my vehicle when his was wrecked or not running. However, I could not worry about that now; I had to capture this opportunity. My uncle and I drove to Whitley's used car lot in his car, where we formalized the deal. I drove my first car away with my wallet $100 lighter and my first book of car payments in my shirt pocket. No insurance was required at that time, and I did not purchase any.

I was extremely proud to have my first set of wheels and everything went well for a week. Then Bud came back. Then the car started bouncing excessively whenever a bump or dip in the road was encountered; and the front wheels started to shimmy. The steering wheel play I discovered during one of my inspections could not be adjusted out because the steering gear was worn out. By now, I realized that this was not such a great deal. I made my first payment and was reminded that all sales were "as is" and final. I was stuck.

I went to Chilton's to research what caused the shimmy. I learned that that model Chevy had knee action shock absorbers as part of the front suspension system. It was a problem design, one to avoid. I checked replacement costs, which turned out to be economically unfeasible. Therefore, I devised a solution that was safe and cost effective: I replaced the recommended shock absorber oil, which was thin and quickly leaked out, with 90-weight hypoid oil that lasted at least two weeks and provided sufficient damping to maintain safety.

The play in the steering wheel had no easy solution. I replaced the adjustment screw with a longer one, which helped some. Then I replaced the steering sector oil with grease used to lubricate a car's chassis, which, of course was much, much thicker. This measure somewhat further decreased play in the wheel. Driving a car with this much play in the steering wheel dramatically increased the workload of the driver. I had to anticipate and literally wind up the wheel in advance to make a right or left turn.

After three weeks of ownership, I discovered something else. The vacuum-assisted shift mechanism that was supposed to make the steering-column-mounted shift lever float through the gears effortlessly actually made shifting much more difficult. Worse yet, there was no way to repair, disconnect or remove the device. It was part of the upgrade luxury package.

Of course, I had to suffer Bud's wrath for making such a foolish decision. Not only that, Bud, while at Fort Sill, had found a nice, cheaper 1940 Ford four-door from a fellow guardsman. It was available immediately and mine if I wanted it. Bud was willing to sign for and register it for me.

Clearly disappointed at my decision, he never made that offer again. What did I learn from all of this? My inspection system was good, but flawed. I should have insisted on driving the car to the station to inspect the car on the lift. I should have taken the front wheels off for a closer look, and I would have seen the knee-action suspension, which would have alerted me to research it. In short, I would not have bought the car. That hard lesson was well learned. I knew how to avoid these mistakes on subsequent car purchases.

With all its flaws, the car was still a girl magnet. It was 17 years old, older than its passengers. However, it had a special charm; it was almost an antique. Girls loved cruising in it. They loved the town and country horn, which sounded normally in the town toggle and like a freight train in the country position. They also loved the tube-type radio that resonated like a jukebox. With the car, I assumed the persona of "Little Eddie Joe" after Little Richard, who at the time had big hits with *Tutti Frutti*, *Long Tall Sally* and *Slippin' and Slidin'*. The car allowed me to travel to all the remote extensions of the county and beyond when necessary. I met girls from North Little Rock, McAlmont, Jacksonville, and Sweet Home.

One night after working late, I decided to cruise through downtown for no particular reason. I noticed a girl, Ella Mae, aka Doll Baby, and her older sister walking south on Main Street. I pulled alongside them and Doll Baby asked me to give them a ride home. I agreed to do so when she said, "Buy me a foot long hotdog and a milkshake before you take us home." I knew that meant buying the same for her sister, too. I said, "Ok," and headed for the malt stand at 15th and Main. I bought the foot longs and shakes and planned to quickly drop them off at their house and head for home. I knew where they lived on East 21st from my walking and bicycle tours, but I never went inside their house. We always just talked outside.

Doll was short in stature but had grown considerably in the chest. She was not beautiful, but had sex appeal. When we arrived at their house, Doll sent her sister inside and asked me to talk to her a few minutes in the car. She said, "Do you notice anything different about me?"

"Yes, those two grapefruits on your chest."

"Man, they are all mine, too. Check 'em out!"

I did. At that point, I knew everything she had on: one cotton dress, brassiere, panties and black patent leather high heels. Still, I thought I would be leaving in a couple of minutes. For some reason, I was extremely nervous. She seemed to sense my urge to leave.

"Come on, walk me to my door."

Sensing closure, I said, "Sure."

I walked her to her door, but somehow she coaxed me inside. There was no one else downstairs. In the blink of an eye, she pulled me into a small closet and shut the door. She tiptoed up to kiss me. By now, I knew the deal, but I was scared. She asked, "Do you want to take off my bra?" While I was stammering, she said, "Here I'll do it for you." She obviously knew I was nervous. She literally took things in her own hands. She took out my wallet and removed the rubber that she saw when I paid for the dogs and shakes. With the deftness and sleight of hand of a skilled magician, Doll installed the rubber and navigated the proper geography of her person. In a few seconds, it was all over. Of all people, Doll Baby had vanquished my virginity. Through no fault of my own, I had just made Dr. Robinson proud.

Section Three: Pegasus Profiles: People, Places and Predicaments

During the Pegasus period, I met hundreds of personalities at the filling station. They came from all walks of life: no collar, blue collar, professional and multicultural. Some were friendly and frequent, others candid and casual; to an extent, they became surrogates to me – my Pegasus family. The characters, places and predicaments in this section were so interesting, influential, and memorable that they command detailed profiles.

13

Oscar Lane – Pegasus District Manager

Oscar Lane, the district sales manager for Mobilgas, was an interesting and knowledgeable person to me. He looked as if he could have been the father of *CBS Evening News* Anchor and *60 Minutes* Correspondent, Scott Pelley. The backseat and trunk of his 1955 blue Plymouth was jammed full of marketing and promotional items like pencils, pens, key chains, maps and flying red horse stickers of numerous sizes.

Oscar was my first marketing teacher. He explained institutional advertising and corporate sponsorship in a way that I understood. We discussed Mobil television advertising and its impact on our filling station. He explained corporate tie-ins and sponsorships like the race up *Pike's Peak*, the *Indianapolis 500* and the *Mobil Economy Run*. Oscar also discussed the renowned *Mobil Travel Guide*, which annually rated hotels and restaurants on a system based from one to five stars according to assessed quality. All of these promotions hosted the flying red horse, the corporate logo.

Oscar took questions and problems from local filling station proprietors and provided them with answers and solutions. He seemed to know everything about the oil industry. One early evening, after he finished a discussion with Bud and the Old Man, I followed Oscar to his car for my own Q&A session. He always took time to answer my questions. I remember this session because Oscar gave me a mini-history lesson in Greek mythology.

"Hey, Oscar," I called out.

"Yes."

"A question for you."

"Ok, go ahead."

"I heard the Red Horse has a name. Is that true?"

"Ok, let me explain," said Oscar.

"The horse's name is **Pegasus** from Greek mythology. In Greek mythology, Pegasus was a beautiful, winged horse capable of flying up to heaven. Look it up at the library, and we'll talk about it next time I see you."

"Ok, Oscar, see you," I said, just as a customer drove up to the gas pumps. Oscar and I talked numerous times after that very short conversation, but that one was my favorite. About two years later, Oscar took a new job at the regional level, and I never saw him again. There were two other district sales managers during my filling station career, but neither one was as memorable as Oscar Lane. Two names I never forgot; they belong in the same breath: Oscar Lane, our first district sales manager, and Pegasus, the flying red horse. Pegasus became the obvious name for this book.

14

Urinating Man – Forbidden Toilets

On a slow lazy, hazy summer afternoon in 1956, a 1954 Oldsmobile sedan drove up to the west pumps where I was standing, anticipating the next customer. The driver was a well-dressed Negro man who said in an articulate baritone voice, "Fill my tank with Mobil gas Special and check under the hood, please."

"Sure," I responded as I placed the automatic gas nozzle into his tank's filler tube. I checked all the fluids under the hood of his car and found everything in order, and I told him, "Everything under the hood is fine."

While cleaning his windshield, I noticed a brown briefcase in the front passenger seat. Everything about this person indicated that he was a professional, doctor, lawyer or businessman. By the time the gas nozzle clicked off, the driver was standing outside his car. I topped off his tank. His tab was an even five dollars, and he paid me in cash with one bill. As I thanked him for his business, I noticed he started to move around nervously.

After a few moments of erratic movement, he said, "Young man, do you have a restroom that I can use?"

I answered, "No."

"Please, I have to go urgently!"

"I'm sorry, but I don't have a restroom you can use."

At that moment, a white man walked out of the men's restroom and returned the key to the office. Moreover, the Negro driver of the Oldsmobile, which I had just filled with gas, saw him.

"Young man, can I just please go in there?" I knew our policy. Negroes could not use the restrooms. I answered the man, "I'm truly sorry, but I can't give you that key. Negroes aren't allowed to use the restrooms."

The man was dancing and skipping around the pumps. I felt like a heel. He bounced and skipped through the lubrication bay and saw our deep sink in the back room. "Can I use that sink? Oh, my God, can I just use that sink? This is serious. That sink, please!"

"Sir, I can't do that. I'd be in trouble if I let you go in the sink."

"You don't understand! I have to go!" he said as he stepped outside the rear of the grease rack.

"Oh no, oh no," he said as he slowly started urinating on himself. His eyes were closed, and he had a grimace on his face. His hands were up about shoulder high as if he were reaching for something. I watched as his urine flooded his groin area, slowly creeping down the inside of both pant legs into his shoes and spilling onto the ground. Time was in slow motion, and it seemed like he urinated forever.

"Oh, my God! I'm so embarrassed," the man said, as he quickly high stepped back through the lube bay on the way back to his car, still parked at the pumps. I wanted to offer him one of our fender covers to put over his velour seats to keep them from being stained. However, I knew we only had four and received only two new ones each week, so we needed all we had. I wanted to do something, anything, but my mind was blank. I had just witnessed, first hand, the consequences of our restroom policy and my actions (or inactions). Relieving one's self was not supposed to be this melodramatic or public.

He got into his car and drove away. I noticed his Arkansas license plate as he drove south on Chester Street.

I stood at the pumps, momentarily stunned, digesting the last few minutes. I imagined how it would feel running back to your car with your urine dripping from your expensive pants and sloshing in your fancy shoes, and then sitting in a nice car with pants and shoes saturated with urine to soil and stain the seats and carpets – and the smell in the summertime.

I ran back to the spot where the man initially relieved himself for a retrospective view of this event. I wondered, who was this guy? Where did he come from? Was he from the area? Where was he going? Did he recognize that he drove right by the community center, which had plenty of Negro-friendly bathrooms? Did his make-water emergency come upon him in an instant? Didn't he have a personal water management plan like most Negroes? Most of us, out of necessity, knew where all the public restrooms that we were authorized to use were located. I had so many questions and no answers.

Then I pondered the ultimate question. Why didn't Urinating Man just whip out his water cannon behind the filling station and relieve himself? I could not answer that question. Maybe it was because the area was very open; therefore there was no opportunity for complete cover or concealment. In addition, I am sure he understood one of the cardinal rules of the segregated South: a Negro man never exposed himself in front of a white person, especially a white woman, lest there be dire consequences, including a fine, jail or worse. I assume he considered all of this before his bladder just gave way.

If the Old Man was aware of any of this as it played out, he never tipped his hand. It was a slow day and Bud was off. The Old Man was preoccupied by his bookkeeping chores, well aware that I would handle all routine tasks. He may have seen the man running through the lube bay, but since I was right behind him, assumed I was explaining something to him. Moreover, on occasion he nodded off.

I never saw the man before that day, and I never saw him again. However, I never forgot him. A video of his indignity is permanently etched in my brain. I mused several questions for weeks. What did I learn from this incident? What can I do to preclude its recurrence? Could I convince the Old Man to alter the policy? After all, why could itinerant Mexicans use the restrooms and not Negroes?

After about three weeks, time ameliorated the issue. I decided not to discuss a new policy with either Bud or the Old Man. I arrived at a different solution. When the next Negro asked me for the key to the restroom, I would simply give it to him. And I did just that. There were no repercussions. About a year later, we left the restrooms open all the time. Even today, I wish I knew the identity of the dignified man, who in 1956, was forced to relieve himself in such an undignified way.

15

Carl Tullos – Immoral Hustler

Carl Tullos' life was rife with immoral, illegal and unethical practices, yet he was an interesting man to me. During his many stints of transitional unemployment, he often worked temporarily at the filling station, so I got to know him well. He often told me he was slicker than the motor oil we sold. After listening to and witnessing some his exploits, I was convinced that he was at least as slithery as a snake.

Carl was white, rotund, with a large pavilion (as he called it) covering his working tool. He was married, although he said only his wife was. His wife was a cute, shapely blond lady, who did not seem to be a good match for him. Her appearance was immaculate; she was graceful, looked great in her clothes. Carl was slovenly, bowed over, knock-kneed and disjointed. His wife, the breadwinner, always had a great job; Carl never had a good one. They never had kids.

By his accounts, he was a ladies' man. When we worked together, I personally watched him try, to use the parlance of the day, to make out with every female filling station patron who was not universally ugly. "Joe," as he called me, "I know I'm an ugly S.O.B., but the women love a big working tool. And I have a big one. Why do you think my old lady stays with me? She loves what I do to her in the bed. I throw the meat to her with my sweet peter. She loves me. I can't run her off," he told me as we washed a car.

Carl had been a self-professed master door-to-door salesman. He sold

129

encyclopedias, vacuum cleaners, ladies' shoes and Fuller brushes. Actually, he sold almost nothing; he merely offered them for sale. According to Carl, his masquerade got his foot in the door and, more often than I could imagine, got him the opportunity to sleep with the woman of the house.

He explained it to me this way. "I prey on BUWYKs – bored, unemployed, white, young and kidless. There are four major apartment complexes in Little Rock that I frequently work and one in North Little Rock. These places are full of married, horny slut women. I go door-to-door about nine in the morning on weekdays. The unsuspecting husbands have gone to work. Many of the women are still in their nightgowns. No makeup, no panties, no problems. I levee's all."

"Tullos, did you ever sleep with a Negro lady?" I asked. "Many times in the back seat of my cab. My favorite Nigra gal was a maid who worked in Pulaski Heights. I picked her up late at night after work, drove her home, and made out in the back seat of the cab. Man, she had great tits. We did it all in that back seat."

Tulles sometimes drove a taxi for the Yellow Cab Company. Unlike the West 9th Street Cab Company, the Yellow Cab Company hired only white drivers. Tullos often stopped by the filling station in his cab when it was out of service. During such stops and stints as my co-worker, he explained the cab business to me – both the legitimate and seedy sides. Tullos drove a cab – on and off – longer than any of his other moneymaking ventures, so he knew the business well. I remember his first cab, a 1955 Plymouth built at the factory to be a cab (like all those he drove) with a heavy-duty suspension, electrical system and a very durable interior. That cab was not radio dispatched and did not have a fare meter. Fares were determined by the number of zones crossed at 25 cents per zone. Tullos' later cabs eventually had two-way radios and fare meters, which greatly increased productivity and the money he earned. He owned one cab, which was later repossessed.

During one of these out-of-service stops, Tullos opened the trunk of his cab. "Joe what do you think I have in here?" he asked.

"I don't know. What?"

He showed me several bottles of moonshine and several bottles of legal booze with unbroken seals. "What do you do with this stuff?" I asked.

This is where I make the real money. I pick these guys up late at night at Missouri Pacific or Rock Island train station. They want some whiskey and everything is closed. I sell them some at a huge profit. In addition, I know where all the whore houses are. If a guy wants a gal, I fix them up; take them to the whorehouse. I get a fee from the john and a fee from the house madam. Sometimes, I take some out in trade from the whores."

"Some gentlemen want to gamble," he said. "I know where all the action is. I know where they take bets on the dog track in West Memphis and the horse track in Hot Springs. I know where the big poker games are played, and I know where the hot bones are rolled. Whatever their pleasures are, I know just the place. That information is valuable. For an extra fee, I take them to the action."

He explained that one passenger asked him to take him to a massage parlor, one with only masseurs. Tullos said he asked,

"Are you gay?"

He said the passenger responded, "Yes."

"I know just the place. I will take you there; it will cost you an extra two bucks off the meter."

"Great," said the passenger.

During another conversation, Tullos told me about a train station passenger from Chicago. This man wanted to stop by a house of ill repute on the way home to his wife. Tullos said he expected to drop the man off at one of the whorehouses, which paid him a referral.

To his surprise, the man said, "Wait here. Keep the meter running. I made a lot of money off him that night," Tullos recalled. "That guy was in that house for over two hours and then I took him home. He paid me full meter as well as my off-meter fee and a huge tip," said Tullos.

When Little Rock's unionized city bus drivers went on strike, the transit system hired replacement workers to keep the buses running. The intrepid Tullos crossed the bully picket line at the bus yard and became a scab. As such, he drove many bus routes, including the West 15th Street-Prothro Junction course. One night, I met Tullos on the West 15th Street leg and boarded his bus, sitting in the back, of course. It was his last run for the night. I rode with him to the Prothro Junction turnaround and back to the bus yard to park the bus for the night. During the run, Tullos endured many taunts from passengers and agitators, such as goddamn scab, strikebreaker and much worse. At one stop, I thought he was about to be assaulted by a worked-up group. He maintained his composure and managed to pick-up passengers, close the front doors and drive away, escaping potential violence.

Tullos parked the bus at midnight. The bus yard was quiet. The picket line Tullos encountered at the beginning of his shift was gone. He secured the bus, and we walked to his car. He drove me back to my car. He talked about the daily explosive encounters with the union drivers and their supporters at the picket line. He did not expect to drive the bus any longer, not because the strike ended, but because the constant death threats made him feel mortal. He ruminated about what his wife would think if he were killed. I had never heard or seen him this pensive. Then he quickly reverted to the Tullos I knew.

"Joe," he said, "During the few weeks I drove these buses, I met two women I really enjoyed. I slept with both of them. One was a young college student, who I asked if I could come by her apartment after I put the bus to bed. She was lonely and said ok. I did not go home that night. My wife was pissed. The other was a married mother of six, who said she was happily married but willing to trifle a bit. I worked her over, or she worked me over, right behind you in the back seat. I could not tell she had six kids. I would like to meet up with her again."

Tullos dropped me off at my car. As I drove home, I felt I had a much better understanding of the emotions surrounding pickets, scabs, unions and men like Carl Tullos. However, I also felt that, since he lived in a "Bible Belt" state, maybe he needed to join a Bible-based church. On the other hand, maybe not. Religion was one subject we never discussed.

16

Gary St. John – Blue-eyed Soul Brother

Gary St. John was a long, lanky blonde who projected the reckless, bad boy image of James Dean. He was tall in the saddle like Randolph Scott. His hair was styled in the typical Duck-butt, which was popular at the time. His swagger was a blend of Marlon Brando and Reese "Goose" Tatum of the Harlem Globetrotters. He drove a black 1950 Ford convertible, which had been modified to host a 1953 Chrysler Hemi engine with a four-barrel carburetor, mated to a four-speed transmission with a floor-mounted Hurst stick shift. This car had a twin exhaust system, which included straight-through glass pack mufflers. It was loud and very fast. It could peel rubber for half a block.

One of Gary's favorite pastimes was luring other daring drivers into a stoplight drag race. Most drivers took the bait, not realizing that his car was a Chrysler Hemi masquerading as a Ford flathead. Gary issued a challenge by gunning his engine to a low rumble. The other driver, if interested, gunned his engine to a slightly higher roar. This continued back and forth until the light changed. Whoever peeled the most rubber, made the most noise and had the lowest elapsed time to the first intersection was the winner. After work, I was cruising in the car with Gary during one of these encounters. He won handily, but it was dangerous and scary. He was clearly braver than I was.

One thing that set him apart from other whites was the fact that he loved black, rhythm and blues, or race music. During the day, his radio was always tuned to KOKY, the local Negro radio station. It was a sight to see: this tall, blonde white guy with his convertible top dropped and the radio loudly emanating Jimmy Reed's classic *Going to New York*. At night, Gary switched to more of the same from clear channel AM stations broadcasting from Shreveport and Nashville.

After work, Gary and I sometimes met at a watermelon stand at 12th and Park Streets. This stand, which sold only watermelons and soft drinks, was owned and patronized mostly by Negroes. It had outdoor chairs and tables covered by a canvas roof. A nickel jukebox was constantly pumping out rhythm and blues songs. Gary was right at home. In a sea of black folks sat this blonde guy devouring melon and spitting seeds. One night, he asked me, "Eddie, when are you going to set me up with some colored girls? I want to date them, dance with them. You know I'm cool; I'm not afraid."

"I'm working on it," I answered.

"I know a really beautiful colored girl, high school senior, who would really love to meet you, be with you – but not here. Maybe in New York or L.A., where she can be herself. She said she was afraid to do it here. I told her all about you."

"Listen, I'm not afraid to be seen with colored girls in public in Little Rock."

"I understand both situations," I said.

We departed while listening to Hank Ballard and the Midnighters singing *Sexy Ways*.

If Gary saw me when he was out on the town, with one of his lady friends or just hanging out with the guys, he always acknowledged and introduced me as his friend. Unlike some of my customers in those situations who rendered me invisible or unrecognized, Gary was always proud to speak to me.

Late one summer night, Gary's luck ran out. He fell asleep and ran head-on into an overpass abutment on the way to Hot Springs. His car was totaled, and he was severely injured. He did not come into the filling station for weeks. When I finally saw him again, he had a different car and subdued demeanor. The old adventurous Gary was gone. Eventually, he drifted away from the station, and I never saw him again. Someone told me he moved away.

I always thought of Gary as a white man with the soul of a black man, a white façade hiding a black physical being. He was perfectly content mingling and connecting with Negroes – anywhere – including church, clubs, and concerts. In another time or place, we might have been great friends.

17

The Parker Family

The first time I vividly remember seeing the Parker family was in the spring of 1956. Daddy Parker worked on the railroad and Momma Parker was a businesswoman, operating a beauty salon adjacent to the family home on West 20th Street.

They were loyal white customers since they lived only about four blocks from the filling station. The family had three vehicles: a 1956 Oldsmobile, an older straight eight Pontiac and an old pickup.

Mother Parker never said much to me, but Daddy Parker talked to and around me often. His normal dialog, other than car jargon, was his concern that a Negro would move into his neighborhood and cause its social and economic demise. His campaign was so candid at times that I thought maybe he forgot I was Negro.

At least a hundred times, I heard him say something like, "We have got to keep the niggers out of my neighborhood. When niggers move in, the integrity of the neighborhood is destroyed. Property values go way down. Customers will stop coming to my wife's shop. Her business will be destroyed. Niggers should stay in their own neighborhoods. The races were not meant to be together."

There were three children in the family: Sammie Dean, who was about my age; middle child, a brother, Bobby; and younger sister, Sally. All three were drivers who often came into the filling station alone. All of them talked incessantly to me except when they were with their parents. The Parker siblings, whether together or alone, were always very friendly and cordial to me, including before and after the Central High School integration crisis.

I was very surprised when I saw Sammie Dean on national television disparaging the Negro (Little Rock Nine) students who integrated Central High School. I had never heard her speak that way. In fact, I never discussed the Central High issue with any of the Parker children.

Sammie introduced me to her fiancé, Eddie, a Michael J. Fox look-alike, one day at the filling station. Eddie, like Daddy Parker, worked for the railroad. Eddie and I often discussed the railroad and cars. Eddie drove a light-colored 1949 or 1950 Chevy.

Sammie Dean and Eddie expressed maximum gratitude and respect for me after I intervened in what they described as a very dangerous and scary experience. I was cruising downtown Main Street about 11 p.m. one hot summer night. As I approached Sixth Street, I saw a Chevy that I recognized as Eddie is being chased west on Sixth Street. Eddie had panicked and his car struck two street light poles. His car came to a halt after he hit the second one.

The pursuit car, a 1955 Mercury Montclair hardtop was occupied by five Negro males. The Mercury stopped, and two men headed towards the Chevy, when I pulled in behind it. One of them said, "Nigger, what are you doing here? You want your ass kicked? Get the hell out of the way! I'm gonna hurt these peckerwoods."

Scared to death, I just drove away. Somehow, though, I mustered enough nerve to get out of my car. One of the men was tall, stone-faced, and cold looking, like Snoop Dogg. He said, "What's your stake here? I'll slice your ass up like warm butter."

"I know this guy," the steely-eyed man said as he looked at me at a distance. This guy came into the filling station, I thought to myself. As he got closer to my face, he said, "I know you, you work at that filling station on Wright Avenue, right?" I said, "Right."

"Nigger, this is your lucky day. Get these crackers off my street," he said. The two guys walked back to their car. The Mercury burned rubber and sped west on Sixth Street into the night.

I walked up to the Chevy and realized that both Eddie and Sammie Dean were in the car. Sammie was obviously scared and crying uncontrollably.

They were glad to see a familiar face. Sammie said, "Thanks, can you help us get out of here?" Eddie said, "Will you escort us to the malt stand at 15th and Main?"

"Sure," I said as I directed Eddie to back away from the light pole. I followed them to the malt stand, which was a safe haven for them, but could be a dangerous location for me, a lone black male.

Once there, Eddie, Sammie and I exchanged informal pleasantries. They had regained their composure, but I was losing mine. I realized how close I had come to being seriously hurt or worse. I decided that I had enough excitement for that night and headed home around midnight.

I reflected on the incident while driving. The most perplexing thing about this episode was that the chase took place in the heart of downtown, and there was not a cop in sight.

I saw the Mercury at a distance several times after that night. I never encountered, that I recognized, any of its occupants again.

Bobby Parker was the most affable of the Parker family. We often talked about our fondness for girls. These girls were generic and devoid of color. Then we talked cars, mostly dragsters. Many times, Bobby invited me to accompany him to the Carlisle Drag Strip in Carlisle, Arkansas, for weekend drag races. He was always charitable that way. We both knew I could not go; Negroes were not allowed to attend. He also continually invited me to go with him to play Snooker at the parlor on South Main Street. Once again, he knew I could not get in. However, I believe in his heart he really wanted me to go with him. Sometimes he came to the filling station just to hang out, talk to me, and smoke cigarettes. I always enjoyed his company.

Sally Parker was the youngest and perhaps the freest spirit. During slack periods, she came up and talked to me about music, movies and boys behind the filling station. On several occasions, these public meetings got us in trouble, especially when she wore shorts. Some of the customers thought we were too cozy, that I had forgotten my place. One customer threatened to tell Daddy Parker. I was told, by Bud, it was not good for business or my safety, to cease and desist. I did.

Daddy Parker also expressed concern to others and me about some nigger sleeping with his beautiful daughters. Once, he remarked to another customer, "Every nigger's dream is to sleep with my beautiful daughters." I knew that possibility was Daddy Parker's worst nightmare.

Sammie Dean and Eddie were later married and had at least one child. No,

I was not invited to the wedding. Several years after the Central High School crisis, I saw Sammie Dean with her kid on South Park Street. We had a friendly chat for about 15 minutes. I have not seen or heard from her since.

18

Casket Man – Impersonating a Nigger

Another one of my interesting customers was *Casket Man*. He was self-described as a highly educated Negro, who made a very good living selling caskets in Mississippi. He enjoyed explaining to me how he lived *down* to his white customers' expectations. He had two distinct personae: one for Little Rock and another for Mississippi.

In Little Rock, he was a Negro bourgeois owner of various items of personal property, including several new automobiles, numerous expensive jewelry pieces and a trendsetting wardrobe. Casket Man told me he also had several pieces of real property, including rentals, parcels of unimproved land and an upscale home in the South End.

Said Casket Man: "In Little Rock, I am an uppity nigger; in Mississippi, I am a good nigger, who knows his place. You see, Eddie, I'm an actor who plays his role very well. In Little Rock, I play a Ralph J. Bunche role; in Mississippi, I play a real-life Stepin Fetchit, a bumbling, deferring nigger. I sell my soul to the white man, but I also sell a huge number of caskets."

Casket Man and his trophy blue-vein wife each drove new Cadillacs. His business vehicle was a 1949 Chevy pickup, which looked dilapidated, but was in excellent mechanical shape. This was the vehicle he drove to, from and in Mississippi.

He often explained and complained to me about the travails of living, traveling and doing business in the state of Mississippi, which he labeled the racist state in America. His sales route kept him in the state from four days to a week at a time, usually two times a month. He never risked buying gas or stopping for a restroom break at a filling station in Mississippi. If he approached a white female of any age, he kept his eyes glued to the ground. During transactions with customers, he only wore denim overalls, work boots and shirts. He used a liberal number of slowly executed *yessurs* and *yessums* to indicate agreement but inflected to indicate subordination. To make sure there was no mistake, he also used animated body language to show deference to his white clients. He occasionally performed some of this routine for me at the gas pump island. "Eddie," he said, "Learn this well, boy. You will likely use it one day to beat The Man at his own game."

"Some people, including some of my in-laws, think of me as an Uncle Tom. I tell them, until you surpass my success, keep quiet!" Casket Man was the first person to explain to me that perception is the white man's reality; true reality is bull hockey to them.

"In Mississippi," he explained, "I am who I am perceived to be, not who I really am. Sometimes life has to be an illusion to level the playing field. Just be sure you make the illusion work! I am testament that it does work. Use it wisely."

I never knew what to make of Casket Man. I certainly could not argue with his apparent success. I never had to use his techniques to any extent, but I never worked in Mississippi either.

19

Miss Fairlane – aka Marilyn Monroe

It was a late, hot summer night in 1957. I was cruising alone south on Main Street, listening to the radio, when the 14th Street light changed to red. When I stopped, I noticed a 1956 pink and white Ford Fairlane two-door hardtop in the lane to my right. The young white female driver was signaling to get my attention. I initially tried to ignore her gestures and gave little indication that I even saw her. There were other cars around us, so it was the prudent thing to do.

When the light changed, she slowly drove alongside me for the next two blocks and blatantly signaled for me to pull over. After the intersection of 17th and Main, along a very dark stretch of road, I pulled over. She pulled in behind me.

I was very reluctant to get out of my car. I seriously considered driving off. Before I could do so, she got out of her car and approached mine. "Hi, I'm Marilyn Monroe, want to go somewhere alone where we can talk?" she said. Before I could answer, she said, "Come on, I'd like that." She was a well-endowed blonde wearing a wide skirt filled with petticoats. The whole situation was nerve wracking to me. Several cars drove by. I thought what if the next one was a police car?

In a fraction of a second, I made an impetuous decision to accompany her.

"Where are we going?" I asked.

"Get in my car. You know a secret place where we can park and talk? Some place where we will not be discovered? You are not afraid of me are you?" she asked.

Quickly my fear vanished, and I meekly climbed into her car. I thought about the two most popular black lovers' lanes in Little Rock, Blueberry Hill and Shangra-La, but neither offered the secrecy required for this tête-à-tête.

I told her, "Just continue south. We'll head to a place called Arch Street Pike." This was a newly discovered, seldom used lovers' lane.

"Great!" she replied. Several times during the drive, I had to Huck below the window line, and once I had to crawl under the dash to avoid being seen when the ambient illumination was intense. We both thought it was safer that way.

We drove across the Arch Street Bridge and over to the spot I had previously reconnoitered. There was no other activity in sight. As we stopped, I had two concerns: what someone could do to my parked car and what could happen if the State Police caught "Marilyn" and me back here.

I understood from the beginning that Marilyn was a pseudonym, and she confirmed that later. In fact, I never learned her real name, although she knew mine. I vividly remember how she introduced herself: "Please don't ask too many details about me because I really can't answer. I know you will understand, ok? I am a senior at a state teachers' college in Arkansas. My dad is a successful businessman who bought me this car. I enjoy driving to Little Rock. I would love to have you as my good friend. I enjoy being around colored guys. I can't do this at home."

For some reason, I bought into all this anonymity and did not press her for specifics, although her purse was in the seat between us before I tossed it on the floorboard. When the purse was in my hand, she pleaded for me not to look in it, fearing, I suppose, that I might use the information to get her in serious trouble. I acquiesced.

I told Marilyn my short history, about the filling station and gave her the number to reach me there. By now, the moment was awkward, and I was not sure why we were there, so I asked her, "What are we going to do?"

"Eddie, just have fun with me. Don't worry about anything. I know how to take care of myself," she said assuredly.

I wiggled around the front cabin of her car trying to get comfortable while keeping a nervous eye and ear for any headlights or car sounds on the horizon. Suddenly, she turned to face me and said, "Eddie, it's time to have some fun." We began to canoodle (today's term), all in one continuous motion. Then I *counted* her petticoats.

She drove me back to my car about 1 a.m. It was still intact. As Marilyn drove away, I noted her license number and wrote it down after I got into my car. I began to ruminate about my adventure with Marilyn and its potential consequences. She had a lot of information about me, including my license number, car description, place of work, work phone number, and my real name and description. I thought of all the things that could happen to me. I remembered what happened to Emmett Till for a lot less. It was scary.

Marilyn made me swear to keep our episode top secret, and she swore to do likewise. I was so scared; I did keep it to myself. I never told even my best friends.

In the days that immediately followed that night, I wondered why I had trusted someone I had just met. Who was she, really? I did not dare try to find out. As days passed, I became less fearful. Still, when I serviced new customers at the gas pumps, they all looked suspicious. One older white man had cold, piercing eyes that looked like laser beams. I imagined he knew everything.

One day at work, the pay phone rang and Bud answered. "Joe," he said, "There's a sweet-sounding honey on the phone for you. That's a new voice. I haven't heard that one before." I was not expecting *any* calls, so I was suspicious, especially about a voice that Bud had not heard. I picked up the phone, and it was Marilyn. She said she disguised her voice until I came to the phone.

"I'll be brief. Have you thought about me lately?"

"Yes," I answered and for more reasons than she would ever know.

"I want us to meet again this Saturday night at 10 p.m. I will slowly drive by where you left your car last time. I will have a blue ribbon tied around the top of my antenna. You pull in behind me as I drive by, then overtake me and lead me to where you plan to leave your car this time. Then I will drive us back to Arch Street Pike. Ok? Just be there!"

"Ok," I answered and she was gone. I thought to myself, I do not believe I agreed to that again after all the angst I felt after the last time.

I followed her instructions. We linked up and headed back to our same rendezvous spot. Once again, I was somewhat nervous but completely vigilant. I asked Marilyn, "What would you do if a state police trooper caught us back here? Cry rape?"

"Of course not," she said.

"You and I both know that if that happened, I would be dead," I retorted.

She fired back, "We would both be dead! Eddie, forget the grizzly talk for now. Let's have some fun. You have to play a game with me."

I listened but remained silent.

"You have to find my two garters. They're on my body somewhere. No petticoats this time. On your mark, get set, go!" She pulled the lever on the front seat bottom to let it slide all the way back. She wanted to turn on the radio. I vetoed that idea; too much noise. The game began. I found her garters.

On the way back, I asked her how old she was. She would only answer, "Not quite 21."

The last words she said to me before I left her car were "Thanks for another great night. I hope you learn to trust me. I will call you again when the time is right. Goodbye, Eddie." I told her goodbye, and she placed her right two forefingers on my lips. Then mysterious Marilyn was gone again.

I saw her four more times that summer. Marilyn always employed the same modus operandi: more creativity, more games – same result. I did learn to trust her more. Still, I kept our bombshell friendship secret. Young Negro man plus beautiful blonde young lady plus an intimate relationship in Little Rock, Arkansas, equaled a lethal combination.

I remember well the last time I saw Marilyn, especially her parting words: "Eddie, I have something to tell you." I stiffened a bit in anticipation of what she would say next. "I will not be able to see you again. I'll be graduating this summer and moving to another state." I listened intently, actually somewhat relieved. She went on, "Maybe a different time and place, things could be different. I am truly sorry for the things we had to go through just to be together. I am hopeful for a change for the better. Goodbye, good luck. Remember, this is our secret forever." She made me lock my little finger with hers to seal our secret pact. One last time, she placed the two fingers on my lips. Then she was gone. I never saw Marilyn or her 1956 Ford Fairlane again.

After that personal experience, I better understood the fears of Daddy Parker, Old Man Heitman and others. Young white women and young Negro men in Little Rock got together intimately at all costs. Our tryst was just one of perhaps hundreds. And from some of these unions, children or, as whites called them, mulatto monkeys, were born. I remember what another old white man at the pumps said to me, "Those mulatto monkeys will dilute the white race. It ain't fair. God didn't mean it to be."

In retrospect, I ponder the circumstances that allowed Marilyn and me to stop simultaneously at the traffic light at 14th and Main Streets. What if I had cruised through the East End like I originally planned? What if I had ignored her signal to pull over? Then, I wonder, why did I trust her? What if we had been caught? Would I recognize her today, more than 50 years later? Would she recognize me? I will never know the answer to those last two questions – unless she reads this book and contacts me. I may not recognize her face or voice, but I could identify her after a short series of questions. Miss Fairlane, aka Marilyn Monroe, should be able to respond with details known only to the two of us.

20

Vernon Walker – The Great Pretender

Vernon Walker was a tall, dark and handsome Negro man. With his processed hair and sunglasses, he could have been B.B. King's brother, but he did not sing. He lived in a rooming house half a block away, so he was a frequent patron of the filling station.

The first time I met Vernon, I noticed there was something different about his speech. First, he sounded like he had a Caribbean Island accent. I asked him where he was born, and he said, "In the southern United States." Secondly, his grammar, pronunciation, enunciation and inflection were always perfect – English textbook style. I took note of this every time we talked. I knew I did not speak as well as he did, but talking to him made me strive to emulate him.

Initially, he drove a 1946 blue Chevrolet 2-door coupe with skirts. The car had a split exhaust manifold to accommodate an after-market dual-exhaust system. The tailpipes were clamped to twin glass-packed mufflers, which gave the car a loud, mellow, purring sound. You could hear his car long before you could see it and long after you saw it.

His car was a girl magnet. His female passengers were some of the most beautiful young black ladies I had ever seen. They could have been models in Tan and Ebony magazines. When I cleaned his windshield, I was amazed that the clothes and makeup of these women always appeared to be perfect. I wondered where he found these women. In my view, they were in the same league as one of my favorite black actresses, Dorothy Dandridge.

I was impressed every time I serviced Vernon's car. His lady of the day was sitting shoulder-to-shoulder next to him in the front seat. His radio was more likely playing Ray Conniff than Ray Charles. Impeccably dressed, he always jumped out of his car, walked around to me with a confident swagger, and said, "Fill it up." However, I knew from a standing agreement that the real amount to place in his tank had to match the bills he ripped from his gold money clip, which was usually one to three dollars.

In time, Vernon bought a 1952 Oldsmobile Super 88 sedan with an external sun visor for the windshield, wide whitewall tires and a Hydra-Matic automatic transmission. The car was much bigger than the Chevy, and the loud mufflers were gone. The gorgeous girls remained. Vernon continued to be a local fashion visionary.

Vernon never told me his age, although I assumed he was in his mid-twenties, about ten years older than I was. For obvious reasons, I wanted the pleasures he seemed to have. I talked to him often – with and without the women – but really knew very little about him. I never knew where or if he worked. I saw his car at the rooming house down the street during working hours and in the evenings, so, if he worked, his hours were irregular. He said he had gone to college, but there was no evidence of it. Vernon was somewhat of a mystery. Where did he get his money? Why were so many girls attracted to him? The girls did not appear local, so where did they come from? I was never able to answer these questions.

The more I looked at Vernon, the less I saw. No degree. No visible income. No career. What I did see, his cars, clothes, abode, after a while no longer impressed me. The women who accompanied him were less beautiful and I saw fewer and fewer new faces. I realized that with education and planning, my success could easily trump his.

After several years, I saw Vernon less and less frequently until he disappeared completely. In retrospect, Vernon was an enigma. I did not really know him at all. However, he did leave me a great legacy – the gift of speaking correct English. During the Pegasus period, most of us spoke the popular black vernacular of the time, which sometimes defied the tenets of correct grammar. Nevertheless, Vernon was different. He always spoke correctly, and I took notice. In addition, he corrected me when I spoke incorrectly. Vernon is gone but his legacy lives on – even to this day. Because of his influence, I was able to sharpen my verbal and written skills, which have served me well.

21

Professor Townsend – Fantasy Lady

Professor Townsend was my favorite college faculty member, but I was not her student. In fact, I was still in high school. The professor taught summer classes at Arkansas Baptist College in Little Rock and was a frequent filling station patron.

My fondest memories of the professor were from the summer of 1959. She had been coming into the station for at least a year but never seriously aroused my interest until then. She usually drove in on Fridays around 8:30 or 9 at night and, if necessary, waited until I was free to service her car. She indicated to other attendants that she was my customer exclusively. Her car was a 1957 Dodge with the expansive wraparound windshield and no air conditioning. Because of the hot Arkansas nights, her clothing was usually skimpy. When I cleaned her windshield, she made sure I saw every stitch she wore and as much of her chocolate skin as possible.

Each time she came in, I learned a bit more about her. She told me she was the estranged wife of singer Ed Townsend – a one-hit wonder who had a big 1958 hit song called *For Your Love*. She taught summer classes at the college and on weekends drove home to Pine Bluff, Arkansas, about fifty miles away. She had a credit card that bore the name E. Townsend. She was the first black woman I saw with a gasoline credit card.

However, she was still a mysterious lady. I really did not know much about her. For instance, was she a tenured professor at another college or university? How old was she? Where did she live? Was she a PhD? What was her first name? What was her relationship with her estranged husband? Those questions were never answered.

The professor was a beautiful woman; she looked a lot like Brenda Sykes, the famous actress in Blaxploitation genre movies. Before long, I thought she was my sex goddess – a black Athena. I was in love and lust – at least every time she drove in. Her image always lingered in my mind long after she drove away.

"Fill 'er up!" she said during one of her stops. "Ok. By the way, what's your first name?" I asked.

"I'm your sweetheart, just call me sweetheart, ok, honey?" "Oh, yes!" I answered, although I never called her that. I was afraid to.

Then she said, "Come ride to Pine Bluff with me tonight."

"How will I get back to Little Rock? I have to work tomorrow," I said to her.

"That's no problem, I'll drive you back tomorrow morning."

"Where am I staying?"

"With me, dummy," she said, placing her face so close to mine that I could smell her sweet breath, which had the effect of an aphrodisiac.

One of my favorite encounters with Professor Townsend was during another hot summer night at the pumps. She offered me another invitation to go to Pine Bluff, but this night was different. She got out of the car, complaining how hot the evening was.

She walked up to me and said, "It's so hot."

She turned around and said, "Unbutton the back of my dress and unhook my bra. Now pull it out." I nervously removed her cream-colored bra.

"Put your hands inside my dress and touch the front of my chest."

My hands shakily found their target. She was not well endowed, but that did not matter. At that moment, every one of my 18-year-old hormones was raging like a Texas tornado downtown. I did not know how old this woman was, but I knew she was old enough to take my personal knowledge of the birds and bees to a much higher level.

Another favorite encounter occurred on a misty summer Friday night when Buck and I were just waiting for closing time when he said, "Joe, here comes your favorite lady."

I immediately recognized Professor Townsend's 1957 Dodge, perked up, and headed for the pumps. The routine was completely familiar.

"Fill it up, baby," she said, as soon as she rolled to a stop.

I started pumping the gas and quickly moved to the front of her car and began cleaning her huge windshield. As always in the past, she showed everything, lots of eye candy. I cleaned the windshield much longer than necessary and, the few short moments that I glanced up at her face, I saw that familiar wicked, yet seductive look. As always in the past, she got out of her car and stood in front of me, toe-to-toe, face-to-face, eye-to-eye, almost cheek-to-cheek and literally presented herself to me. I felt her warm, sweet breath on my face and remembered again, why this mature woman was my fantasy woman. It was her lips, stance, look and smell that simply blew my mind.

As always in the past, she asked the question, "Sweetheart, are you going to ride to Pine Bluff with me tonight? The night has something good for us." As always in the past, I equivocated and graciously declined her invitation. The real reason I declined was sheer fear. I simply did not know how to deal with a separated, mature, experienced professional woman.

The professor was visibly disappointed that I did not agree to ride to Pine Bluff with her. However, just as she had done numerous other times, she voiced empathy and concern about my fear of spending the night with her. She simply said, "Maybe the next time. One day you will be able to trust me." I thought, maybe. Professor Townsend drove to Pine Bluff without me.

I did not see the professor after the summer of 1959. She just stopped coming. Like most teenage boys, I had numerous fantasy ladies, including Lena Horne and Dorothy Dandridge. However, I only saw them on the screen and in print. I actually talked to and touched the professor in person – an experience I will never forget. I never did ride with her to Pine Bluff. I always wondered what would have happened if I had.

22

Reverend Cotton – School Bus Sanctuary

An interesting Negro businessman that I met at the pumps was a customer I called Reverend Cotton. I never knew his real name, but the moniker I assigned him was descriptive.

He owned and drove a yellow 1941 Dodge school bus, which was too old to transport schoolchildren to and from public schools. I often serviced his bus with gas, air and oil, which gave me lots of face time with Reverend Cotton, who was also the pastor of a small church. He explained to me that the church was God's will, but his livelihood came from the cotton fields just outside North Little Rock, Arkansas.

Reverend Cotton was tall, rugged, dark, affable and engaging. During our conversations he routinely engaged me with Bible speak. He especially taught and quizzed me about the order and meaning of the *Ten Commandments*. One day during a scheduled maintenance service, he showed me the gear pattern and let me drive his bus around the filling station – twice; but never on the street. It was my first experience with a transmission with low and double low gears and a two-speed differential. It was also the first and last bus I ever drove.

On Sundays, Rev. Cotton also used his bus to transport his small congregation to and from church and church-related outings.

"Praise the Lord, little man," the reverend always said to me after he pulled alongside the gas pumps and dismounted. "Fill 'er up, check the oil, tires and clean the windows." I always cleaned the front and rear windows, and he cleaned the side windows. "Tomorrow, I am going to Cotton Plant, Arkansas, to the cotton fields. I should have about 25 to 30 cotton pickers," he said.

In the back of the bus stood four cases of assorted Barq's sodas, the so-called belly washers. There was also a 15-gallon water can. In the early mornings on the way to the cotton fields, the reverend stopped at the ice plant at 14th and Chester to pick up a 50-pound block of ice to cool the water and sodas. The water was free to the riders; he sold the sodas for a profit.

"Little brother," he said to me once, "I have two churches, one stationary and one on wheels. The bus is my rolling sanctuary, and it is a full service church, too. Even do communion. So far, I've done one Baptism. Stopped at a creek on the side of the road, performed the service."

"While driving to the fields early in the morning, I preach a little sermon to the passengers. Then the riders and I sing praises. Make a joyful noise to the Lord. Lord have mercy! Some passengers, when they exit the bus, put a little something in the plate."

I asked, "You mean you collect tithes?"

"No, they just put something in the plate. Maybe guilty. Maybe the only church they go to," he said.

Reverend Cotton was a real entrepreneur, but not an educated one. He made money several ways. He charged a round-trip head fare to his cotton field passengers. He sold drinks, snacks and sandwiches that his wife made on the bus and at the fields. He sometimes received tithes, and he picked cotton. He said he was a seasoned picker and could bring in up to 300 pounds a day. He provided exactly the same services during cotton chopping season. Reverend Cotton demonstrated to me, just as Allan Jones had, that, if you tailor a reliable service to market needs, you could always make money.

23

Little Rock Nine – Circle of Friends

By now, the world knows the tremendous accomplishments of the Little Rock Nine, originally known as the Negro Nine. Numerous books, films and newspaper accounts have detailed their contributions to the civil rights movement, and I will not attempt to add to that. However, I will share my personal interaction with each of the Nine before, during and after they integrated Little Rock's Central High School. I will also share my personal experience with their leader and Arkansas State NAACP President, Daisy Bates.

One sunny day in 10th grade, I was summoned to the office of Mr. Otis T. Harris, Dean of Boys at Horace Mann High School. My initial reaction was one of trepidation because usually an audience with the Dean was not a positive event. However, it turned out that he wanted to inform me that I had been selected as one of the first 25 (a number that would grow much higher) students to be considered to potentially *volunteer* to integrate Central High School during the 1957-58 school year. He explained to me that all the students would come from our school, Horace Mann High School. I knew the students who *volunteered* had to have grit, grades and a Gandhiesque approach to make this challenge successful. I came away from the meeting elated, but surprised that I was being considered, yet fearful of losing my great job. However, after I thought about how unselfish Jackie Robinson was when he integrated baseball, I knew I would *volunteer* if I had the opportunity. I never had the opportunity.

Long before that day in the dean's office, I, like most high school students, knew the NAACP and the Pulaski County Board of Education were preparing to test Brown v. Board of Education by integrating Central High School. I knew from a number of sources, including from Arkansas State NAACP President, Daisy Bates.

By all accounts, Daisy Bates was a beautiful fair-skinned Negro woman and, by some accounts, her husband, L.C. Bates, was an articulate, smart, dark-skinned man. L.C. Bates was the editor and publisher of a local Negro newspaper called the Arkansas State Press, which I sometimes read. He always drove Chrysler cars, a 1954 model when I first met him, and 1957 model later on. He patronized the filling station, so I had the honor of servicing his car at the gas pumps, as well as on the grease rack, lubricating the chassis, and changing the oil and filter. He and Daisy once told me they were customers primarily because I worked there.

The Bateses usually filled up weekly. I had the opportunity to discuss NAACP issues in his newspaper while dispensing their gas and sometimes afterwards, depending on customer load. I had longer conversations with L.C. (I called him Mr. Bates.) during his monthly oil and lube jobs. Therefore, I was well versed on current NAACP issues and concerns.

I knew every member of the Little Rock Nine long before they integrated Central High School. They had been fellow students of mine at Gibbs, Capitol Hill, or Dunbar High School. Some I knew very well, others less so. I will discuss them by order of familiarity, from very well known, then in descending order.

By far, I was most familiar with **Terrence James Roberts**. We had been best friends since elementary school. In sixth grade, he was, like me, one of the Four Musketeers. He wore his hair very short, almost shaved, spawning nicknames of Monk and Nicodemus. Sometimes, we wrote poems together; other times, we competed to see who could write the better poem. He usually won.

I personally knew and interacted with his entire family. I spent lots of time at their house, which was just a few blocks from the filling station. I had a double motive for spending so much time with his family. First, he was one of my very best friends and, secondly, I had a serious crush on his older sister Juretta. Juretta, who was older than Terrence, was smart, articulate and beautiful. Despite my best efforts, I never won any attention from Juretta. However, I continued to try.

In one of these efforts, Terrence and I planned to ring in the New Year by cruising Little Rock in my 1939 Chevy and ending up across the bridge at North Little Rock's Novean's Drive Inn just prior to midnight. There we would celebrate, eating a hamburger and drinking a soda.

I talked Terrence into convincing Juretta to join us. If he knew about my crush on his sister, he never admitted it; he just played along with my game.

About 10 p.m. on New Year's Eve, 1955, I picked up Terrence and Juretta at their house on 17th and Izard Streets. I had ten dollars in my wallet, which I had deemed sufficient to impress Juretta. We did not get very far. As usual, I stopped at the stop sign at 16th and Cross. Almost as soon as I started up again, I saw the flashing red light on the police car behind me. I quickly stopped again, just clearing the intersection.

The cop got out of his car and walked up to my window. "Didn't you see that stop sign?"

"Yes sir, officer."

"Then why didn't you stop?"

"Officer, sir, I did stop."

"Listen, boy, you didn't stop. Are you disputing my word?"

"No sir," I said, hoping he would just give a ticket, so I could salvage the night and still impress Juretta. The cop shined his flashlight into the face of Juretta, frightening her and embarrassing me.

"Nigger, you just lied to me, an officer of the law. You ran that damn stop sign," he said, turning around as if to convince an invisible jury of his truthfulness.

"That's bad, very bad. I'm running your ass in. You're under arrest! You drive straight to the police station at Markham and Broadway. And I will be right behind you. I have your license plate number and, if you try anything funny, I'll put out an APB on your ass. Now go!" he barked.

I drove to the police station amid dead silence. I parked the car and told Terrence and Juretta that I would be right back, although I was not so sure that would be the case. The police officer escorted me inside and left me waiting to be processed. I had no idea what to expect next. Would I be thrown in a jail cell? What about Terrence and Juretta?

The desk sergeant who processed me was poetry in very, very slow motion. More than an hour and a half passed before he turned his attention to me. Finally, at about 15 minutes before midnight on New Year's Eve, he looked at my paperwork. After much quiet deliberation, the sergeant looked at me and said, "Eddie, you have two choices: pay a ten dollar fine or go to jail. What will it be?"

I thought to myself, he must have looked into my wallet. "I will pay the ten dollars, sir," I replied. I put a ten-dollar bill on the counter. The desk sergeant finished processing my fine at five minutes after midnight. I thanked him and left. It was 1956. Had I impressed Juretta? Almost certainly, just not the way I had in mind. If nothing else, it was unforgettable.

I returned to the car and found Terrence and Juretta anxious after the long wait. They had no idea whether I would or could come back. It was apparent to all of us that the night was ruined. We just returned home. Few words were spoken among us during the drive home, but several instances of celebratory gunfire ringing in the New Year were heard. The three of us got home without further incident.

Terrence and I remained best of friends, but I never had the desire or opportunity to pursue Juretta's attention again. Sometime just before or after Terrence entered Central High School, his family moved to a corner house near the livestock grounds, a few blocks from Allan Jones' shack. One night, while he was a Central High School student, Terrence and I were talking in the street adjacent to his house, when a pickup truck with two white passengers slowly drove by. A few minutes later, they drove up again and the driver tossed what appeared to be a stick of dynamite, which landed under Terrence's house. One of the occupants shouted racial epithets as the truck sped away. Terrence and I looked at each other and, without much thought, took off in a full-speed run, finally stopping several blocks away.

After we caught our breath and realized there was no explosion, we slowly walked back to his house. I do not recall now whether the device was an inert stick of dynamite or something else, but I do remember it evoked collective terror.

All Little Rock public schools were closed (See the J.C. Cook chapter for an explanation.) during the 1958-59 school year, and Terrence left Little Rock to attend high school in California. I never saw him again.

When my mother died and I went to live with my aunt and uncle, I joined a comity of friends, which included Milton B. Smith, **Jefferson Thomas** (affectionately known as Horn), and his older brother, Granville Thomas (better known to us as Bubble). Horn was one year younger and a grade behind me, while Bubble was one year older and a grade ahead of me. I spent lots of time at his house and therefore knew his entire family well.

Jefferson's house, which was located at 20th and Pulaski Streets next to Powell's Grocery Store, was very accommodating. There, Jefferson and I spent lots of time listening to his radio. Our favorite shows were *Sky King, Bobby Benson & the B-Bar-B Riders* and *Gang Busters*. We also spent countless days patrolling the concrete ditch behind his house.

A strange thing happened to me one night as Milton and I stood in front of Jefferson's house. An unknown person threw a golf-ball-sized rock that struck me in the middle of my forehead, producing a scar, which I still bear. Jefferson walked outside his house and escorted me inside where his mother cleaned my wound and applied a large Band-Aid. The three of us played Boston Blackie (the detective) but never found the culprits.

One day, during a game of chicken, all of us: Bubble, Horn, Milton and I took turns holding a small lit firecracker in our hand until it exploded. If you held it carefully at the very bottom with the tips of your fingers, you escaped injury. It was Little Rock roulette. Fortunately, we were not injured.

Thelma Mothershed lived at the intersection of 14th and Chester Streets. We knew each other well, and I visited her house frequently. She had sisters Grace, Lois and Gloria. I really enjoyed being among these beautiful young women but I was mesmerized by Gloria, who was just gorgeous. Thelma was frail and, other than school, did not participate in many activities. Therefore, I often stopped by her house at night, and we would talk for hours. I had a mild crush on her. During one period, she had a boyfriend, Billy Joe Hart. He sang; I could not. My crush was crushed.

Earnest Green lived at 21st and Pulaski Streets, a block away from Jefferson Thomas. While Earnest and I were fellow students at Dunbar and Horace Mann High Schools and knew each other well, I socialized primarily with his brother, Scott, who was the same age as I. I was a guest at Earnest's house numerous times and had many relevant philosophical discussions with his mother and aunt, both of whom were teachers. In fact, his aunt, Mrs. Gravelly, was my eighth grade history teacher at Dunbar.

Earnest's household impressed me as being imbued with order, intellect and affluence. Both his mother and aunt were college graduates.

For a number of years, **Gloria Ray**, Earnest Green and I lived on or near West 21st Street. I lived at 21st and Ringo, Gloria at 21st and Cross and Earnest at 21st and Pulaski, one block apart respectively. Gloria's father once owned a 1954 Chevrolet four-door sedan and patronized the filling station where I worked. Gloria's very nice house faced Cross Street.

I knew Gloria's mother and father and occasionally visited her house. Gloria and I socialized in our neighborhood, but it was her brother, Harvey, who impressed me the most. He joined the Navy and, while home on leave, explained all the important aspects of his military training and job to me. Wearing his crisp Navy uniform, he looked and sounded like a VIP.

Minnijean Brown and I once had mutual crushes on each other. We shared with each other mutually embarrassing elementary school secrets: we were both digit suckers – I sucked my left thumb, and she sucked her right fore and middle fingers.

Minnijean was always just Minnie to me, and we were friends for the entire time we lived in Little Rock. I personally knew her mother, father and younger brother and talked with them often. For a time, her father and mother drove a green 1951 Pontiac and patronized the filling station where I worked.

Melba Pattillo lived on Ringo Street, a couple of blocks from Philander Smith College on Ringo Street. I remember Melba from my earliest elementary school days. When I walked home from Gibbs or Capitol Hill schools, I passed her house, which was very nice. Unlike most females my age at the time, I considered Melba a sophisticated young woman. She dressed fashionably and immaculately. While many of us struggled with our language skills, Melba was very articulate. I never visited her house.

Unlike the other members of the Little Rock Nine, I did not meet **Elizabeth Eckford** and **Carlotta Walls** until Dunbar High School. Neither attended Capitol Hill or Gibbs Elementary School, so I have a shorter history with them. Although I knew specifically where they lived in the west end of town, I had little social contact with them outside of school activities.

Every member of the Little Rock Nine was a passenger in a car serviced by me, either at the gas pumps and/or the service bays on several occasions between 1954 and 1958. Since I left Little Rock in 1962, I have not seen any of them.

24

Three Cool White Cats – Girls, Man-Toys and Rock 'n' Roll

Jack McCuin, Jim Page and Freddie White were three cool white cats, short for tomcats, or in today's parlance, players. They always seemed to be in the company of the most willing, wildest and wickedest women in Little Rock. Most of the men around the filling station, including me, wanted a lifestyle such as theirs. For a teenage Negro boy, it was, of course, a pipe dream.

Jack, Jim and Freddie had everything – all the boy-toys and man-gadgets one could imagine. They had love boats and land chariots. They had sex, drugs (just cigarettes and alcohol as far as I know) and early rock 'n' roll. The trio had the finances, fortitude and noses to chase and conquer the most beautiful and sophisticated skirts. Vernon Walker was still my real hero, because I could achieve his status, but he was dwarfed by these cats. Sometimes, I had the pleasure of servicing all three of their cars at the pumps at the same time. Listening to their capers, exploits and conquests of the women became my impossible bellwether. They were a jovial bunch, talked a lot, mostly about football, jobs, girls and cars – never race.

They were alike in many ways – all three were in construction. Jack and Jim, who were about 30 years old each, were journeymen electricians and union members. Freddie, the youngest of the group at 21, barely made the list at number three, was in general construction. All had convertibles; Jack and Jim had rather large boats, which they towed to the popular lakes and rivers all over Arkansas. All tanked up every Friday about 5 p.m. at the station, cashed their checks and discussed their weekend plans.

Jack had an Orchid 1958 Oldsmobile 98 convertible with a white vinyl top that had all the bells and whistles – power everything, including automatic transmission, air conditioning, power seats, remote trunk opener, towing package, fender skirts, factory-installed trailer hitch, optional portable transistor radio that was embedded in the dash and an automatic headlight dimmer. The car had the biggest Rocket 88 V-8 engine available with a four-barrel carburetor and a dual-exhaust system.

My favorite toy of his was an aftermarket 45-RPM record player mounted underneath the dash just above the transmission hump. This chrome-cased marvel, which played music through the car's sound system, impressed everyone – it was a jukebox in a car! You stacked up to ten records on an upside-down spindle. The tone arm played the bottom of the record, which dropped off the spindle when it finished playing to a shelf below. A full stack played about 30 minutes, and then you restacked the spindle and started over. In the summer when the top was dropped, Top Forty tunes were always blaring. One of his favorites, which became one of my favorites, too, was *Run Samson Run* sung by Neil Sedaka. Jack always addressed me as Joe. He took a picture of me that is included in the readpegasus.com photo gallery.

Jack introduced me to college football during this time. He was a big fan of the Arkansas Razorbacks and, whenever he could get tickets to a home game, he and a date were there. He was always cheering the Razorbacks or Hogs to earn a berth in the Cotton Bowl. He would point out on-field accomplishments of the team's biggest star, Lance Alworth. Before Jack, I had never heard of him; after Jack, I never forgot Lance. Jack was right about his playing ability. Lance went on to become a member of both the College Football Hall of Fame and the Pro Football Hall of Fame.

Jim's car was a Red 1957 Oldsmobile 98 convertible with a white vinyl top that had fewer bells and whistles than Jack's, but nonetheless attracted the women. He, like Jack, had a large towable boat and a car record player. Jim turned the tables on me and called me "Cat." He knew I really wanted to be one.

Freddie White had an even smaller chariot. His ride was a 1958 baby-blue Dodge convertible with a factory-installed Continental spare tire kit and fender skirts. His car did not have a record player, and he did not have a boat. He called me Eddie, always said it rhymes with Freddie.

I often saw their distinctive vehicles trolling the town looking for quail (attractive young women) or parked in places off limits to Negroes, like Snappy Service at 7th and Broadway, the Center Theatre, downtown on Main Street, or the swimming pool at Fair Park. They always had a great looking girl with them.

My biggest pleasure was having the opportunity to service and drive these nice powerful cars. Just to watch the scores of vacuum servos, electric motors and hydraulic-powered convertible top mechanisms operate flawlessly was a real treat for me. I also, to a limited extent, serviced their boats and trailers. I learned about outboard motors, their oil/gas mixtures and various types of trailer brakes and towing packages.

I remember meeting several of their female guests, as I gassed up cars and boats for weekend getaways on the lakes. Most of them exchanged small talk with me. I offered small guarded responses in return. They often were dressed in water attire, usually a swimming suit or shorts, which revealed more skin than normal, including cleavage and well-defined impressions of nipples. Like most Negroes of the time, I had learned to look without leering, that is look peripherally or obliquely at white females, lest you make even your white friends angry. Up close, some of them looked less glamorous in beach attire and without full makeup.

I learned labor union basics from Jack and Jim. Jack once offered, "I can go on the worksite, lie down, and sleep all day, still get paid for a full day. Plus, I cannot be fired. I just have to keep my union dues up to date." At the time, I thought that was great until I found out that Negroes could not join that union.

By 1960, the glory days seemed to be gone. Both Jack and Jim had white 1960 Oldsmobile convertibles with the record players and still had boats. Jim was slower and balding. Jack's hair was thinning, and his paunch had grown. Freddie, the most handsome of the trio, who had a dreamy Tab Hunter look, was married. The Tomcats had taken a final bow and exited stage left.

After I had a chance to observe, interact with, and analyze the performance of the Tomcats over time, two interesting facts emerged: not one member of the 'Cats attended college and, during the Tomcat era, every one of them lived at home with their parents. These facts caused me to give extra respect to Vernon Walker – he lived in a boarding house and not with his parents. However, overall, they taught me a lot about women, fancy cars and boats, and life in general from a perspective dramatically different from mine. In addition, I learned to enjoy college football. Although Jim continued to call me Cat right through our last meeting, I was never anything but a wannabe. In time, I traded my desire to be a cool cat to be a cool college graduate.

25

Little Rock Air Force Base

The Little Rock Air Force Base, which is actually in Jacksonville, Arkansas, officially stood up amid great fanfare in October 1955. The base was home for the B-47 Stratojet, a long-range bomber capable of delivering nuclear weapons and the KC-97 Stratotanker, an aerial refueling aircraft that usually supported the B-47, extending its range all the way to the Soviet Union.

In the beginning, there was an acute shortage of on-base housing. Therefore, many airmen, including those with families, found housing a half-hour away in Little Rock. The situation was especially dire for Negro airmen and their families because segregationist practices at the time reduced their options. Many of these military families were relegated to renting rooms with local black families, both crowded into single-family residences. A number of these air force families, both black and white, lived nearby, and patronized the filling station. A young black airman lived with his wife and young child in a very small garage apartment next door. He told me he could not afford a car. He carpooled to the base with two white airmen.

These airmen were very interesting to me. They brought geography, technology and news to me at the gas pumps. They were multi-cultural, multi-racial, and multilingual. They hailed from all over the United States, including Alaska, Arizona and Arkansas. They had been stationed in Germany, England, Hawaii and Libya. They were officer and enlisted. There was a B-47 pilot, a very young B-47 copilot, and a master sergeant who had flown the KC-97 as a boom operator for 22 years. But the airman I spent the most time with and got to know very well was Roger "Buck" Buchanan, a young, tall, lanky white guy from a small town in Tennessee.

After Buck completed basic training, he was assigned to Little Rock Air Force Base. He worked for what is now known as public works, which was responsible for, among other things, the safety and habitability of base housing. Most of the time, when he talked about his job, it was about patching nail holes, repairing light fixtures and replacing light bulbs.

The first time I saw Buck, he was in the car with two other airmen from the base. As they drove away, I heard for the first time his signature so long, "I'll be sawing you."

Since Buck was soon hired as a part-time employee of the filling station, I heard it probably a thousand times. He and I alone operated the business, usually nights and on weekends, for many hours over the next several years until he left the air force. Then he was my full-time coworker for several months.

Buck's favorite entertainer was Elvis Presley. He bought every record and saw every movie Elvis made, as soon as they were released. Elvis' movies, starting with *Love Me Tender,* usually premiered in Little Rock at the Center Theater, and Buck was always in the audience. By the time his movies appeared at a theater that I was allowed to attend, I knew the entire plot, courtesy of Buck. Viewing the movie was anticlimactic.

Even though we were friends, Buck and I never discussed racism, segregation or integration. I never visited his house or rode in his car. I was not invited to his wedding. It was easy for me to tell he was completely comfortable with the racial status quo at the time. Buck's big aspiration was to be a Coca-Cola-route truck driver. He watched the delivery process first hand when Cokes were delivered to the filling station. The driver was white and the bouncer, who bounced out of the truck and humped the wooden cases filled with glass bottles of Coke, was Negro. They even wore different color uniforms. The driver settled the account, while the bouncer delivered the order.

For most Negroes in Little Rock, the new air base was a glimpse into racial equality. Those of us who had the opportunity to visit the base saw all integrated public facilities. Blacks and whites swam together in the base pool, competed together in the bowling alley, sat together in the movie, shopped together in the Base Exchange, and drank together in the Airmen's Club.

Then there was the darker side. Young black high school men like me, could not compete very well for the affection of our female classmates. We were outclassed and outgunned by the young black airmen from the base. They were usually between 18 and 21-years-old, had more money, new impressive cars and were able to dress like recording artists when they were out of uniform. They usually won the favors of the beautiful girls, who enjoyed the integrated activities on the base, especially drinking and dancing at the Airmen's Club. There were no drinking restrictions then; if you wore the uniform, you and your guest could drink.

The aviators were everywhere, even at our junior and senior high schools. They waited at 3:30 p.m., when schools let out. They offered the girls rides home or to the base. They were there after the close of nighttime school activities like socials, talent shows and sock hops. Some girls enjoyed being seen with their airmen; it was one-upsmanship.

One very beautiful girl whom I knew since elementary school said this to me: "Eddie, I love you, baby, but you guys are pipsqueaks compared to the airmen. They have means, I mean money, honey. They have cars, I mean love chariots. They take you to the base. They can entertain a woman. You can hang out, get drunk. A girl gives so little to get so much." I fully understood the quid pro quo!

Eventually, those relationships contributed to sharp increases in truancy and to unwed pregnancy rates among 15 to 18-year-old female high school students. This caused the base commander to put at least my school, Horace Mann High, off-limits. That alone did not solve the problem, since the girls and airmen simply met off campus.

Airmen who patronized the filling station hinted that B-47s always flew with nuclear bombs aboard. I could never verify this, but there were many purveyors of nuclear intrigue, which created some local paranoia.

About 6 a.m. on or about 31 March 1960, I was on my way to a physical education class at Philander Smith College, when I witnessed a thundering explosion and huge fireball high in the southeastern sky. The shockwave was tremendous and felt throughout most of Little Rock. I immediately knew it involved a plane from the air base. I saw a severed wing and sheets of flaming jet fuel falling from the destroyed aircraft. It was a clear day with a blue sky, so I saw everything in high resolution. I felt helpless when I saw a crewmember descending in a parachute with the silk canopy in flames. I never learned his fate, but I think he survived.

Curious, I started driving towards the wreckage's likely impact site, which appeared close by. I managed to get to a location where a piece of debris had fallen, dug a deep crater, and was still burning. Someone at the scene said it was one of the plane's jet engines. No one could verify that, and all of us feared a secondary explosion, so we were afraid to get too close. Ironically, this crater was in the middle of Battery Street, directly behind one of the schools I attended, Capitol Hill Elementary School. In just a few minutes, the police cleared and roped off the area. As I left, I saw plane debris strewn over a wide area, and I was not even close to the main impact area. Several houses were burning and numerous stores had broken windows.

The crash occurred in the middle of the cold war civil defense era and civil defense posters were conspicuous everywhere. Citizens who could afford them had well-appointed home fallout shelters. Community fallout shelters for the public were designated with the standard yellow and black fallout shelter signs. Rumors were abundant about radiation that had been released because of the crash. Two customers had Geiger counters used to measure radiation levels, and one had what he called a Roentgen meter, which also detected and measured radioactivity. As far as I know, it was never determined whether the crash aircraft carried nuclear weapons or any radioactivity was released.

26

Sidney Moncrief – Honorary Economics Professor

Sidney Moncrief was a security guard at the Little Rock Branch of the Federal Reserve Bank of St. Louis, which was located on Center Street downtown. Although he worked full-time for the bank, it seemed he was always hanging out at the filling station. He was about six-foot-two, big with a Santa belly, but looked dapper in his two-tone blue uniform. Sidney possessed a mellow baritone voice suitable for radio. His belly projected an infectious roaring laugh that was heard all over the station's grounds. He was a verbal jokester and, like funnyman Red Skelton, he laughed at his own jokes.

I learned a lot about him while performing scheduled maintenance on his car, a 1955 two-tone gray Pontiac. The color was unusual and so was the fact it was V-8 standard shift; he hated automatic transmissions. He was always teaching me something new about the Federal Reserve Branch Bank, where he worked. For example, he explained to me how long each denomination of currency lasted before it was replaced. I remember the one-dollar bill wore out the fastest and the hundred-dollar bill lasted the longest for obvious reasons. Sidney told me the Federal Reserve banks only provided coin and paper currency directly to banks, not individuals. I learned how the Federal Reserve destroyed mutilated and worn currency that had been removed from circulation.

However, I remember Sidney most for his indelible sexual innuendo quip - "That's what she said!" He stood around inconspicuously waiting for someone to unwittingly prompt his retort. On one occasion, while performing an oil change and grease job, the customer and I were discussing how to operate a mouth-powered siphon device his sister had given him. He wanted to remove stale gas from an old car he owned. We had talked about this device for at least ten minutes through all the ambient noises, including bay, pump, road and aural noises. Then suddenly everything was still and quiet. Precisely at that time the customer said with conviction, "I can't put this thing in my mouth and suck on it!" About a millisecond later, Sidney walked out of the office into the lubrication bay, pointed his right hand at the customer and quipped, "That's what she said!" and immediately broke into his contagious barrel laugh. We all laughed several seconds, and Sidney was gone. I explained to the customer there was another siphon device that had a built-in rubber bulb to generate the suction; he would not have to use his mouth.

One day, I was servicing Sidney's car at the western island of gas pumps. Sidney was standing between the regular and high-octane pumps, pontificating as usual. A flatbed truck drove up on the other side of the island loaded with junk items stacked precariously high. A passenger in the vehicle got out, noticed all the attention the cargo was receiving, turned and said, "Damn! That's a big load." Sidney with the comedic timing of Bob Hope, said, "That's what she said!" We all laughed, and Sidney drove away.

Once a young graduate engineering customer was in the office discussing a fluid dynamics course he was taking and made a comment about a formula he had to remember: "It's just too long and hard!" Sidney, who also was there, very much alert and smooth as ever, raised his arm, pointed his finger and said, "That's what she said!"

During my military career, I earned undergraduate degrees in business from Methodist College (now Methodist University), University of Maryland, and a Master in Business from Boston University. However, I consider Sidney Moncrief my very first economics teacher. Roger "Buck" Buchanan got to know and like Sidney much better than me. He became his son-in-law.

Section Four: Horace Mann High School Years

27

Horace Mann High – Opening Act

I was among the first group of students to attend the new Horace Mann High School at the beginning of the 1956-57 school year. Mann had about 40 classrooms, each of which had a two-way intercommunications system and opened into an outdoor breezeway. There was also a gymnasium, library and cafeteria, but like Dunbar, there was no sports stadium. Now Dunbar and Mann, too, had to use the stadium at Central High School for track activities and football games. Although I really enjoyed having a brand new school, Mann never had the ambience and excitement of Dunbar.

Academically, Horace Mann never interested or challenged me like Dunbar. In class, often found myself daydreaming, giving less than full attention to the teacher. I recognized that I could devote only 25% of my attention and still capture the full essence of the class. The other 75% was equally divided among fantasizing about girls, glory and my dream car, a 1955 Mercury. When I stared out my classroom window, I saw myself riding on the back of the mighty Flying Red Horse – Pegasus. It was up and away to glory. Just where was glory? Glory or glory land was an imagined, magical, mystical place where race and ethnicity were invisible, energy was boundless, and opportunities were unlimited. In reality, glory for young Negro boys of my era was the West Coast, specifically Los Angeles.

My fantasy car was a 1955 black and white Mercury Montclair, two-door hardtop with red and white leather interior and fender skirts. I drove this car from Little Rock along Route 66 to the West Coast or, in the parlance of the day, the Coast. There was a new girl in the Merc with me every day. The total experience was just sand, surf, song, sun and sex. I also acquired a chopped and channeled coupe with a rolled and pleated naugahyde interior. Then I snapped out of the trance and came back to class. I had not gone to the Coast. There was no Mercury; I was extremely fortunate to have my 1939 Chevy.

I saw how the Coast was touted as a mecca for Negroes. Eight young blacks that I knew very well, including one female, moved to Los Angeles and on a staggered schedule returned to Little Rock for vacations. Each came back driving a new car, wearing the latest fashions and flashing scads of cash. The young lady brought her handsome West Coast boyfriend to Little Rock; one guy brought his beautiful West Coast girlfriend. In each case, the West Coast/Los Angeles mystique grew exponentially. The Coast took on a life of its own. Those cheesy Frankie Avalon and Annette Funicello beach movies also helped characterize Coast life as ideal. I, like my fellow students, wanted a piece of this action.

Then two brothers of this group shared some secrets with me. No one had great jobs. They all worked low-level, low-paying jobs in LA. Most worked a minimum of two jobs and sometimes three. Some of the group lived with relatives; other lived in squalid housing. They were all terrified by the LA gangs. The brothers both saved for the car they bought together. They drove back to Little Rock tag-team style in less than three days. The engine was turned off only while getting gas. One brother drove while the other slept, and then they switched off. They lived on coffee and fast food. They did not have money for motels or hotels. The clothes we saw them wearing were all they had, and they had just bought them for the trip home; likewise with the car. Even so, I still wanted to go to the Coast. I reasoned they had failed because none of the group had any skills; some did not even finish high school. However, I had service/filling station skills, and it would be different for me. It took a couple of years for reality to set in.

As a tenth grader, driving my own car to Mann every day was awesome, even though the car was two years older than I was. I was often teased by other students for having the oldest car in the parking lot. One of my friends said my situation was analogous to driving a Stanley Steamer to the Indianapolis 500; another likened it to trying to enter a Roman chariot in a drag race at Carlyle, a local drag strip. Nonetheless, it was my short (urban slang meaning car) and I was very proud of it, faults and all. My friends, Herman Jones and Sam Tenpenny, also drove cars to school. Herman drove the family car, a 1956 persimmon and white Mercury four-door hardtop, and Tenpenny, or Dime for short, occasionally drove his older sister's blue and white 1955 Oldsmobile.

The obvious benefits of having a car were mobility and flexibility. However, I also learned there was tremendous responsibility associated with the well-being and safety of the souls I transported. This car afforded me the opportunity to place others and myself in harm's way, including traffic and/or vehicular accidents, gang-related activity, crime and malicious mischief. Despite all the potential liability issues, insurance was not required, and I had none.

I was known over Little Rock as the young Negro kid who was a knowledgeable, responsible and reliable filling station attendant. As a result, I was a trusted agent with some parents' most precious commodity: their young sons and daughters. I was simply amazed at the number of parents who trusted me to repeatedly pickup their beautiful daughters and keep them out until the wee hours of the morning. I seldom gave an itinerary, most likely we were just going cruising, a destination anywhere and nowhere at the same time. I often thought about the possibility of doing something while driving to accidently cause a fatality or maiming of a fellow student. On the good side, I never drank, smoked or did any drugs, so I was always in total control of my faculties. I was also a very slow and deliberate driver. However, I recognized that bad things often happen to good people.

There were jealousy issues with fellow students thinking a car gave me an advantage, especially with the girls. Some students threatened me with bodily harm; others threatened to damage or disable my car, including putting sugar in the gas tank. I recognized the opportunity cost of riding around listening to a bunch of screaming girls and a blaring radio. About two months into my first school year at Mann, I drove the car and one of my young neighbors into my first slippery and dangerous situation. I wanted to impress my long-term girlfriend, May Helen Coakley, by going to a juke joint called Over the Levee. This place, as the name implied, was located between the Arkansas River and an earthen levee, which protected the neighborhood where May Helen lived from floodwaters. My plan was simple: surprise May Helen by parking my car in front of her shotgun house at 213 John Street and hope that she saw it. Theartis Hunter, my intrepid neighbor and acquaintance, and I were going to visit Over the Levee.

I parked the car that Sunday night, and we started walking towards the joint, which was about three blocks down Second Street, a mostly dark, empty road. We had gone about two blocks when out of nowhere appeared Johnese Wright, a student at Mann and alleged gang leader. She called my name and said, "What the hell are you doing over here?" Instead of answering, I said to Theartis, "Let's turn around and go back."

Johnese was not alone. She commanded six thugs, who seemed to appear from the bushes. As we tried to walk quickly back to the car, she said, "Get them niggers." About a millisecond later, I felt rock-hard fists pounding my head, back and stomach. I took off like a marathoner in a 100-yard dash. Johnese and her gang followed in hot pursuit. I ran right across John Street, where my car was parked. In fact, I ran a quarter mile through a pitch-black field, where I lost my pursuers, to the back of a local furniture-manufacturing factory. Then, I doubled back and hid in an open boxcar on a spur track. From the slightly ajar door, I heard the gang shouting, "Come on out, nigger, or we'll turn your car over." I thought, how did they know we were there? Did Theartis somehow sell me out? Where was he now? I did not remember him being hit, but things were a blur. What will May Helen think of all this? Was she watching all of this go down?

Then I heard and watched them count, "One, two, three, rock!" They rocked my car up on two wheels. Then I heard someone shout, "Let's cut his tires!" Then there was silence. I saw no one, heard no one. Two hours went by; it was almost midnight. I knew I had to get to my car. I low-crawled through the field, with the stealth of a tiger stalking prey, until I saw that my car was upright with all tires still inflated. The challenge now was to get inside the car, start it, and get away.

After about ten minutes of deliberation, I decided to make a run for it. I made it to the car, unlocked it, climbed inside, and started the car as quickly as I could. At that moment, all hell broke loose. The stillness of midnight was shattered with loud shouts, "There the coward bastard is. Get the nigger!"

I drove off as fast as I could, only to be bombarded by a hail of rocks, which cracked my right windshield and passenger side rear window. When I reached the bright lights of downtown, I noticed huge dents in the roof, hood, right passenger door and the trunk of the car. I was extremely sad. My 175-dollar car was severely damaged but still running. What would students think tomorrow when they saw the car? And, again, where was Theartis?

I was so disenchanted over the damage done to my car that I kept driving past my house and headed southwest for an hour. My goal was to find Barbara Reid's house, although I only had general directions. She always told me to come out to her house for some mature, matronly comfort and loving. After such a disastrous night, she was the remedy to cure my ills. I arrived in the vicinity and took a serious pause: I had no specific address and she had no phone. In addition, it was after 1:30 in the morning and the neighborhood was devoid of moonlight and streetlights. It was stupid even to even think of knocking on doors. Reluctantly, I gave up and drove home.

I slept very little that night, and I was up very early. In the light of day, I was able to assess clearly the serious damage done to my vehicle. I did not want to drive it to school this Monday, but I had no choice. I was at the station when Bud opened and showed him the car and explained what happened. Bud helped me by bumping out some of the dents in the roof, using his hand through the headliner, which made the top look a lot better. I put a flying red horse adhesive sticker over the locus of the cracks in the passenger windshield. Then I drove my corpse of a car to school.

As I parked my car that morning, I knew what some students would be saying, "You now have the oldest and most battered car in the parking lot." It took only a few minutes to find out I was correct. My walk towards the school was painful. My butt had been thoroughly kicked the previous night, and I was sore all over, head, back and rib cage. Word of my assault arrived at Mann before I did, and some students heckled me upon my arrival. Within minutes, I encountered Johnese Wright in the breezeway. With the crazed stare of a voodoo queen, she said just two words to me: "Black bastard!" To this day, the other assailants in Johnese's posse remain unidentified. Neither they nor Johnese ever did physical harm to me again.

I met Theartis Hunter later that day and learned he was unscathed. In fact, he said he walked back to Over the Levy and someone later took him home. He claimed he did not recognize anyone but Johnese because it was pitch black and the posse took off after me, and he never saw them again. I suspected that Theartis was a coconspirator of Johnese and he was never a passenger in my car again.

At work after school, I used some body-shop tools to suck, pop and pry out more dings and dents from the hood, passenger door and rear body panel. I could not get the car back to its original condition, but I improved its condition to a point that I could tolerate. I never did replace the windshield or the right rear passenger window. Neither was economically feasible. A flying red horse decal, which I replaced periodically, from then on graced the windshield. A custom aluminum insert, which I made from a five-quart Mobiloil can, patched the rear window. Those modifications remained until I switched cars.

I told Barbara Reid about the incident and the fact that I had been in her neighborhood looking for her, but was lost. She gave me exact directions to her house and again extended her invitation to drive out and spend some time with a mature woman – but somehow she dropped off my map. I never went back to her part of the county again.

Remarkably, May Helen and her family were asleep inside her house and oblivious to the entire incident. I certainly surprised May Helen, but not the way I intended. She said her father, Erastus T. Coakley, could have defused the situation, and at least saved my car, since it was parked directly in front of his house. However, he, too, was unaware. Although she tried to soothe my bruised ego, which was hurting as much as my body, she said the incident was routine for that part of town. I returned often to May Helen's neighborhood without incident, but never to the juke joint, Over the Levy.

Sock hops and socials at Mann were very popular. There was at least one every month, usually Friday night. They were sponsored and promoted by and held at the school. They were very well attended, chaperoned by teachers, and only students could attend. Parents considered them safe and often dropped their kids, especially girls, off for the hop and picked them up when it was over. Students were sly, cunning, alert, and way out in front of their parents. Numerous girls, after being dropped off at the entrance, made their way to the room hosting the hop, flashed their faces to be seen and danced to a couple of songs before heading to the girls' bathroom. Of course, they did not come back, at least not right away. They made their way out one of the side doors, while the guys did likewise, or were waiting for them in the side or back of the parking lot. Once there, they hooked up with boyfriends to make out in the parking lot or somewhere remote, like Blueberry Hill (a real location), after the popular song of the same name by Fats Domino.

Once I saw two sisters, one in the tenth grade and the other in the eleventh grade, both making out in the back seat of the same car. What I witnessed that night was truly a family affair. These events were about two hours long and anybody who had been dropped off briefly passed through the social or hop again and was available to be picked up at the proper place on or before time. Parents were none the wiser.

At the conclusion of a late fall sock hop, I waited in the side parking lot for my pal, Willis White. Willis came out the side door with Elnora Nixon, a thin brown-skinned girl with an interesting mole near her mouth. He rushed her into the back seat before she had time to put on her coat. Willis was kissing and getting under her clothes before I started the car. By the time I got out of the parking lot I heard her rhythmic oh, oh in sync with his gyrating body. About two blocks from the school, he stopped and asked me, "Hey, man, got a rubber? I don't want to drown this young lady." Elnora said nothing. I passed him a rubber from the glove compartment. Quickly, the gyrations started again.

I heard her tell Willis, "I have to be home by eleven! My mother will kill me if I'm not."

I looked at the clock in my car. It was a quarter to eleven. I told Willis, "I'll head to her house now, and we'll get her home on time."

"No, man," he said and kept hogging her body. He used three of my rubbers. All of a sudden, Willis said, "You can take her home now, man. But drop me off at home first, I have to get up early tomorrow and go someplace."

We were within five blocks of his house. I dropped off Willis at ten minutes after midnight. I really did not like what Willis had done to Elnora and me. I asked her to get in the front seat with me. I asked her what all that was about. She explained, "Eddie, I told Willis that I would go one round apiece with each of you and he had to get me home by eleven o'clock or I would be in serious trouble. He promised me he and you would do just that. Now I'm in a real mess." She started to cry.

"Why didn't you say something to me?" I asked her. "I heard you tell Willis you had to be home by eleven. However, I had no clue about any agreement the two of you made. I will drive you directly home now, ok?" When we got to her house, it was half past midnight. She said, "I can't go in now. Please take me to my aunt's. I'm in big trouble now."

I apologized to her and told her we/he should have kept our/his promise, although I did not know the deal. "Elnora, I was cheated. I never got my round," I told her.

She said, "I understand, and I'm sorry about that, too. You're a nice patient guy, but in this case, you should kick Willis' ass. He won't get on me again. Eddie, I'm not in the mood for any more of that tonight. I'm tired."

She promised me a rain check. We arrived at her aunt's, and she gave the most tender and passionate kiss I think I ever had and said, "Next time, it will be just you and me, ok?"

"When is that?" I asked.

"As soon as I'm allowed out of the house again." She quickly got out of the car. I waited until she went into the house and drove off for home.

I was sleeping soundly in my bed at about 3 a.m. Saturday morning when my aunt woke me up. When I got my eyes focused, I saw my aunt and a uniformed white city police officer hovering over my bed. The cop said, "Son, where is Elnora Nixon? A young man named Willis Hiram White said you were the last one known to be with her. Is that true?"

"Yes, officer. Elnora is at her aunt's house," I said. Then I told him where the aunt lived.

"Don't leave town. I may have to talk to you again," he said.

"Yes, sir." The officer departed my house. I thought to myself, Willis strikes again. I got up and went to work at 7 a.m. After that episode, I had had enough. I never ran with Willis again.

During football season, Wayman Barnes and I decided to attend one of Horace Mann's away football games, a night game at a rival high school in Hot Springs, Arkansas. The drive was about sixty miles south on Highway 70, not a challenge even for a 1939 Chevy. The plan was simple, the two of us, no girls, would drive over to the game, support our team and be back home by midnight. By pure happenstance, I picked up two other guys at a friendly juke joint at 24th and High Streets. They were Mann students, but distant acquaintances of mine and Wayman's, but not people that I would normally transport across town, let alone to another city. Somehow, I relented and agreed to let them ride with us. They offered gas money, which I declined. Once underway, Wayman and I did most of the talking and only to each other.

We were approximately fifteen miles into the trip, when out of nowhere in the distance, I noticed the flashing light of the state police. I was not speeding, so I reasoned there was no justification for alarm. I thought the trooper would just pass me by in pursuit of real violators. After he passed a few cars, trailed me at a distance for a couple of miles with his light still flashing, I became nervous and afraid to pull over. In a couple of minutes, he was directly behind me. Now I was really scared and signaled that I was trying to pull over at the first opportunity.

Just as I pulled over, something slid from under my front seat up against my right foot. I knew there was nothing under my seat, so I reached down to determine what it was. It was a gun, a revolver. As I rolled to a stop, I pushed the gun back under my seat. Where did this gun come from?

Which one of these two last-minute passengers brought this weapon into my car? Now I was really scared. I started to shake. What if this state trooper searched my car? I did not know what kind of gun it was. It did not matter now. I had a much bigger problem.

The trooper now stood about five feet from my front door with his hand on his gun, which was still in his holster. He said, "Boy, get out of the car."

"Yes sir," I said respectfully.

"Where you going, boy?"

"Hot Springs, sir."

"What's in Hot Springs?"

"Football game, sir."

The trooper noticed that I was shaking uncontrollably and remarked, "What are you so nervous about, boy? You're shaking like a Georgia cow shitting peach seeds."

"Yes, sir. I am a little bit nervous, sir."

"Shit, you're a whole bunch nervous, boy. What have you got in that car? Anything illegal?" He shone his flashlight in the car. I knew he would search the car next. Instead, he asked to see my driver's license and found no issues with it, even though my chronological age had not caught up with the age listed on my driver's license. The trooper gave me my license back, shone the flashlight straight into my eyes, and said, "I don't want a bunch of you nigger boys out here on my highway. Turn your shaky ass around and take this contraption back to Little Rock. Is that understood, boy?"

"Yes, sir!" I got back into my car and found the first place I could turn around and headed back home. I had no further desire to attend the game. I turned my attention back to the gun.

One of the guys in the back seat reluctantly claimed the gun, which was loaded. He said it was protection in case a fight broke out at the game. Two things really angered me about this situation: first, I had no idea there was a gun in the car. Second, he slid the gun under my seat to look as if the gun belonged to me. I knew this guy would have denied ownership of the gun if the trooper had searched the car. What I learned from this was to stick with a known circle of friends, no matter what.

Why did that state trooper stop me? Why did he trail me for so long? When did he notice my car? Where was he parked? Finally, why did he choose not to search my car? Why did he let me go without trumping up some charge? I never got those answers, but I was extremely grateful for the outcome.

Clyde Jones was a very interesting customer. He was a diminutive man who wore a felt fedora like the Indiana Jones character in the movies. His hat, glasses, and the omnipresent cigarette formed an indelible caricature of this man. Clyde was a state employee who logged more than five thousand miles a month – all in the state of Arkansas – more than any other customer of ours. Since he bought so much gas from us, he was given a fleet discount of two cents per gallon. I have long since forgotten the nature of his job, but I have not forgotten the lessons he taught me about the geography and topography of Arkansas. I knew about the larger cities of Arkansas, like North Little Rock, Hot Springs, Pine Bluff and Texarkana.

Clyde introduced me to some obscure city names, which I still remember because they have self-explanatory characteristics, like Heber Springs, Eureka Springs, Mineral Springs and Siloam Springs. Then there were others like Cave City, Mountain View, Mountain Home, Walnut Ridge, Bald Knob, Hickory Plains and Crows. Some sounded presidential like Harrison and Van Buren. A couple were inspirational, such as Hope (President Clinton's hometown) and Strong. Others reminded me of plant life, including Black Oak, Dardanelle and Magnolia. Two cities, Gould and Paragould, had names reminiscent of the occult. I believe that Clyde's tires rolled through every city, town, village and molehill in Arkansas, and from him I learned a little about each of them.

Clyde Jones wore out three cars, all Fords, while I knew him. I loved servicing his car at the pumps or in the bays. He was my virtual tour guide. I always felt that I had also been to all the locations that he had visited. When I had the opportunity to visit scenic landscapes like the Ozark Mountains, because of Clyde, I felt I had been there before. In every case, it was exactly as he presented it. Over time, Clyde stopped coming for gas and service, and I have no idea what happened to him. I missed him. He taught me more about the landscape of Arkansas than anyone else.

John, no last name known, was an important customer to me and for good reason. He was a young driver, the same age, build, and grade as me. The important difference between us was that he was white, a virtual fraternal twin to Ricky Nelson, the popular singer. He lived about a mile away in a well-established middle-class neighborhood with his parents and siblings. We were pump friends, and I saw him infrequently away from the station, usually at his place of work, a local Safeway Store.

John and I had a common interest in each other's socio-economic status, race, high school, curriculum, jobs and opportunities. He attended Catholic schools until tenth grade when he entered Central High School, which was the same time and grade I entered Horace Mann. We comprehensively compared everything, including gangs, girls and grades. When Central was integrated, I had his perspective as a white student and Terrence Roberts' perspective as a Negro student, which proved to be some very interesting insight into racial issues in Little Rock. I do not think John was racist. I just think he was like many whites, comfortable with the status quo. From our discussions, he recognized and accepted the inevitability of racial progress but would never be an activist for change. However, he also made it clear that he would do nothing to impede it.

John, like me, had a job that he worked part-time during the school year and full time in the summer. He worked at the Safeway Grocery Store at 24th and High Streets as a cashier, which meant he wore a white shirt and tie. The only jobs that I could get at Safeway were not visible: unloading trucks at the rear warehouse ramp or stocking shelves after hours. Even the baggers were white. We discussed the contrast of job opportunities at Safeway. I could never be a white-collar worker there, only a low-level blue-collar worker.

We often talked about our respective schools. Central offered high-level math and science courses like calculus and physics in earlier grades than Mann. In some cases, the courses were simply not available at Mann. For example, he was taking a course called Rhetoric in tenth grade. That course was not available at my school. In fact, at the time of that discussion, I had not even heard of rhetoric. He attended kindergarten, which I did not. At an early age, he was on the roadmap to college, specifically the University of Arkansas at Fayetteville. I do not know whether he went to college, since I never saw him after eleventh grade. John's friendship was a very important barometer for me; it helped me understand the weather map of success and chart a course for a rainbow.

After two and a half years of chasing down the Old Man, Bud or Buck to make change after selling a customer gas, I decided to ask the Old Man for a key to the cash register. Then I could make my own change. I was very nervous because I had no clue what he would say, but I thought it was a fair and practical request. Buck worked only part-time but he was given a key as soon as he was hired. I had far more seniority than Buck and worked full time during the summer so I, too, deserved a key. At least I thought so. By now, he must consider me trustworthy. I hoped so. Then there was the matter of race. What about my age? I was only fifteen. What would I do if he said no? On the other hand, would he consider letting me go? I had never seen a Negro man in any cash register he did not own. Robert, my filling station attendant mentor, had worked at filling stations for decades and did not have that privilege. However, I thought, this is 1957. Perhaps the time is right.

After weeks of contemplation, I waited for the right moment. One afternoon when Bud was away, and the Old Man and I operated the station; I decided the time is now. For some reason, I considered him an easier sell on this matter than Bud. Based on what I learned in school during debates, I carefully crafted my strategy. I would simply ask the question, "Can I have a key to the cash register?" Follow that with justification and be prepared to counter any negative responses. So I blurted it out, "Can I have a key to the cash register? It will fit well with all the other business practices you've taught me." I prepared myself for the worst.

He stood up with a perplexed look on his face. He was silent for what seemed like an eternity. Then without further hesitation, he unlocked his desk and handed me a circular retractable keychain with belt clip holder. I simply said, "Thanks." It seemed that the Old Man had the key set assembled, just waiting for me to ask for it. At that moment, two customers drove in, and we went outside to service them. There was never any further discussion about that key.

By the spring of 1957, I was performing major tune-ups using two electronic tune-up and engine diagnostic machines, including the popular Sun Model 500. Once connected, I could monitor and adjust timing, dwell, idle speed and manifold vacuum. I tested spark plugs, spark plug wires, coils and valve performance – all electronically. I thought of myself as the whole car mechanic, excluding body and fender repair (I had no talent or interest for it.), and rebuilding engines, which I learned later.

Mrs. Barber, a cute black homemaker and the wife of a barber (hence the name), regularly had her 1956 Pontiac serviced at the station. Every week, she reliably drove in to purchase gas. Every quarter, she called and had me pick up her car and bring it in for oil, lubrication and filter service. Mrs. Barber only lived a block and half away on Izard Street, so I just walked around to her house to retrieve her car. I knocked on the door, and she always told me to come in. Once inside, she always greeted and handed me the keys completely in the nude. I was stunned the first few times I saw her this way, and then I got used to it. For three years, I only saw Mrs. Barber wearing clothes when she came in for gas. I never figured out what to say to her, so I said and did nothing. That way, I assumed she could never say

I said or did anything. I just concluded that she was an exhibitionist or maybe another coquette. It was great eye candy for a 15-year-old boy.

One block in the other direction on Chester Street, I performed a similar pick-up service for a white woman who owned a 1955 Packard. She had a Jewish name that I could never remember so I just called her Mrs. Packard, after her car. Mrs. Packard also always invited me into her house, but she always wore a nice ankle-length pink robe that she held together with one hand. When she reached to get her keys from the breakfast room table and turned around, the robe always fell open revealing her naked front. Her chest was far less ample than Mrs. Barber's was, but she had an unusually hairy-looking (at least to me) pubic mound, which drew my attention. She always made me nervous when she said something like, "Boy, did you expect me to have underwear on?" Scared of what she might say to Bud or the Old Man, I did not respond. I always just wanted to leave as soon as possible. I considered her a greater threat (to my job) than Mrs. Barber, probably because she was white. It was impossible not to mentally compare their bodies.

Mrs. Packard also paid me very well to disconnect her speedometer cable when she made her monthly clandestine visits to Hot Springs, Arkansas, and reconnect it upon her return. I do not know why she asked me to do such a thing. Was it a mere coincidence or did she somehow know Mrs. DeSoto? Maybe Mrs. DeSoto told her that I performed the same service for her. As far as I know, neither of these women mentioned their shenanigans to anyone, including their husbands, Bud or the Old Man. I did not either.

One day, I had a mild altercation with Mrs. Terry. She and her husband were very good customers. Mrs. Terry was an older, frail woman probably in her late sixties. The Terrys had a Negro domestic worker whom she picked up and took home every weekday. The maid always sat in the back seat, reverse-chauffeured style. At the pumps, Mrs. Terry never made eye contact or spoke to me. That day she wanted someone to ride with her and bring her 1956 Dodge back for servicing. Bud and the Old Man were gone, Buck was servicing a car on the lift while a customer waited and could not leave now. I was working the pumps. I was the obvious person to accompany her and return her car. I attempted to sit in the front passenger seat. Mrs. Terry said, "You can't sit there. You have to sit in the back seat like my maid. Darkies can't sit up here with me." I thought to myself, I am not your darky, and I am not sitting in the back seat.

I responded to her in a soothing, diplomatic voice, "I'm sorry, but you'll have to wait until Bud or Mr. Price comes back."

"I'll wait for Mr. Price."

She lit a cigarette and waited about twenty minutes until the Old Man came back. I told him she needed someone to ride with her and bring her car back. He climbed into the front seat and they drove off. Whatever they talked about during their short ride, the Old Man kept to himself. In fact, as far as I know, there was no further discussion of the incident by anyone.

I played an intimate game, or more precisely, a game of intimates, with a bespectacled young white lady named Marie Tells. She was very easy to remember because of two very unusual things: her 1951 Ford had a hybrid body – a 1952 Ford front end from the doors and windshield forward. The engine, drive train and the rest of the body was a 1951 Ford. The windshield was one piece like 1952 models; the 1951 model had a two-piece windshield. She said she bought the car used and had no idea about its history or origin. Maybe it was involved in an accident. I saw Bud and his brother-in-law replace a 1954 Plymouth Belvedere front end with that of a 1953 Plymouth, so it was possible.

She had her car washed often. That alone was not unusual, but what I found under the passenger front seat was. The first time I cleaned her interior, I blew (Then we blew out the interior, now we vacuum it out.) a pair of green panties from under the front seat. I picked them up, planning to place them back under the seat, and noticed that they were heavily perfumed. For some reason, I took the underwear to the battery room and placed them in a box in a drawer. Every subsequent time I washed her car; there was another perfumed pair of panties under the front passenger seat.

Each time, I added underwear to the box in the battery room. I was surprised that no one discovered the box and its perfumed contents. One day, I counted thirteen pair of underwear in the box. I thought the game had gone on long enough, so I tossed the box in one of our refuse cans to be hauled away by a trash pick-up service. The next time I washed Marie's car – more underwear. This time I left them under the seat. During the car wash after that, I found no underwear; in fact, I never found any again. Maybe the joke was on me.

By now, Reverend Ogden and his family no longer lived next door, adjacent to the filling station. The house was now owned by a very friendly black family (husband, wife and mother-in-law) that patronized the station. They were impressed by my youth and ability to the extent that they picked out the perfect girlfriend and potential wife for me - their niece. The lady of the house, Rose, described her niece as very light skinned, with light eyes and good hair, which meant her hair was naturally long, thick and wavy.

The niece, who was the same age as me and lived in a very small town, was coming to live with them in the big city of Little Rock, graduate from high school and attend Philander Smith College. The family's goal was to find her a potential husband.

Rose, her husband and mother tried to pique my interest in the niece through photos and food. Whenever they fed me on the porch at lunch time or at their dining room table after work, a picture of the niece was always in eyeshot. They arranged for me to converse long distance with the niece. She had a wonderful phone voice but our conversations never exceeded small talk. They promoted her so often as my girlfriend that I began to believe it was my destiny. They even went to the extreme of predicting how beautiful our kids would be. At one level, I could not wait to see her in the flesh; on another I could barely get excited about the niece's arrival. About three months out, Rose started a countdown calendar and told me daily the number of days remaining until her niece, Nancy, arrived. When Nancy's arrival was imminent, the level of anticipation at Rose's house was at its apex. I was just anxious for the Nancy hype to end. In reality, this was really just a gloried blind date.

Nancy arrived by car in the afternoon on the day scheduled. I was servicing customers at the pumps when she and her family clan arrived. I noted her arrival by returning a scripted wave. I walked over to her porch and formally greeted Nancy as soon as I had the opportunity. The next day, I was scheduled to have dinner with Nancy and her family. She was far more beautiful in person than her photos portrayed; her aunt's description of her was pale compared to what I saw in the flesh.

I took Nancy on several cruising dates in my Chevy, showing her the landmarks of Pulaski County. From one young teen to another, I introduced her to Little Rock. After a few dates, I realized there was no chemistry between us and there never would be. It just was not meant to be. Nancy was still starry-eyed and propelled by all the contrived hyperbole and excitement generated to promote our relationship. Now, I had to spin her slowly back to reality. I explained to her that we were far too young to be serious, which she had difficulty understanding. In the end, Nancy's family was more disappointed than she was that our relationship did not work. The sad/awkward part for me was that I had to see them all day, every day, while I was at work. Anyway, Nancy and I remained friends until I moved to the Esso Service Center.

One of my teachers at Mann, who was also a customer, had a niece and thrust me into a similar situation, this time with less hype. However, the results were identical. After that, I stayed completely away from those situations. I learned valuable lesson. Always let the nature of mutual attraction rule in matters of the heart.

28

Horace Mann High – Middle Act

I made hundreds of service calls during the Pegasus period. I helped stranded customers with numerous issues, including flat tires, flooded carburetors, vapor lock, empty gas tanks, dead batteries, shorted points and wet ignition systems. I carried a standard bag of tricks in the service truck, which included a can of gas, numerous batteries and battery cables, a floor jack, a compressed air tank and an assortment of tools. Most service calls were a challenge because of a vehicle's location (bridge or highway), traffic and other situations, such as multiple problems (such as flat tires and a dead battery), yet those were routine. However, I did have two very memorable service calls:

A very loyal customer, Harriet Pann, a mid-to-late-forties white registered nurse with a twenty-something son, called Bud and requested a mid-afternoon service call. She was attractive, with short salt-and-pepper hair, a nice figure and looked angelic in her white cap-to-shoe nurse's uniform. She told Bud her 1952 Ford hardtop was dead, and she needed a new battery. Bud told me to get a new battery and make the service run. Harriet was waiting for me at a filling station located at Asher Avenue and Fair Park Boulevard, about ten miles away.

I thought it was strange that she was at a filling station and called us. I wondered why she had not bought a battery there or had the attendant jump start her car so she could drive it to our station for a new battery. However, we had serviced her car since we opened, and I thought maybe she wanted to keep it that way. I put a battery designed for her car in the truck and departed within five minutes of Harriet's call.

I arrived at her location, drove around the station looking for her car, so I could drive over to it, but I did not find it. I found Harriet sitting in the filling station's office, and she said, "Eddie, my car's not here, but I'll guide you to it."

She climbed into the truck and, under her direction, we drove north on Fair Park Boulevard for a short distance and turned left on an obscure dirt single-lane road that appeared to be a logging trail. We drove about three-quarters of a mile through wooded, undeveloped forest until we came to a large dirt berm. Her car was behind this berm, literally hidden from view. I must have look perplexed, because Harriet offered this explanation, "I played the radio with the engine off, I guess for too long, and the engine wouldn't start. I asked Bud to send you because I knew you'd understand."

Her explanation sounded plausible. If she played the tube-type radio in her car long enough, it would run her battery completely down. But what was she doing back in here? This place was more like a lover's lane. I told her, "These radios draw a lot of current and will certainly run a battery down in time, if the engine is not charging it."

"My car's been here all night," she said. She was still in her nurse's uniform.

"I'm going to get your car started, so you can drive it back to that filling station where I picked you up, and I'll replace your battery." I knew in this situation prudence was necessary. It would seem odd to someone that we were back in here. She agreed without hesitation. I opened her hood and gave her a twelve-volt boost. Despite her six-volt dead battery, her engine immediately sprang to life. I followed her back to the filling station at Asher Avenue and Fair Park Boulevard and put in her new battery.

Then I told her, "Please drive back to the station, and I'll completely clean the corrosion from your battery cables, then grease and insure the cable ends are snug around the battery posts. I will also completely check out your charging system to make sure all is well there. And I'll write up your battery guarantee."

She said, "Listen; there's something we need to discuss."

"Ok."

"I don't want anyone to know where you found my car," Harriet continued, "That secret is important and valuable to me. I'm willing to buy your silence."

"Are you trying to bribe me?" I said jokingly, thinking I may have said the wrong thing and made her angry.

"Yes, I am. All you ever have to say is that you found my car right here at this filling station. Forget everything else. Here's ten dollars to help you forget where you really found the car and remember that you found my car right here. Is that a deal?" she asked.

"That's a deal. My lips are sealed. I put the new battery in here and I will say no more. But I suggest that you remove all that mud from the tires. It really looks like the car went off road. You can come in today, tomorrow, or whenever, and I'll finish all the battery stuff. Thanks a lot. I'll see you back at the station. Bye." I drove straight back to the station.

Neither Bud nor the Old Man ever asked me any questions about this service call. To them it was just a routine service call, and I kept my secrecy pact. Harriet came in later that day, and I permanently secured the battery and cables. Her charging system, including the generator and voltage regulator, was operating properly. The mud had been washed off her tires. I charged and checked out her old battery. Interestingly, she did not need a new one. In fact, I took her old battery on numerous service calls until we sold it to someone who could not afford a new one.

Another one of our steady customers, a fiftyish Negro man, as I found out later, had been trying to tighten a loose fan belt with the engine running. His wife called the station, and I took the call. She and her husband were on their way to the hospital and wanted me to go check on their other car, a 1952 Chevrolet, parked in the backyard. She also told me to look for part of his index finger, which somehow had been cut off.

I drove the five blocks to their house and found the car still running. I turned off the car. I checked the fan belt and found it extremely loose. I adjusted it to the proper tension. I saw the splattered blood under the hood and tried to follow it to the missing finger. I found about a one-inch piece of finger, including the fingernail, on the ground underneath the car. I picked up the remains and wrapped it in a clean service cloth I had in the truck and took it back to the station. The partial finger could not be reattached, and the customers did not want to see it. I threw it away.

He never explained how he cut off his finger; I don't think he really knew

190

what happened. It was unsafe to even consider tightening a fan belt with the engine running. They were always adjusted with the engine turned off. However, there were at least two ways to cut off a finger with the engine running: inadvertently touching a spinning fan blade or somehow accidently getting a finger caught between the fan belt and one of its pulleys. He told me that his wife forbade him from even opening the hood on either of their cars.

Grocer Hedley operated a small grocery store that he purchased from the Warren family, and it was located just across Chester Street from the station. Because of proximity and convenience, he was a regular customer. Hedley, who had a face with the rugged look, reminiscent of President Reagan, had a curious nervous twitch on the right side of his face. Of the three white grocers located within a half block of the station, Hedley was the friendliest to me. We talked primarily about cars and the grocery business, including how it compared to the filling station business.

Hedley often gassed up his black and white 1956 Ford four-door sedan after he closed his store and before he headed to his home across the bridge in North Little Rock. During those times at the pumps, I learned things about his kids, who I saw twice, and his sickly wife, whom I never saw.

Hedley was a one-man show; he operated his store alone, performing every task, including that of butcher. He was very creative with a meat cleaver. Just as an artist has his easel, Hedley had this huge round wooden meat-carving table, replete with cut marks. He often demonstrated his prowess to me, quickly turning a huge slab of cow into ribs and choice steaks with just a few strokes with his clever (his word) cleaver. If he was sick for a day, his store simply did not open that day; if he went on a vacation for a week, his store did not open that week. In time, an inconspicuous woman sporadically appeared and helped him a few hours on some days. One day I noticed she was there all day, without Hedley.

By summer, when I was out of school, I had more time to observe his store activities. I noticed the woman, who sometimes helped in the store, changed her routine. She no longer parked on the street on the side of the store, but a block away in front of Rightsell Elementary School. As soon as she entered the store, Hedley closed all the shades and closed the store for about 30 minutes. The store reopened and the woman walked back to her car. These episodes continued at least twice a week for a month when Bud and I dreamed up the Dreamsicle Caper. As soon as the store reopened, Bud and I ran immediately to the store to buy a Dreamsicle, a combination of orange sherbet and vanilla ice cream. Often we found the woman sheepishly standing behind the meat-carving table placing her hair and clothes in order. We did it so often that Hedley, when we walked in the door, just retrieved the frozen sicles from his ice cream bar and placed them on the counter before we asked for them.

Bud and I theorized that Hedley was having sex with this woman, either on the meat-carving table or on the floor in front of it. I thought the sex was performed on the meat table because that's the way the poets would write it. If what appears to be obvious was indeed true, then Hedley the Butcher was cutting some meat in the traditional sense, including fine steaks and hams, and cutting some meat in quite another sense – all on the same meat-carving table!

One late summer night at the pumps, I got an earful from Hedley. "Eddie, let me tell you," he started, "I know you and Bud know what is going on with that woman you see in my store. I know you two are trying to catch me, but when I reopen the store, it's all over. Since I've got you all alone, let me explain something. My wife is very ill, in fact dying. I have two young kids who help take care of her. That woman you see in the store when you guys come over for Dreamsicles is my next-door neighbor and my wife's best friend. She helps me take care of my wife and kids. I cannot fully care for my wife or operate this store without her help. Neither my wife nor the woman's husband knows what's going on. That woman does for me what my wife can't; I do for that woman what her husband can't. The safest place for that business is in my store. I'm telling you because I think you're too young to form any firm opinions about me. Always be slow to judge."

I took all that in as well as any young teenager. And he was right; I had not formed any opinion about his morality. I merely thought of it as an old man and woman having sex on a meat carving table, nothing else. I had never seen his wife and did not know whether the woman was married. I never forgot what he said about tempering my judgment with deliberation. That woman continued to come to Hedley's store. However, Bud and I never bought another Dreamsicle while she was there. Not long after that night with Hedley at the pumps, his wife passed away and that woman continued to come to the store.

I lost control of my Chevy and the opportunity to get the girl during the Annual Rodeo and Livestock Exposition when I was persuaded to give some acquaintances a ride home. I had arranged to take Jerri home about 10 p.m., after she spent some time with her girlfriends. However, around 9 p.m., I was asked by Harry Hightower to give him and two couples a quick ride home. I knew him most of my school years, so I decided to do him a favor and honor the request. Harry gathered the couples, who turned out to be distant acquaintances from school: Will Anthony Bush and a female friend, not his girlfriend, and Shelly Bryant and her boyfriend, a guy I knew by sight from school, but not by name. The original plan was to drop everybody off in Tuxedo Court, a black neighborhood a few miles away. Like most plans, these changed before they were fully executed. Now there were three destinations.

Will Anthony was a handsome guy known in girl circles as a gunslinger; Will's friend, Huck, was a slender, attractive senior with a dark-chocolate complexion. Shelly was a blue vein with very light eyes in the same grade as me. I knew nothing about her friend except his complexion mirrored hers; he could have been her brother. The couples were in the back seat. Harry was up front with me. I had barely warmed up the car when I heard Will say to Huck, "How about a little trim?" All I heard Huck say was, "Uh-huh." It was apparent he was kissing her. Harry and I were astonished when moments later a leg with a medium-heeled patent leather shoe on its foot and pink underwear hanging from its ankle, protruded into the space between the front seatbacks. It was a challenge to drive the car, watch this leg jiggle and watch the backseat motion and commotion through the rear-view mirror. Shelly's friend must have tried the same tactic with her, because she kept saying, "Wait until we're all alone." A few minutes later I heard Huck say in a loud whisper, "You bastard." Then she was silent. I knew that could only mean one thing: *non coitus interruptus*.

Huck was the first one to be dropped off at home. Will did not walk her to her door. Next, I dropped off Shelly and her friend near her house. Now only Will, Harry and I were left, and Will started talking, "I'm sorry, guys, to do that to you, but I have to get that snatch while it's available. She's mad at me because I messed up her clothes. Hey, just drop me off at Shirley's place. I'll be spending the night with her." I dropped him off, and then dropped off Harry at his house at 11th and Victory Streets. It was 10:30 p.m. and far too late to think about salvaging my opportunity with Jerri.

That night, I learned another valuable lesson: Benevolence has its price. Be sure you are willing to bear the cost. I enabled one person to get over, and probably enabled another to do likewise. I did not; I missed my opportunity. I never had another chance to get Jerri alone.

Tenth grade Spanish class was usually a bore, but one day the teacher, Mr. King, was late for class. Suddenly, a very interesting, spirited conversation erupted among the girls. The subject discussed was Ride the Johnson bareback, which translated meant engage in unprotected sex. I don't know what initiated the discussion, but the first thing I heard was what Sally said, "I'm a woman and I can take a Johnson bareback like a grown woman."

Immediately, Mary Ann retorted, "I can handle a big Johnson just as well as you, maybe better."

Then five or six other girls chimed in with more audacious claims about their womanhood, such as, "My boyfriend, who's a senior, tells me how much woman I am every day. My man is an airman with the Air Force, and he's twenty-two. I take care of him every night, so I know I'm a woman." One girl said her boyfriend was twenty-six years old and that definitely made her a woman! The tales got taller and taller and spilled over into the dining hall after class.

One girl, who was a year senior to me, told me that she had been pregnant twice and had both babies knocked, which meant aborted. Several of the girls knew all the details about knocking babies, either first hand or from older sisters. They explained to me all the administrative, operational and procedural instructions for terminating pregnancies. This was an important subject because pregnant girls were expelled from school until after they gave birth. Some girls, however, because of the timing of the pregnancy, were shrewd enough to fool the system. Another young woman, who was normally very quiet, explained how she practiced birth control. Birth control pills were not yet available. Immediately after intercourse, she took a warm ten-ounce bottle of Coke and shook it to the point of agitation. She popped the bottle cap and inserted the neck of the bottle into her vagina, where the carbonation forced the Coke into her genital cavity. She said Coke was a very good spermicide. Years later, I learned, in principle, she was right.

A charitable female member of the class said this to me that day: "You wonder why girls don't waste their time with you? You attempt to be mannish, but you are not a man. You are just a punk-butt child. Where is your carnal knowledge? You don't have a clue about the birds and bees; in fact, you don't know birds from bees! Ever had a wet dream? Where is your facial hair? (I did not have any.) Have any pubic hair?" I just listened. Her points were well taken.

I could not verify any of the claims I heard that day. All the girls in that class making claims had boyfriends external to the tenth grade and in some cases external to Mann. The ladies labeled us boys as immature, wet-behind-the-ears wimps, who could not move them with a bulldozer or make a baby with a baby-making machine. One thing was very clear: we were too young and stupid for most of these young ladies. We were simply inferior in their eyes. The claims of some of those girls must have been true. At least four of them became pregnant before the end of our tenth grade school year. That fact made me glad that I was dumb and stupid, but not a father!

I completed my first year, tenth grade, at Mann. Except for the audience with the Dean of Boys, Mr. Harris, explaining that I was under consideration to be one of the students to integrate Central High School; there was little school-related excitement. For whatever reason, I was dropped from consideration and no one spoke to me about attending Central again. Blueberry Hill was my favorite song during the summer. I was prepared for another interesting summer at the filling station. A very high priority was to procure a later model, better car, this time with Bud's concurrence. The 1939 Chevy had served its time and was ready for the pasture.

Red Speirling had a 1949 Plymouth that I really liked. He told me that he could get me one just like it. After weeks of procrastinating, delays refurbishing the interior, clearing clouds from the title and prodding from Bud, Red finally delivered a gray 1949 Plymouth to me in the late summer of 1957. This car was a four-door modern marvel compared to my previous car. It had whitewall tires with full hubcaps and a modern pushbutton radio. There was no shimmy, shocks to refill and no vacuum shift to contend with; this car was just one smooth, quiet, comfortable ride.

As soon as the car was legal to drive, I picked up one of my favorite cruising friends, Dora Moore. Dora was a tall brown beauty with long legs, which she made visible and accessible. We frequently cruised and talked for hours. That night, we rode through Prothro Junction in North Little Rock. Again, she reminded me: "Eddie, baby, you know I love you with all my heart, but if we have sex, you got to use a rubber. My mother says don't have a baby by anyone darker than me. If you were like Johnny or Bill, (who are really fair-skinned, then forget the rubber. I will take my chances." Because I was darker than Dora, I understood. We continued to cruise, but we never had sex.

On separate occasions at the pumps, two good-looking women, one black and the other white, offered me payment in kind (in both cases their bodies) for five gallons and ten gallons of gasoline, respectively. I turned them both down.

I started my fourth summer at work in typical fashion. In a way it was like continually traveling around the same large oval track, the scenery changed very little, yet surprises and opportunities lurked around every corner. I met numerous interesting characters through my job at the station, but none where I was the focus of attention, until I met Candy Man. Candy Man was – as the name implies – a candy vendor. We had two of his candy machines on consignment in the office at the station. Candy Man was a tall, white man, probably in his sixties. His appearance was unusual because one of his eyes was discolored; the eyeball, including the cornea, pupil and iris were all just one shade of gray.

I saw the look of evil in his good eye when he came to service his machines and settle the accounts. He followed me around and stared at me in an eerie fashion without uttering a word. Candy Man's stalking became a concern to me when he started servicing his machines twice a week. During one of his staring episodes, his face turned beet-red, and the two veins on both sides of his neck became enlarged. I thought he was about to spit on me, so I quickly moved out of range. After he left, I talked to the Old Man.

The Old Man told me that he had been watching Candy Man. He explained to me that the man was a member of the local Citizens Council, which opposed the imminent integration of Central High School in the fall. He had a two-fold goal: recruit the Old Man to become a member of the Citizen's Council, revoke my cash register access and ultimately fire me. The Old Man assured me he would do none of those.

Over the late summer months of 1957, Candy Man appeared to acquire the look of a fiend, which scared me. I imagined that, during one of his visits, he would pull a gun and shoot me. The Old Man said he increased the pressure on him to achieve his stated goals. The Old Man never relented.

Finally, Candy Man presented the Old Man with an ultimatum: fire me or he would take his candy machines home. The Old Man said he was tired of this person's shenanigans and told him to take his machines and leave. After some deliberation, he did. I immediately felt safer. I was very proud of the Old Man for his actions and wanted to do my part to ensure that he did not suffer Candy-Man remorse. In a very short time, we got newer, more colorful machines from another vendor with a much wider selection of products.

Old man Martin was a customer who made it impossible to forget him. Everything he did was at half cadence plus slow motion. He said he was 89 years old and was certainly a creature of habit. Martin came in for gas every Tuesday at 2 p.m. He had his 1954 Chevrolet gas tank filled with regular and had everything checked: all fluids under the hood, air pressure in all tires on the ground and the spare in the trunk. When you checked his oil, he wanted you to show him the dipstick. Martin expected me to clean all of his windows and both outside mirrors. He then had me check his door-jam sticker to see if he was due for an oil change. Martin oil was almost never due; he drove only about 1200 miles a year. His fill-ups never took more than two or three gallons. He spent at least 20 minutes at the pumps, but he always gave me a nice tip; he was not so kind to Bud or the Old Man when they serviced his car.

Said Martin of himself, "I am an old SOB. I know I am a pain in the ass. I am far too concerned about minutiae. (That word was not yet in my vocabulary; I had to look it up.) My lovely wife tells me so." His wife was right.

I learned the lubrication charts for two brand new foreign cars for the summer of 1957: a 1957 Volkswagen Bug and 1957 Peugeot. I also had the pleasure to service a classic 1932 Rolls-Royce Phantom II. These cars were great examples to highlight the differences between European and American engineering styles. The Volkswagen was a German example, the Peugeot was French and the Rolls-Royce was British. It was an opportunity for me to think international. It was also a thrill to drive these cars, even the short distances around the filling station. The Volkswagen had a factory installed gasoline heater in the front trunk. The Rolls had a huge crankcase capacity, over twenty quarts. The Peugeot moniker later gained fame on the television series *Columbo*, where the rumpled police detective character drove a weatherworn 403 convertible.

By midsummer, the imminent integration of Central High School in the fall produced tension among the citizens of Little Rock, including our customers. I often felt the resentment at the pump, not necessarily at me, but certainly at the race I represented. This caused me to talk less and listen more. One customer, who was normally mild mannered, was clearly agitated at the prospect of blacks and whites attending high school together. He caught me off guard while I was pumping his gas, "Eddie, what do you think of all this integration B.S.?" I knew from his tone he was angry, and I did not need a confrontation at the pumps. I did not answer.

He went on, "The races are separate in the Bible. They were meant to be separate; they should never mix. It is against God's and man's will. I don't want you living with my granddaughter, producing mongrel kids. You understand?"

I had cleaned his windshield and was topping off his tank, relieved that I was almost finished with him. I answered with all that I could think to say, "I see your point."

He must have realized my tact because he said, "I'm sorry that I went off on you. I'm venting a lot of pent-up anger about this situation. I shouldn't have taken it out on you. Keep what I said under your hat." This customer never talked to me like that again.

Many snide remarks were made about the Pulaski County Board of Education plans to enroll Negroes at Central in the fall. Some of our black customers were also skeptical about this decision; they were happy with the status quo. I was well informed by the Bateses and others; I knew blacks would be enrolled in Central in the fall. The most pressing matter for me was how to defend myself at the pumps, which is where I felt the most vulnerable, especially at night. Without saying anything to the Old Man or Bud, I devised tactics to use the gas nozzle as a weapon. The nozzle was heavy and worked very well as a club; I could also simply squirt gasoline into someone's face, which would certainly incapacitate them.

In the fall of 1957, the Little Rock Nine eventually enrolled in Central High School. The ramifications, even for me, were significant. One night while I was using the outside phone booth at one corner of the filling station's lot, a carload of white boys hurled three house bricks at the booth, shattering the Plexiglas, sending the shards over my head and face. Another night, while walking along the Wright Avenue sidewalk to a nearby malt stand, a pickup truck slowly drove by with two white men or boys standing in its bed. They shouted racial epithets at me and one of them snapped a bullwhip, which ripped my nylon shirt off my back and produced a large welt. Immediately, when I heard the whip's crack and felt its sting on my back, I dived for nearby bushes to conceal and shield myself.

The cops pulled me over on Battery Street one night, near where Allan Jones and I had maintained a client's lawn. I had just changed a flat tire on my Plymouth, and the hubcap and the medium-sized screwdriver I used to remove it were on the rear floorboard.

One cop said, "Nigger, what are you doing in this neighborhood? You fit the description of the black-ass nigger who just assaulted a white woman on the next block. You prowling around here looking for some white rookie? Huh, boy?"

"No, sir."

"What is that big old weapon back there on the floor? You gonna use it to rob somebody?"

"No, sir."

"Get out of the car and put that weapon in the trunk. Do it now!"

"Yes, sir." I complied with the officer's instructions.

"Listen, boy, if you want to live to be a man, stay out of this neighborhood, looking for white ass. You never gonna get any. If I ever catch you anywhere near here, I'm running your ass in. Now get out of here. Run, nigger, run!" They both chuckled.

"Thanks, officer." One officer never said a single word. I was never asked to show a driver's license or registration.

It is well documented that President Eisenhower sent the 101st Airborne Division into Little Rock to ensure the safety and rights of the Little Rock Nine. The 101st patrolled outside the school and escorted the Negro students during school. The soldiers created the most secure 24/7 environment ever around the Central High campus. This was especially noticeable during our football games, which were played at Central's football stadium. During these events, blacks walked to the games in safety. I drove my car to several games. There was not a single fight or case of car vandalism. The soldiers were very professional. At every game, a group of off duty soldiers in uniform enjoyed the game as spectators.

I was extremely proud to drive my Plymouth to Mann and park it on the school campus. It was not quite my fantasy car – a 1955 black and white Mercury Montclair – but I enjoyed driving it. Fellow students discontinued the horse and buggy talk that persisted with the 1939 Chevy. The car, however, did not raise my Casanova factor; I did not gain a new flock of eager girls. I was still not Harry Belafonte. The car did increase my daring.

My daily drive-to-school ritual included a drive through Central High's ground zero, the intersection at 16th and Park Streets. Vociferous crowds gathered at that location. News reporters gathered there. Negro effigies hung there. On a typical day, I picked up Wayman Barnes and headed north on High Street for three blocks, then turned west on 16th and drove the few blocks to the Park Street intersection. We dwelled long enough to observe the corner activities, then I made a slow turn south on Park Street and headed for Wright Avenue, a few blocks away. One crisp morning, as we approached the intersection, we saw a Negro effigy hanging from the limb of a tree. The large crowd there was very agitated. Without thinking or consulting Wayman, I suddenly stopped the car in the intersection. We both jumped out of the car, leaving both front doors wide open. I shouted, "Cut that thing down!"

The crowd fanned back as if they were afraid of us. It took less than a millisecond for both of us to realize simultaneously how vulnerable and stupid we were. There were no cops or soldiers to save us from the crowd. Wayman and I hustled back into the car and managed to drive away without incident. The next morning we drove through the intersection again – without stopping. There was nothing hanging in effigy.

At the station, during the Central crisis, it was business as usual. The Parker family, Daddy Parker and the kids, treated me just like always, despite what was playing out at Central, on TV and in the newspapers. Bobby Parker continued to invite me to the Main Street Snooker Parlor for pool. I continued to wash Ferrell Faubus' (son of the sitting governor) Corvette.

Many nights after work, I spent time with my other cruising friend, Maxine Flowers. She was different from Dora Moore. Dora had long sexy legs. Maxine had gorgeous breasts that were visible and available. We spent long hours together, eating footlong hotdogs and slurping malts. We grooved to such songs as Mickey and Sylvia's *Love Is Strange*, the Dell Vikings' *Come Go with Me* and Larry Williams' *Boney Maroney* as they wafted from my twin rear-seat speakers. The cops never stopped me when I was with Maxine or Dora. They both had curfews like mine: nonexistent.

May Helen Coakley, my on-and-off-again girlfriend had a strict curfew, mainly in the presence of her daddy, Erastus T. Coakley. Nevertheless, necessity and ingenuity provided a solution. One night like many before it, I drove in the field near the boxcars where I once hid and flashed my parking lights three times and waited. May Helen climbed out her bedroom window around 11 p.m. and ran up to my car. In the wee hours, we returned and successfully reversed the process. Erastus T. never knew. After eleventh grade, May Helen did not register to attend J.C. Cook and quit school. In addition, her father Erastus quit the curfew.

During one of our previous capers, May Helen and I drove to a lovers' lane behind the bauxite pits near Sweet Home. I parked the car on what I thought was a deserted road. Within minutes, out of nowhere, a white man with a double-barreled shotgun walked up to my window. "Nigger, don't squat your ass here! You and that nigger gal get off my land. And don't come back here again. I'll use this here piece. Now git!" he said in a deep drawl. I have no idea where this person came from. I drove the entire lay of the land around these pits and never saw any houses. However, that did not matter now. It was time to go and fast. Any amorous thoughts I had that night just vanished. That double barrel was totally convincing.

During our junior year at Mann, Herman Jones, Robert Graham, Dorothy Howard and I formed a singing group patterned loosely after the Platters, one of the great doo-wop groups of the fifties. Graham was the musical director but, in reality, none of us had any musical training. We rehearsed a cappella a few times and thought we were ready to make a hit record. We had no music, lyrics or songs to record and no name for our group, but we thought we were ready for the recording studio. There were no studios in Little Rock, so Herman and I, as the advance party for the group, headed to Memphis to check it out. My research showed that the great bluesman, B.B. King, had an office and recording studio on the most famous music street in Memphis, Beale Street. We planned to meet with B.B. and convince him to sign our unnamed group.

I thoroughly inspected my 1949 Plymouth and pronounced it ready for the 110-mile trip to Memphis. At my driving speed, which was slow, I predicted it should take us about three-and-a-half hours. I studied my map, and we headed north. This was the first trip outside of Arkansas for both of us. About one-and-a-half hours into the trip, just as it started to rain, we came upon a stalled car along the side of the road. A black family was inside the car, so Herman and I decided to stop and help.

The driver told me he and his teenage daughter were driving back to Memphis when the engine just died. I opened the hood of his 1955 Ford and told him, "Let me see if I can determine the problem." I had run scores of service calls, many for this very symptom, so I knew the procedure: First, see if the engine is getting gas. Then, check for spark. The sudden onset of the problem was caused by lack of ignition. I pulled off a spark plug wire and confirmed that there was no spark. Next, I had to find out why. There was a spark coming out of the coil. Therefore, the issue had to be between the coil and the distributor. I reseated the coil wire into the distributor. "Now try to start the car," I told him. The engine roared to life. I closed the hood.

The man and his beautiful daughter considered us heroes for getting them back on the road and because we were from Little Rock. While I was getting wet, Herman got inside their car and got the daughter's phone number and address; I got the man's car running and got dirty. Life was not fair.

The rest of the trip was uneventful. Herman and I played tourist along the way. I drove across the famous Mississippi Bridge. We saw the mighty Mississippi River. I drove briefly across the border into the bigoted state of Mississippi, just so we could say we had been there. Even that little incursion was scary. We arrived in Memphis well within our time budget. I got directions and headed straight for B.B.'s Beale Street Office.

We found his office and recording studio doors locked. We inquired throughout the building about B.B. King's office or studio hours. No one had seen him in months. Most of the people assumed he was gone for good. Once the people in the building discovered we were from Little Rock, they were far more fascinated with us than B.B.

As Herman and I left the building, we were peppered with questions, like "How do you cope? Are you afraid? How does it feel to have the Army in your town? Are things as bad as they look on the news?" Then someone stated, "You guys must be brave."

"The Little Rock Nine are the brave ones, not us," I told them.

We left the building feeling the trip was a bust. I told Herman that we could stop by Sun Records, but we did not have an appointment there either. We decided to walk along the Home of the Blues, Beale Street, which dwarfed our Ninth Street. We apparently looked lost, because many people offered to help us find something. We gave them all the same response: "We're from Little Rock, and we came to meet B.B. King." Most people just smiled about B.B. and queried us about Little Rock. One kind man tried to explain our chance of meeting B.B. was slim – even if we lived in Memphis, "B.B. is always touring. He is not around here much."

About two blocks further down the street, we walked up to a sidewalk shoe vendor, who literally forced me to try on a pair of his shoes. Herman resisted. I tried on a black club-toe, which did not fit very well. "Let me get your size, little brother," the man said. "Sit on that stool and stay right there! I will be right back." He came back with three boxes of shoes. The pair of shoes in the first box fit perfectly. "Those shoes are you. You and those shoes are one," he said in a gruff voice.

"These shoes are ugly," I told him. He looked at me with bloodshot eyes and said, "Little man, let's not make trouble. I know y'all from Little Rock and used to trouble. But I want you to be able to get back home, ok? I put your old shoes in the bag, here take it. Give me seven dollars and kindly walk away." I did both.

I liked Beale Street, but I was afraid of it, too. Herman and I drove around Memphis. I was impressed by the sheer size of the city; Memphis was at least three times as big as Little Rock. This was the biggest city I had ever visited. Soon, we had enough of Memphis; there were too many people and vehicles and too much traffic. We got directions back to the highway and headed back to Little Rock. Paradoxically, we came to Memphis from Little Rock seeking fame but, in Memphis, we were famous for being from

Little Rock.

The three-hour drive back to Little Rock was smooth, but silent and somber. Neither of us talked much. The day was a big downer. We failed to meet B.B., we didn't secure a recording contract, and I was forced to buy shoes I didn't like or want. On a bright note, two teenagers successfully made the roundtrip from Little Rock to Memphis and returned. That trip was over 50 years ago. I have not been back to Memphis since.

Our unnamed doo-wop group disbanded shortly after the trip. Graham, our musical director, quit school after eleventh grade and joined the Navy. Dorothy, our female vocalist, became a mother. Herman and I found other interests that did not include singing.

Initially, I was ashamed to wear the club-toe shoes to Mann. Eventually, Herman talked me into it. I expected to be the laughing stock of the school. However, it was not the fashion faux pas I envisioned. Instead, I turned out to be on the leading edge of a new shoe fashion trend. The guys asked me, "Man, where did you get those cool kicks?" In about a month, the club-toe cool migrated from Memphis to Little Rock. All the fashion conscious guys at Mann wore them. For the first and only time in my life, I was a fashion leader.

29

Horace Mann High – Closing Act

A couple of months after the Memphis trip, at any speed above idle, my Plymouth developed a strange noise that sounded like 10,000 bumble bees in flight. From my experience, I knew it was worn wrist pins, rod bearings or main bearings. The issue, of course, was which one? I got help from an unexpected source - a very elderly white customer, who looked well past retirement age, with a full white beard and missing teeth. Nahlen, the only name I ever knew, was a loner who never mentioned a wife, children or family. He worked at a local dairy maintaining its delivery trucks, some of which had engines similar to the one in my Plymouth. Once while the Central High School issue was under discussion in the station's office, Nahlen strongly remarked, "I don't like what they're doing." He was a man of few words and said nothing else. When I considered his remark out of context and the fact that he often looked at me with what I perceived as disgust, he was not the first person I expected to offer help. He did volunteer his help.

After he finished work at the dairy, Nahlen brought his stethoscope by the station to help diagnose my engine problem. I watched him place the pickup unit on various parts of my engine, including the crankcase. After a few minutes of testing, he said, "Rod bearings!" He let me listen. "Eddie, the crankshaft is probably worn out of spec. Slap in rod bearings and sell the car. Take off the oil pan, and I'll come by after work and we'll inspect the rod bearings," he advised me. I removed the oil pan, and Nahlen came by and brought his micrometer to check the condition of the crankshaft. He was right. The rod bearings were worn out. The crankshaft was also worn and needed to be replaced or reground. I installed new rod bearings and replaced the oil pan. I learned two lessons from all of this: how to quickly replace rod bearings, and people are not always what they seem. Once again, be slow to judge.

Two months later, the sounds came back. I did not need Nahlen this time. I replaced the bearings again and understood that I needed a replacement car immediately.

Thursday, April 10, 1958, 3:40 p.m. was a sad time for me. It was one week past my 17th birthday. I had just left school on my way to work when the KOKY disc jockey announced the death of one of my favorite singers, Chuck Willis. He had died suddenly from a stomach ulcer (My uncle had a stomach ulcer.) He sang one of my favorite songs, *Ease the Pain*, which I always played on the jukebox as soon as I entered the bar and grill at 24th and High Streets. Ironically, two songs released just after his death were *What Am I Living For* and the B-side, *Hang Up My Rock and Roll Shoes*, both became favorites of mine. Were these songs prophetic? A clue to his impending demise? A pall descended over me while the radio played Chuck Willis songs all the way to work. He was one of the few R&B singers who wore a turban onstage.

Laverne Walker, who was my only non-female cruising friend, was interesting to me for numerous reasons. First, I never knew that Laverne was suitable as a boy's name (one of my girlfriends was named LaVerne Lyles); second, he had a beautiful sister, Antoinette, who I enjoyed being around. He was my West End liaison; Laverne lived on West 42nd Street, a couple of blocks from another girl I was wooing, Curtistine Holt. He was as passionate about the West Coast as I was. We spent hours discussing what we could accomplish if we got to the Coast.

Laverne was a chain smoker and by his own admission was not a smart person. He had a gold tooth in the front of his mouth that attracted some girls and turned off others. I did not like his gold tooth, but found it interesting and different. Numerous dudes, including me, befriended him to earn sway with his sister. Laverne's family was solidly middle class with all the trappings: two cars, detached house, multiple telephone extensions, two television sets, and all three siblings had separate bedrooms. The entire family dressed very well.

Laverne worked as a dishwasher for a restaurant on Asher Avenue, but like most dishwashers, he called himself a short order cook. No one wanted to be known as a suds buster. I helped him pursue the girl he loved, Patty Crumpton, and he helped me pursue Curtistine Holt. I never told him that I had a crush on his sister. Whenever he danced a slow dance with Patty, Laverne said he always experienced a spontaneous emission. Therefore, when Laverne knew he was going to be near her, he carried extra shorts.

Laverne's neighbor Billy across the street was a very interesting study. He was deep into an affair with Mattie Benson, who was sixteen when the affair started. He was 27, married with three young children. Mattie was the same age as most of my Mann classmates. She was a very attractive young woman with a great body and she knew it. She made grown men, including teachers, drool when we were at Dunbar and this continued when we graduated to Mann. I had the opportunity to hear both sides of this dangerous liaison, from Mattie at school and from Billy after work. Billy was proud to brag to Laverne and me that he had such a young, good-looking girl under his spell. However, he had forsaken his family for so long and in so many ways that his marriage was irreparably broken.

Mattie, as she explained to me, was just having fun, enjoying all the money, gifts and time she was getting from Billy, who was one of several older men in her life. Billy told me how lucky he was to be able to satisfy such a young girl and his wife at the same time. His wife spun a much different tale. She said there often was not enough money for food and rent. Billy's job was delivering furniture, so he did not make a lot of money. He often did not come home until late or not at all. Laverne and I talked to Billy usually about 11 or 12 p.m., just after he arrived home.

Billy's family and Laverne's family lived on opposite sides of the street and presented me with a study of contrasts: one family, including three kids, was very successful; the other family, including three kids, was severely broken. I knew which model I wanted to represent.

I only knew Laverne for two years. Then the entire Walker family moved to California; so Laverne got his wish – he went to the Coast. Otherwise, there were no winners in this story. Antoinette got pregnant and married before graduating from high school. Laverne never won any attention or affection from Patty Crumpton; I never gained any traction with Curtistine Holt, and Billy's wife divorced him. After Billy's wife filed for divorce, Mattie dropped him for another older man. Mattie told me the new guy, who was a lawyer, had more money and status. Billy told me he wished he had never met Mattie, that his affair with her was the biggest mistake he ever made. It destroyed his life. He warned me not to be as stupid as he was. I took his advice. I never heard from Laverne after he left town.

Ernest Green, senior member of the Little Rock Nine, made history on May 27, 1958, when he graduated from Central High School. At the same time, I completed my junior year at Horace Mann High and started my fifth full-time summer session at the filling station. As far as I was concerned, it was time to move beyond the memory of the 1,000-member 101st Airborne Division detachment, the federalized 10,000-man Arkansas National Guard unit and Little Rock Police Department officers encircling Central High. It was time to move beyond the public rancor, acrimony, hatred and doom that had shrouded the city. I was looking forward to enjoying my senior year at Mann, only driving a different car.

Just like last summer, my priority was to get a more reliable car. My Plymouth threw rod bearings twice, and I replaced them. The crankshaft was worn and needed to be reground, which required oversized rod bearings for a proper reinstallation. That solution was not economically viable, so the hunt was on for another car.

Bud, Red Speirling and their network of friends quickly helped me locate a car, a 1950 Ford two-door sedan. This car was not a cream puff, but mechanically it was sound, although it needed some immediate attention. The interior was a mess, but Red agreed to refurbish the interior in red and white vinyl, including seat covers, door and quarter panels, before delivery for $150. I agreed to the deal, the car was turned over to me in late June and I immediately started work on it. I replaced a leaky water pump, installed new spark plugs and rebuilt the carburetor. The engine, a 100-horsepower flathead V-8 could easily be adapted to a dual-exhaust system. This car had two other interesting features: a 3-speed manual transmission with an overdrive unit that would cut in at speeds above 27 mph and return to normal below about 20 mph. In addition, the car had a second full-sized gas tank in the trunk, which indicated that the car probably had been used by a ridge runner transporting moonshine.

This car was the twin to the car driven by Robert Mitchum in the 1958 cult movie, *Thunder Road*, a tale about running moonshine in the mountains of Kentucky and Tennessee in the early 1950s. In the film, Mitchum drove a souped-up 1950 Ford with a custom tank in the back for moonshine. I did not remove the second gas tank in my Ford, which was not connected to the car's fuel system. That car was part of history.

I spent most of the summer of 1958 re-engaging regular station customers and learning the idiosyncrasies of new ones. Three new customers, all black ministers, became my newest philosophers at the pumps. One was the pastor of a Sanctified Church, another was the pastor of an African Methodist Episcopal Church (usually called the AME Church), but the most interesting to me was Reverend Young, who was new to Little Rock. He was the first pastor of a brand new Seventh-day Adventist (now just called Adventist) church at Wright Avenue and Pulaski Street, just three blocks south of the station. Reverend Young was young, handsome, articulate, newly married, and fresh out of seminary. I liked him for two reasons: He was close to my age, and he philosophized, like Reverend Ogden, without proselytizing. I enjoyed explaining technical things about his 1955 Oldsmobile to him, and he explained biblical matters in a manner that I easily comprehended. He also explained that his church is a Protestant Christian denomination distinguished primarily by its observance of Saturday, the "seventh day" of the week, as the Sabbath.

My other mission, over the summer, was to transform my "new" Ford into the car I wanted it to be. The transformation was done incrementally as discretionary funds became available. The first task was to paint the car black. The original color, a nondescript green was severely worn and faded. That color was a great choice for a ridge runner, who wanted the car to attract no attention, but a poor choice for a senior who aspired to be one cool cat. I negotiated a good deal with a local body shop on West 7th Street and had the car painted black enamel.

Next, I replaced both rear taillight lenses with blue dot tail light lens and added stainless half-moon headlight covers. I painted the inside window frames, dashboard and rims Mobilgas Flying Red Horse red. I installed a powerful spotlight and an eight-inch rear seat speaker kit. One at a time, I replaced the tires on the ground with recapped whitewalls. After saving money for a few weeks, I purchased four new 1956 Oldsmobile Fiesta-style spinner hubcaps. With that purchase, the car projected the look I sought.

This summer, like the previous five that I worked here, Little Rock experienced intense gas wars, which lasted from as short as one week to as long as one month. The average price for gas in the fifties was approximately 30 cents per gallon and very stable. The gas war always started when one station in town, like the People's station at Wright Avenue and High Streets, lowered the price per gallon of gas to twenty cents. Another station lowered the price to eighteen cents; still another to twelve cents. The objective was to see which station could lower the price the most and keep it there for the longest. I saw stations sell their entire inventory of over ten thousand gallons of gas at ten cents per gallon. We could not afford to let our customers patronize those low ballers, so we lowered ours, too, just to stay competitive. In many cases, we like the other combatants, sold gas below cost. It made no economic sense; it was just the cost of doing business.

I was working alone late one Friday night. I do not remember why I was the lone closer that night, but it was common to have just one attendant on duty at night after 7 p.m. We normally had two, but not this night. One of our long-time customers, Bowman C. Kogan drove in. I filled his tank as I did every week about this time. Bowman was a tall, imposing man about 6'4", 250 pounds, a rugged-looking John Wayne type on steroids. His routine was rigidly set: every Friday night, he left the lumber mill where he worked and drove straight to the station, filled the tank in his 1954 Ford, cashed his payroll check, paid his gasoline bill, and with cash in hand, headed to the grocery store to buy next week's food. I added up his bill and presented him with the total. He gave me a very strange look and said, "Where's Bud or Mr. Price?"

"Neither one is here tonight," I replied.

"Well, I'll be damned. I can't cash my check. The little wife will be pissed! I won't be able to buy groceries!" he said.

"There's no problem. I can cash your check and take care of your bill, and you can be on your way before Safeway closes. You still have about an hour," I explained to him.

"No nigger is cashing my check! I worked too hard for the money. Just put tonight's fill-up on my tab. I'll take care of everything when Mr. Price is here."

I told him, "No problem. Thanks."

"Goddamnit! The wife will be pissed!" Bowman said, as he ambled to his car. I never understood the part about he worked too hard for the money. At 9 p.m., I closed the station without incident.

That summer, there were two part-time station employees who were memorable for what they told me. Lemuel Camuel Samuel Antonio MacNeil, L.C. for short, was long on names and short on talent. How he got to Little Rock, I do not know. He was from Sweetwater, Texas. The first day we worked together, a schoolmate of mine, Anna Foley, came in her dad's Mercury and bought one dollar's worth of gas. Anna was a tall, bronze, statuesque brickhouse, who always flashed liberal leg and more than ample cleavage.

This time was no different, except that L.C. cleaned Anna's windshield. He went into spasms and began to babble like an infant. When he was finally able to speak, he said, "Who is thaaat girl? I am just an old cowboy from Texas, but I would give my left testicle to get in bed with her. I can tell you know her, right?"

"I know her from school."

"How can I bribe you? I'll trade you a white girl for her, I'm serious," he probed.

The next time Anna came in alone, I told her what he had said. Playfully, she added, "I will show L.C. some pubes and nipples. I'll drive white boy wild." Anna and her family went on vacation, so she was gone for a couple of weeks. By the time she came back to the station, L.C. had disappeared without notice. He never came back. Maybe he went back to Texas.

The other memorable person was a good old country dude named Merle Denn. During a lull in activity, he explained his method of birth control to me. "I have four kids and a wife. My dining room table seats six. One more kid and I won't have a place at the table. My wife delivered four kids in five years. She is gun shy of sex. If I even look like I want sex, she runs and cries. Sex to her only means one thing, another kid. She talked to her mother about it, and her mother told her to close and lock the front door and open the back door. She did, and now she does not run away and we have had no more kids. Hallelujah!" All I could say was, "I understand." There were no birth control pills in the 1950s.

The station was included in the beat of Morgan, the friendly white cop. Morgan, from his nametag, was the only name I knew. He was extremely friendly to me, and I learned a lot from him. He was always willing to explain things to me. If he did not have an immediate answer, he had one the next time I saw him. He worked some type of rotating shift, because he parked in the station's lot watching for stop sign runners, speeders, and reckless drivers, morning, noon and night. Morgan let me inspect all the details of his squad car, including the high output generator or alternator, high-capacity batteries, two-way radio and the bullet siren.

The Little Rock Police Department vehicles, which were mostly Fords, were factory made to be police cars. He shared some of the unusual activities that occurred during his watch, including the most bizarre incident. He apprehended two criminals rolling a huge safe down the middle of Chester Street, near the station, at 1 a.m. Of course, he sent them to jail. He told me I had immunity if he drove up on me in any of the lovers' lanes on his beat. He never drove up on me.

Just two weeks before I was supposed to return to Mann for my senior year, I completed the final modification to my Ford. I bought and installed a dual-exhaust header kit, two tailpipes, one right and one left, and two fiberglass-pack flow-through mufflers, which produced a pleasing rounded low frequency rumble. The car now had the perfect look, feel and sound. With this new sound, my Ford was often heard before and after it was seen.

A week later, I performed one last set of tweaks to the car in anticipation of driving a cool car to school. I added one-inch lowering blocks between the rear springs and axle to lower the rear end, which gave it that "squatty, ready to launch" look. I also added eight-inch chrome tailpipe extensions and pointed them slightly inward towards each other. I was extremely proud of the way this car turned out. I was ready in all aspects to return to Mann for my senior year.

I never attended another class at Horace Mann High School. In September 1958, Governor Orval Faubus ordered all public high schools in Little Rock closed for the school year, creating what became known as "The Lost Year." The Lost Year refers to the 1958-59 school year in Little Rock (Pulaski County), when all the city's high schools, including three white high schools: Central High, Hall High, Little Rock Technical High and, of course, Horace Mann were closed in an effort to thwart further desegregation.

The entire student population of Mann had to find educational alternatives or succumb to the consequences of "The Lost Year." White students had alternatives in Little Rock, including several Catholic schools, a Baptist school, and a newly formed private school. Negro students had none. Displaced Negro and white students enrolled in nearby in-state public schools where students lived with friends or relatives, out-of-state public and private schools, General Education Diploma or GED courses, correspondence courses and early entrance college programs. A sad fact was that about half of the more than 700 displaced black students simply dropped out, quit school altogether. I successfully enrolled in J.C. Cook High School (Negro) in Wrightsville, Arkansas, about 25 miles away, which enabled me to continue my education and maintain my job at the filling station.

Section Five – Post Mann

30

J.C. Cook High School – Disappearing Hubcaps

During the 1958-59 school year, I was extremely grateful to be able to attend J.C. Cook High School and maintain my great job at the filling station. I was also fortunate that I had a reliable personal car. Former Horace Mann High students, who still lived in Little Rock and attended Cook, had a major transportation issue. There was no organized public or commercial mass transit to or from Wrightsville. Transportation-challenged students used their ingenuity and devised ways to get to school. Students like me, who had cars, participated in carpool caravans; some caught rides with Cook teachers who lived in Little Rock; others caught rides to Sweet Home, Arkansas, a direct waypoint to Cook, and caught school buses to school; and a few students rode with employees of the Reform School for juvenile boys, which was down the road from Cook. One student from Little Rock rode to school on a motorcycle.

Of my inner circle of friends, only Herman Jones joined me and attended Cook. Samuel Tenpenny, Wayman Barnes, and my long-time girlfriend, May Helen Coakley, did not.

Compared to Mann, Cook was a different world. Academically, Mann was like a major university, while in comparison, Cook was like a small liberal arts community college. Cook offered no high-level sciences or math courses like calculus, biology, chemistry or physics. There was no football team or marching band. Classrooms were very crowded; sometimes there were as many as forty students per class. There was also a shortage of classrooms; even the library was turned into a classroom. Although all faculty members worked very hard to accommodate those of us from Little Rock, classes were often not very stimulating or challenging. While this environment was not very conducive to learning, we were able to demonstrate mastery of the lesson objectives quickly with very little effort, which created some tension between the native students and us. Despite all of this, the school had a special rural charm that grew on me. I actually enjoyed being a Cook student.

Cook had no Bamboo Inn like Dunbar, but it had Gerard's, which was much better. It was an integrated convenience store, gas station and post office in a building located directly in front of the school - so close that it appeared to be on the school grounds. It was not open 24/7, but close to it. Gerard's was a hangout for students before and after school, during lunch, and whenever they cut class. This place had the coin-operated toys to attract students, including a bank of four pinball machines and a jukebox with R&B music. It had all the food staples we liked, including all our favorite sodas (Royal Crown, Pepsi Cola, Barqs, and Coca-Cola), chips, pastries, shakes and burgers. The featured sandwich was the Doggie Woggie, a cheap baloney-based sandwich that was prepared in advance, which was a very big hit with students. My favorite jukebox songs there were *So Long* and its flipside, *When My Dreamboat Comes Home* by Fats Domino.

Perry, last name unknown, was the Negro general manager of Gerard's. He was a hands-on person, a trusted agent, who was the soul of the enterprise. The students at Cook, including me, held Perry in very high esteem. Mr. Gerard, the owner, practiced the laissez-faire approach to his business, and it thrilled the students to see a Negro man in charge, the keeper of the keys to the bank. Perry reminded me of my situation at the filling station in many ways, except he was much older than I was. Perry always looked out for the welfare of all of us students, even sending us back to school when we were not authorized to be in the store like hooking class.

My carpool passenger list included Frances Simmons, Alma Jones, Delores Hubbert, Carolyn Peters and Evelyn Scoggins. For various reasons, group members rotated in and out of the pool, so on average I transported four passengers. The fact that the passengers were all female was pure happenstance; they all contacted me. Being boxed up with all that estrogen for the two-hour roundtrip to and from Cook produced some interesting conversation and situations. For me, the eye candy was awesome. It appeared that they had a contest to see which young lady could attract the most attention from me, even though Delores and Evelyn had very steady boyfriends. My favorite passengers, though they did not know it, were Frances and Alma, two sophomores.

A typical commute to school started the day before at work at the filling station with a preventative maintenance inspection: check oil, tires, repair any previously detected deficiencies, and top off gas tank. On commute day, I was up and out of my house at 6 a.m., heading to the West End, where all my passengers lived. I picked up Frances first or last, because of where she lived – outside the tight cluster of houses where the other passengers lived. Although the order in which the ladies were picked up or dropped off, was often a point of contention, I did what made logistical sense to save time, especially after school, since I had to go to work. As soon as I picked up everybody, I headed straight for Roosevelt Road, which was also State Highway 365 which I followed south through College Station, Sweet Home, Higgins and finally to Wrightsville. En route, I kept the radio tuned to KOKY, which played R&B greats such as *Oh What a Night* by the Dells and *A Thousand Miles Away* by the Heartbeats. When we ran out of the range of KOKY's signal, the young ladies often serenaded me a cappella style with the songs, *Eddie, My Love*, fashioned like the Teen Queens, and *To Know Him Is to Love Him*, fashioned like the Teddy Bears.

Along the route to Cook, we also drove by three very noticeable landmarks: Horace Mann High School, Granite Mountain and the bauxite pits. The iconic school was only two years old but a lifeless shell of its former self. It stood there in golden splendor, devoid of students. It seemed paradoxical to drive right past a perfectly good high school to attend one that was not as good. Delores, a senior like me, and I mused how life as a returning student might have been; others in the car thought about what entering Mann as a new student would have been like. In a couple of minutes, Mann was gone from view, and we all returned to the present and reality. On the way home from school, we passed by Mann, again invoking emotions. After a few weeks, we all became oblivious to Mann, the landmark.

In Sweet Home, Arkansas, there was a 90-degree turn in the middle of this small town, which required me to slow down to about 20 mph. We usually came through about the same time Sweet Home high school students were waiting for the school bus, which gave me the opportunity to demonstrate how cool my car was. About a quarter mile from the turn, I came out of overdrive, shifted into second gear and let the engine slow the car down. The smooth, mellow rumble projected our presence before we arrived at the turn. Once I made the turn, I always accelerated sharply to let the loud rumbling sounds of my twin glass packs signal my egress.

We usually arrived at school early enough to spend about fifteen minutes mingling with students at Gerard's. We listened to a play list of R&B greats sustained with an endless supply of nickels fed to the jukebox. We watched expert pinball players rack up thousands of points and free games. We swapped news and rumors from the last 24 hours. We drank coffee and tea and ate pastries. When the morning school bell rang, we headed for class.

Some of the guys from Mann moved around the school with a swagger that won sway with the native Cook young ladies to the consternation of the Cook men. Relationships that were solid before the arrival of Mann students collapsed. Survival of the fittest, flashiest and richest in this case, prevailed. This situation was very similar to what we experienced at Mann when the young airmen with money and flashy cars alienated the affections of the Mann young ladies. As a result, Cook men and Mann men often looked at each other with disdain. That combination of circumstances ameliorated with time.

I had just reported to work after school one afternoon, and my first customer was Reverend Young. We talked briefly about Little Richard, my favorite singer. The reverend was very well aware of this fact, but he surprised me at the pumps this time with the depth of his knowledge about him. "Remember when Richard quit rock 'n' roll to, quote, make his peace with Jesus?" he asked me.

"Of course!"

He went on, "Richard enrolled in seminary, my alma mater in Alabama."

"What? You never told me that before."

"I wrote him and asked him to speak at my church. If he accepts, maybe you can come to hear him speak," the reverend said.

"That would be awesome. I sure would like to see him in that role," I told him. Then I topped off his tank, and Reverend Young drove away.

Another day after dropping off my passengers I reported to work and learned about a bizarre incident. For some strange reason, the Old Man left the cash register unlocked, which meant it could open without a key. After about two hours, he discovered and corrected his error. He also performed a reconciliation of the cash register and found $110.00 cash missing. During the period that the register was unlocked, Bud saw a strange man lurking in the office. He did not realize the register was not locked. Bud did not recognize the man, which was not unusual or cause for alarm. Many anonymous walkups bought cigarettes from our machine located inside the station's office. The Old Man reported the incident to his business's insurance company. To his surprise, the loss was not covered. It was not considered robbery or theft, which was covered, but mysterious disappearance, which was not. That drama made an interesting day; I wish I had been there. However, on the other hand, I was glad I was not.

"Red" Donahue ran a neighborhood drug store at 15th and Chester Streets and was a steady customer. Red was the nickname he acquired because he was a virtual clone of "Red" Schoendiest, the great St. Louis Cardinal second baseman. He was my pharmacist at the pumps and shared interesting anecdotes about prescription drugs with me. "I'm going out of business and moving away. I can't compete with Walgreens and the other big drug stores. The fun is gone," he explained to me one day while getting gas in his 1955 Pontiac.

I had mixed emotions about Red Donahue after I showed him one of my feet, which had a severe itch. He looked and said, "Athletes foot. It's a fungus. Come up to the store. I'll sell you an antifungal powder. It'll kill the bacteria, and the itch will be gone in a couple of days." I believed him. Over the next several weeks, I applied his salves, sprinkled his powders and soaked my foot in his solutions. My itch turned to infection and spread to the other foot.

The infected feet were threatening my ability to work, so I showed them to the Old Man. He looked and said, "Nasty. My doctor will take care of it. I will give him a call." He got me an appointment the next day at 10 a.m. The doctor's office was in the middle of downtown. I checked in with the receptionist, who said, "Mr. Price referred you to the doctor. The doctor will be with you shortly, just take a seat in the waiting room."

"Ok. Thanks." I saw no other Negroes in the area. I knew without the Old Man's phone call, I would have never gotten this appointment. Moments later, I was in the doctor's examination room.

"Mr. Price said you had some foot problems. Let me take a look," the doctor said. I took off my shoes and socks. "That's bad, probably painful, too," the doctor commented. "Athletes foot?" I asked. He thought for a few seconds before he answered, "I don't think so. I don't know what it is. Nevertheless, I'll take care of it. You need some x-ray treatment." I had no idea what that meant. The doctor swung a boom with a gimbal-mounted gun-looking device over to my feet. The device made a very low frequency hum for no more than 2-3 seconds. "That's it! You're all done. Always wear clean, dry socks," the doctor advised. I checked with the receptionist on the way out for the doctor's fee. She responded, "Mr. Price took care of it. Thanks."

"Thank you."

My feet started healing immediately and, within two weeks, everything was gone. It has been over fifty years, and I have not had a recurrence of that or any other foot problem. I still do not understand what x-ray treatment does, and I have not heard of anyone being treated with it since. However, it worked for me.

Donahue closed his store and moved away as he predicted.

I regularly serviced at the pumps and service bays three customers who owned Nash cars. One lady drove a small green and white 1955 Nash Metropolitan. Another lady drove a 1954 red and white Nash Ambassador. Lastly, a man who drove a 1955 tan and white Nash Ambassador. Anyone who drove a Nash was interesting by association with the car, but the man who lived across the street from the station was the most interesting of this trio. He was an unmarried, retired state government worker, who lived with his sister. This man spoke with a slight British accent and had a Polish name that I could not spell or pronounce, so to me he became Mr. Nash, after his car. Mr. Nash had the handsomeness of Howard Keel, patriarch of the nighttime soap drama *Dallas*, when he was sober. However, when he was drunk, which was most of the time; he had the shakiness of Foster Brooks, the great drunk on the *Dean Martin Show*.

Mr. Nash's breath and pores always reeked of alcohol. He was a chain smoker, and I was fearful of the blowtorch effect, because of the high alcohol content in his breath vapor. Whenever he had his car serviced, he wanted to drive his Nash onto the lift rack. I always talked him out of it. I was afraid he would drive too fast, jump the mechanical stops at the front of the lift, and run right through the back door of the bay. One day, he ran into the pumps on the west island; another time, he could not find his sister's driveway, so he just jumped the curb, drove diagonally into the front yard, and stopped just inches from her porch. One night, because he was so unsteady on his feet, he drove his Nash 100 feet across the street to buy cigarettes from our machine. Once he made his purchase, he forgot he drove over and staggered back to his sister's house and barely escaped being hit by a car.

Mr. Nash was the first white alcoholic I met and that alone made him an interesting study. To him, going fishing meant going drinking. His tackle box and his cooler were stocked with beer and hard liquor, some of it illegal. I never understood how Mr. Nash kept his driver's license; but as far as I know, he never lost it, despite many DWI's. One day after driving from Cook, Bud told me that Mr. Nash was found dead in his bed. By all accounts, he simply drank himself to death. I prefer to remember him as the aficionado of Nash automobiles that he was and all the revealing history he told me about Charles Nash, who was once president of General Motors.

Another customer, Sammy Adams, a Buddy Holly look-alike, was married and had two small kids. He worked in the parts department of the Pontiac Dealer on West Capitol Street and drove a very hot new 1958 red and white Pontiac Chieftain two-door hardtop with twin four-barrel carburetors. Sammy was one of several customers who talked performance at the pumps – high performance. He drove the hottest Pontiacs he could get from the factory and made them perform even better – faster. Sammy knew all the tricks of the day to make stock car dragsters turn the lowest times, including shaved heads, skirted pistons, domed pistons, high-lift cams and twin four-barrel carbs or one barrel per cylinder. I never understood how he afforded these high performance toys with kids and a stay-at-home wife.

One fall Saturday morning, I rode with Sammy to his job to bring his car back to the station for an oil, lube and car wash service. He gave a demonstration that I can never forget. He said, "Eddie, let me show you something."

He placed a hundred dollar bill on the dash on my side of the car. He continued, "From a dead stop at this intersection, I'm going to floor the accelerator. Reach for the bill." I could not reach the bill without leaning forward in the front passenger seat. He said, "If you can retrieve the bill in the first block while I'm accelerating, it's yours." He floored the gas pedal and the rate of change of velocity was so great, I could not reach the bill within the first block of travel. The thrust was so great I was pinned to the seat; I could not move forward. There were no seat belts. I could barely reach the C-note as we sped through the intersection of the second linear block. Sammy repeated the experiment, now that I knew what to expect. The result was the same. I did not win the hundred dollars. I drove Sammy's hot Pontiac slowly, legally and safely back to the station. I was not tempted to duplicate Sammy's experiment. It was the most powerful car that I ever drove for such a long distance alone, about one mile. It was a huge thrill.

Sammy introduced me to something that I did not master until many years later – how to make a motorcycle sing. One time during the early fall Sammy met one of my former Mann friends, Eben Ingram, at the pumps. Both bought gasoline, Sammy for his car and Eben for his motorcycle.

Sammy asked Eben, "Do you really know how to ride that thing?"

"I think so, I have a paper route and been riding about a year now," Eben said in a halting drawl.

"Can I borrow your bike for a ride? I want to show you something," Sammy said.

"Yup! Go ahead," Eben answered.

Sammy hopped on the bike, which was about 200 cc, and took a familiarization ride around the station. Then, he took off south down Chester Street as Eben and I stood in amazement listening to the smooth sound of the bike. The harmonized sound was fine and tempered like an expensive musical instrument; the shift points were blended, transparent and mesmerizing. Seconds later, Sammy came back and found Eben and me astonished after witnessing such coordination. Fourteen years later, with lots of practice on my Honda 350, I learned to shift gears with the same precision as Sammy. However, I never had anything close to his hot Pontiac.

On an evening in mid-October, Reverend Young pulled his Oldsmobile up to the pumps. With great excitement, he announced, "Eddie, guess what? Richard accepted my invitation. He agreed to speak at my church at 2 p.m. Saturday after next. I expect a huge crowd. I sure hope you can come. Should be great."

"Of course, you mean Little Richard?"

"That's right. Isn't that exciting?" he asked.

"That's a workday for me, but I'll try to be there. This is a once in a lifetime thing. I really hope I can see him. Thanks for the invite. I really appreciate the opportunity," I said to the reverend.

I did talk Bud into letting me go to hear Little Richard speak at Reverend Young's church. I arrived at 1 p.m., thought I would be early, and found the church packed with no standing room left and a huge overflow crowd outside. There were no loudspeakers outside to broadcast what was taking place inside. The only space left was dangerously close to Wright Avenue, a major truck route at that location. With absolutely no chance to see or hear Little Richard, I had no choice but to return to work.

About 8 p.m., long after Little Richard had spoken and gone, Reverend Young came by the station to talk to me: "Eddie, I'm sorry you didn't get a chance to see Richard. Would you believe the church was two-thirds full by 9 a.m.? I didn't know Richard was so popular. I didn't advertise much; it was all word of mouth. He promised to come back again."

Little Richard did come back again – this time unannounced. I came to work after school, and the Old Man walked over to greet me. The fact that he walked out to meet me was different; it was to tell me something – good or bad. He said, "Guess who I talked to today, just a few hours ago? I had no idea, but before I could guess, he said, "Little Richard."

No way, I thought. The Old Man went on to explain: "Reverend Young had Little Richard with him when he came in to get a vacuum hose replaced. Little Richard's hair was cut short, and he was shorter than I anticipated but he did not do anything outrageous. He was very soft spoken. He had this record, *Good Golly, Miss Molly*, which we tried to get autographed for you. However, he called it devil's work and smashed the record. Hell, I was impressed! Bud and I shook his hand."

It would have been great to have an autographed copy of the 45-RPM single of *Good Golly, Miss Molly*. Molly was a top ten hit on both the R&B and pop charts back in the summer. Specialty Records continued to release Little Richard singles for a year after he quit rock 'n' roll. Molly was his last big hit on the label.

The next time I talked to Reverend Young, he corroborated everything the Old Man said about Little Richard and added other details. "Richard called me out of the blue and asked me to pick him up at the train station. We came back to the church and discussed some of Richard's personal spiritual matters, had lunch and I brought my car up here for repair. I don't know where he got that record that he smashed, but he has divorced himself from his secular past and now plans to sing only gospel songs. Records that are coming out now were already in the can. Richard has no control over those. The Little Richard you know no longer exists." I was not so sure. The reverend returned Little Richard to the train station and at 4 p.m., he headed back to Alabama.

I thought to myself, what are the odds of my two favorite singers, Fats Domino and Little Richard, setting foot in my workspaces at Price Mobil Service? Fats Domino came here in 1954 and gave me my first one dollar tip. Little Richard came in 1958, although I was at Cook that day and did not get a chance to meet him. What are the odds of this? Incalculable. As far as I know, Little Richard never returned to Little Rock before I left in 1962. I saw Fats Domino in concert at the State Fair Grounds one more time before I left.

After an intense encounter with Professor Townsend at the pumps one Friday night, where I again declined to ride with her to Pine Bluff, I decided to score with a mature woman on my terms and on my turf. After work, I went home, showered, and headed for North Little Rock to the "meat market." The meat market was a place where usually older Negro women, divorced or just down on their romantic luck, lined up on Washington Street to wait for a date to drive up and take them for a night on the town. As I drove over the bridge, I wondered what would make this tour different from those of the past. I did not wear the latest suit, hat or shoe fashions. I thought I had a really cool car – it was a young girl magnet. However, it was not the Cadillac, Buick or Oldsmobile the thirty-plus ladies liked.

I turned onto Washington Street, drove past Square Deal Pawn Shop, and slowly cruised by the lineup of women, which stretched about three blocks long. These were so-called "honorable ladies," not prostitutes, although I knew there were some camouflaged in the crowd. My first drive-through, with my loud mufflers howling, produced screams, howls, whistles and some ceremonial dances to get drivers' attention. I never drew that much attention in previous drive-throughs, but those were always with other cars, not this Ford. To test whether the ladies' reactions were a fluke, I drove through again. The results were the same. Three women were interesting, because they had a shape similar enough to that of Professor Townsend. to warrant a closer inspection. I parked and decided to do a walk-through.

As I walked among the ladies on Washington Street, I found my perceptions far different from just driving by. For instance, now I smelled the unpleasant stench of fried hair and halitosis. Even the streetlights and illuminated display windows of the storefronts clearly revealed the cheap wigs and faux furs and eyelashes, as well as the stockingless legs that shone from liberal applications of Vaseline. I clearly heard and saw the offers for dates. One well-endowed mature woman shook her breasts in front of me and said, "You wanna play with these, hon?" Others said:

"Hey, young 'un, want some of this?"

"Sporting, honey?"

"Want a hot date?"

"Where we going, baby?"

"What kind of car are you driving?"

"Hey, tenderfoot, go home to your mama!"

One lady said nothing, just blew smoke rings in my face, which was a quick turn off. Another one decimated the English language to such an extent that my ears rang. Two of the ladies of interest, upon close inspection, became disinteresting. I walked up to the last potential woman of interest, who was thin and, with heels, was about the same height as Professor Townsend. However, when I saw her close-up, my hopes were quickly dashed. Her big liver lips were painted fire engine red, her face was as wrinkled as the washboard my mother used to use and her shiny gold tooth was reminiscent of the one Big Joe Turner sang about in his R&B hit, *Flip, Flop and Fly*.

This night, I struck out completely here. If there were any Professor Townsend clones at the meat market, they were picked up before I got there. In reality, I knew the professor was in a class of her own. I went to visit a sexy girl I knew in North Little Rock, a blast from my past, and made a good night of it after all. I never considered the "meat market" again.

I was very proud of my fabulous 1950 Ford, it was a girl magnet, but it was also a magnet for malicious mischief and vandalism. I parked my car near 20th and Ringo Streets; one early fall afternoon, got out and talked to a group of girls a short distance away. One of my former classmates, John Trammel, was lurking stealthily near my car and acting suspiciously. While I did not see Trammel do anything to my car, I returned to it to find a huge "X" sliced in the bottom of the driver's seat, ruining my colorful custom vinyl seat cover. There was no one else around my car.

I took the facts of the incident to my Executive Council, aka my gang, Herman Jones, Sam Tenpenny (Dime) and Wayman Barnes. They also served as judge, jury and administrators of punishment. Trammel was tried in absentia, found guilty and sentenced to one complete butt kicking. He went into hiding and was on the lam until I granted him a unilateral pardon.

In the fifties, some casual high fashion pants and skirts for teens had a partial belt and a metal buckle in the rear. One guy wearing a pair of these pants, near the Tastee Freeze stand at Wright Avenue and High Streets, along with a bunch of girls (no buckle skirts), backed up against the driver's side of my vehicle to give several cars more room to pass. I was at the Tastee Freeze about 10 p.m. and did not notice the random scratches, about belt-high on the driver's side rear panel until the next morning. I confronted the guy about the scratches and, of course, he pleaded not guilty.

One night, while driving the car, I was exposed to sheer terrorism. Around midnight, while driving alone south on Main Street, I was unprepared for the events about to unfold. A green and white 1955 Ford, full of white teenagers, pulled alongside to my right. The teens were shouting racial epithets, including the refrain, "Black car; black nigger!"

Our two cars were aligned perfectly and positioned directly in front of Madison Cadillac Company, to my left. I looked to my right and saw a muzzle flash, heard a firecracker-like pop and heard the whiz of a projectile passing the open front windows of my car, narrowly missing my head. The other Ford sped off. It took a minute to digest what had just happened. I decided to get home quickly. However, I recognized the shooter's car; it had been in the station at least once; I could easily recognize it again.

The next day after school and before work, I walked along the sidewalk in front of Madison Cadillac to inspect inconspicuously the showroom window for bullet holes. Just like in the movies, there it was, the incriminating bullet hole, and I knew exactly how it got there. I went back to my Executive Council for action. Verdict: guilty; punishment: immediate forfeiture of the 1955 Ford's windshield. Just after dark, Wayman and I found the shooter's car parked on a side street just off Main Street. Wayman exited my car with a house brick and told me, "Blow (my nickname), I'll see you tomorrow. I have some punishment to administer." Two days later, I saw a teenager driving the shooter's car with the windshield completely missing. I knew Wayman had a successful mission even before I talked to him a few days later. About a week after Wayman administered the punishment with the brick, the 1955 Ford had a brand new windshield.

During work, after school one evening, I decided to attend a basketball game that night at Cook. Alma Jones was temporarily living at her sister's house at 9th and Ringo Streets. I drove there to pick up Alma to ride back to Cook with me. She was babysitting her sister's children and could not go. So I told her I would see her later and that I was going alone.

Alma's reaction was frightening, she said, "Stay here with me. Help me babysit. You don't have to go back down there tonight. If you go there, something bad will happen. Please don't do it." She gave me a kiss and slowly walked me to my car and pleaded again, "Don't go down there without me. I'm afraid for you."

"Don't you worry," I told her, "I'll see you tomorrow morning."

I arrived at Cook and parked directly in front of the principal's office, an area that was very well illuminated and next to the main entrance. The basketball game was unlike the ones at Mann; in fact, it was extremely boring. I went to the boy's room and considered going back home. For some unknown reason, I did not leave; instead, I walked around the school to see what else was going on. In a remote part of the school, I was accosted from the rear by a native Cook student, Dave Thomas, who was better known as Dave Junior.

He quickly grabbed me in a chokehold, placed a linoleum, or hook knife, on my neck, and proceeded with an angry, vulgar diatribe: "Nigger, you black mother*****, I will kill your black ass. You come down here from Little Rock stealing women and breaking bad. I am the baddest SOB in this school. You ain't sh**! Nigger, you gonna give me some respect or your ass is dead. Understand? You understand?" He tightened his grip with two quick jerks and I nodded yes. Dave shoved me onto the floor and quickly fled down the hallway.

Now I was angry and really ready to leave. I went straight to the main entrance on the way to my car. There I discovered another surprise - my genuine Oldsmobile Fiesta spinner hubcaps were gone, stolen. Suddenly, I became even angrier. There was no one around outside, so I went back inside the school. Everyone claimed they saw, knew, or heard nothing. At that moment, I was very alone. Dejected, I went back to my car. The basketball game was still in progress.

Alma's prophetic words resounded in my head all the way back home. I thought, this would not have happened if I had stayed with Alma; then I reasoned it *still* would have happened, just at another time. In my mind, there were lots of questions: What would have happened if I had left the game immediately after I initially considered it? Why was everyone mum about my hubcaps? Was Dave Junior complicit?

It was tough, but I drove my car to school the next day without my hubcaps. My 1950 Ford was emasculated. Everybody at Gerard's and Cook knew before I arrived what had happened to my car and me during the basketball game, but no one identified the perpetrator. Their mass silence supported very loudly the notion that I got what I deserved. Then, several school days later, someone anonymously slipped a folded, printed note into my locker that read simply: Dave Junior did it. Dave was the chief suspect because he threatened me, although there were never any previous indicators of this behavior. Later, several native students implicated Dave Junior with the proviso that I never reveal the source of information. One girl told me she had seen my hubcaps at Dave's house. She also described the house and its location.

Once again, I went to my Executive Council. Dave Junior was indicted, tried in absentia, found guilty and sentenced to one full restoration of my Ford, which meant the return of my hubcaps. In addition, a double butt kicking, one for threatening me and another for stealing my hubcaps. We decided to make an immediate night raid on his house, recover my hubcaps and take him outside and soften him up.

The next night we made an orchestrated raid on Dave's house. Doris Tyler, Herman Jones' girlfriend, drove his car, a 1956 Mercury four-door hardtop, to Dave's house. We had good information that he was home. Herman, Sam Tenpenny, Wayman Barnes and I got out of the car, walked up on the porch, and Wayman kicked the front door in. A very pregnant woman screamed. I asked her, "Does Dave Junior live here?"

"Yes, please don't hurt me," she answered.

"Where is he?

"He's in the next room," she told me. I went into the next room and found him cowering in a corner. I commanded him, "Get your butt up here and face me like a man." He got up, and I noticed that the veins in his neck were big as garden hoses.

"Where are my hubcaps?" I asked. "I don't know," he said as he started to panic. "I don't have them. Please don't hurt me," Dave pleaded.

"You are pretty much a yellow coward without your linoleum knife at my neck," I told Dave.

Wayman interrupted, "Blow, this bastard is lying through his front teeth. After what he did to you, I say let's break his jawbone, smash both his lips and take out some teeth. This maggot needs to be taught a lesson."

Wayman pulled out of his pocket a set of brass knuckles and placed them on his right hand, made a fist and lightly tapped the knuckled fist into the palm of his left hand to demonstrate the action he wanted to use on Dave. "Blow, just say the word and I'll smash his face in, I'm itching to break some bones," Wayman continued.

The pregnant woman, who witnessed all this drama, was crying uncontrollably, pleading for her baby's safety. "Please don't hurt me; I'm due to have this baby in a week. I am innocent. I have no idea what this is all about. Dave Junior, if you know what this is all about, give him the hubcaps. I don't want anybody to get hurt."

I asked her, "Who are you? Girlfriend, wife, what?"

"Sister."

"Oh, yeah. Have you seen a new set of hubcaps around here?" I asked.

"I'm not sure," she answered. I became concerned about her condition when she started shaking violently and her nose began to run profusely.

"Let's take him out front, away from his sister, and kick his butt. I don't trust this idiot," said Tenpenny. I thought to myself, we need to be sensible here.

I went over, got in Dave's face, and said, "If you have my hubcaps or know where they are, I strongly suggest you retrieve them and return them to me by tomorrow."

"I swear I don't have them," he said. I was angry that he did not produce my hubcaps but, because of the sister's condition, I was not up to any violence. My final words to Dave were, "If I have reason to, I will be back to see you. Just keep that in mind."

"I understand," he said in a spineless tone.

I told the sister, "I'm sorry that you had to witness this. I just wanted my hubcaps back, nothing else. Good luck with your baby."

Then, I told the Executive Council, "Let's blow this scene." We walked out to rejoin Doris, who was waiting in the car and acting as a lookout. She had turned the car around, so we had a straight shot to the highway, in case we had to make a quick getaway. We hopped in the car Mafia-style, and Doris sped away.

On the way back home, Wayman assured me that he would requisition some identical 1956 Oldsmobile Fiesta flipper hubcaps in about a week. He said, "Blow, I'm gonna tighten you up with the hubs in about a week. I think Dave had your hubs, but already sold them. I'm going shopping for you as soon as I get back to my crib. Maaaan, your short will be back to normal. Just trust me, I got the deal. Don't ask me any questions, and I will tell no lies. Ok?"

Simply put, that meant that I had to promise that I would ask no questions about the source of my replacement hubcaps. All of us in the car knew that this was going to be a surreptitious, sticky-finger, midnight-hour type acquisition. The Executive Council unanimously agreed this action was justified.

Wayman brought the hubcaps to the filling station one night in pairs – in large grocery bags – spanning two trips. I inspected the hubcaps, which were identical to mine, but not mine. They were genuine, not an aftermarket knockoff, in very good shape, but not as pristine as mine. They had no identification markings; mine did. True to my word, I asked Wayman no questions. I graciously accepted them and thanked him. He just said, "No problem, maaaan. I'm on my way to chill and spend the night at this new hammer's crib." Then he disappeared into the night drinking Thunderbird.

The next morning before heading to Cook, I tapped on the replacement hubcaps with a rubber mallet at the filling station. My Ford was again whole. Everyone, passengers, other students and teachers were amazed that in less than two weeks, the hubcaps were back. Yet, no one asked me any questions and, like Wayman, I told no lies.

Dave Junior never did return my hubcaps. I knew he had them, but probably fenced them before we went to his house. For the rest of the school year, he treated me with maximum deference. I saw him very sparingly after high school. I saw his sister once in a drug store, and she thanked me for having a cool head. She thought the others were really spoiling for a fight. I explained to her that I just wanted my hubcaps back. I explained all the details about Dave wielding the linoleum knife to my neck. She said she had no knowledge of my hubcaps, but she also said I can't tell you he is innocent either.

I went to another basketball game at Cook and parked in the very same spot. Wayman climbed up on the roof of the school and observed my car for the duration of the game. I walked around the school, unchallenged, unprovoked, and unconquered. After the game, which was lackluster, but entertaining, everyone was over-the-top with friendliness. Word spread about our raid on Dave Junior's house and produced positive results at school. Wayman saw no suspicious activity around my car that night. I went to numerous other school activities at Cook and experienced no further acts of violence, vandalism, mischief or mayhem.

The rest of the school year at Cook was mostly routine. There were a couple of dramas. The first occurred when my favorite teacher there, Mrs. Draper, ran off the highway into a water-filled bauxite pit on her way to school one morning. My passengers and I drove up on the scene and recognized her submerged 1954 blue Buick, its rear bumper sticking partially out of the water. We learned on the scene that she had been rescued by a brave white man who saw her car run off the road, stopped his car and dived into the water to saved Mrs. Draper's life.

Later in class, she told us about the accident. "I don't remember how I ran off the road. I just remember hitting the water and the car sinking. I could not open the door underwater, so I accepted the fact that I was going to die. In a few seconds, my entire life flashed before my eyes. And, just as I expected to meet my maker, I saw this white arm forcing the door open and a man pulled me out of the car and then out of the water. I'm very thankful to be alive." The students were thankful, too.

The other drama occurred when an eighty-five-year-old woman ran into my 1950 Ford. I had just picked up my final passenger, Carolyn Peters, and headed towards Cook, when I stopped at a "T" intersection. My passengers and I waited at the stop sign for a slow-moving1958 tan and white Mercury to clear the intersection. Meanwhile, we enjoyed the Five Royales, singing *The Feeling Is Real*, on the radio. Suddenly, without continuing through the intersection, and without warning or turn signal, the driver executed a wide sweeping right turn onto my road. From the driver's seat, the Mercury's actions were surreal and in slow motion, continuing across the centerline until the left front of her car grazed the length of my rear quarter panel. My car rocked slightly during impact, but no one was hurt. The elderly black lady stopped a short distance away, so I walked over to her car. She asked me, "Were you already there or did you drive up just before I hit you? I just did not see you. I'm sorry. I'm just old."

"No, ma'am. I was there as you drove down the street, prior to your turn. We're on our way to school at J.C. Cook, in Wrightsville. We're going to be a bit late, but we have to call the police," I told her.

The police came, did a routine traffic accident report, cited her to be at fault and left. She had auto insurance; I did not. None was required in 1959. My car was wrinkled, but drivable. Because of slack time built in for a few minutes at Gerard's each morning, we arrived at school just a few minutes late.

The elderly lady's insurance company repaired my Ford, but it was on the cheap. The body shop filled the wrinkles with Bondo and painted the entire left side of the car. The rear-quarter panel should have been replaced because, upon close inspection, the panel was wavy, not smooth. One good thing, the scratches left by those rear-facing belt buckles were gone. However, my fabulous 1950 Ford never looked quite the same after that accident.

In the spring of 1959, my tenure at Cook and "The Lost Year" ended. Although former Mann students, like me, completed all senior year requirements at J.C. Cook, the Board of Education allowed us to graduate from Horace Mann High School, Class of 1959.

During my time at Cook, I became friends with a six-foot-tall native Cook senior, Pearl Ann Johnson, nee Whitfield. Pearl lived in Sweet Home, Arkansas, and was one of the girls waiting for the morning school bus as I came rumbling through in my Ford, made the 90-degree turn in the middle of town and headed to Cook. Our relationship endured, even prospered, long after I put Cook and Gerard's in my rear-view mirror for the last time in 1959.

31

Another Car, Another Love

Nineteen fifty-nine was a great year for me for many reasons: It was the year of the tall automobile tail fins, perhaps the tallest ones were on the Cadillac. It was the year of the end of my relationship with May Helen Coakley. It was the year I graduated from high school. It was the year that I matriculated at Philander Smith College. Most significantly, it was the year that I parted ways with my beloved 1950 Ford.

There was no trauma or drama at the filling station that summer; everything was clean, serene and routine. There were some new customers, but no exciting new philosophers at the pumps. For the first time, I saw limits to my professional growth. That summer, there seemed little new for me to learn.

I started college classes at Philander, encouraged by a 100-dollar scholarship, which was the only money I ever got; I paid out of my pocket for everything else. I was proud to attend the college that I once lived across the street from, where the then-president, Dr. Lafayette M. Harris, taught me how to spell Mississippi. I went part-time until I ran out of money. I met no philanthropists at the pumps.

The big event of the summer, just like the two previous ones, was the purchase of a newer and better car. On a car lot just a couple of blocks away from where I bought my first Chevrolet, at 9th and Center Streets, I bought my second Chevrolet. This time it was a 1953 sea-blue convertible, with a Powerglide automatic transmission and a hydraulically operated canvas top. Unlike the Ford, this Chevy was a six-cylinder because Chevrolet did not make a V-8 until 1955. It also came with factory rear-fender skirts, full-rim hubcaps and whitewalls. This car was clean, a virtual cream puff. It was no the loaded convertibles the Three Cool Cats drove. However, it had a very special charm.

This car was different to me for reasons other than just looks or age; it was the most expensive ever for me. It cost $795.00 and it was the first car where I had monthly payments. It was the first where I had car insurance, both liability and comprehensive, which was required by the finance company. It was my longest duration payment plan – 12 months and my biggest loan payment ever, at $48.10. At sixty dollars a week before taxes, it was extremely tough for me to make the car payment and pay college tuition at the same time. It was a tough year economically.

I painted the rims Mobilgas Flying Red Horse red and transferred the headlight half-moons and my genuine Oldsmobile Fiesta spinner hubcaps to the Chevy to give it some of my personality. While the 1950 Ford announced its presence long before you saw it, this in contrast was stealthy; it was upon you and gone and you never heard it coming. It was extremely quiet, and for some reason I liked it.

After graduation, the only one of my former passengers that I saw regularly was Alma Jones. We had a torrid but brief fling. This occurred after Alma went to Chicago to have a baby and returned to Little Rock. Her child's father was Dave (Junior) Thomas, the same guy who held a linoleum knife to my neck at Cook. The guy who allegedly stole my hubcaps. The person who cowered and sniveled when the Executive Council confronted him at his house one night.

The love light that shone brightly between May Helen and me started to flicker and the nighttime rendezvouses tapered. By the end of 1959, the light dimmed and abruptly snuffed itself out. After five years, the tumultuous relationship was over. I remember the last night we saw each other as an item. Little Richard's latest release, *Boo Hoo Hoo Hoo (I Cried Over You)*, was playing on the radio. I thought, how ironic, except there really were no tears, just quiet resignation. I never saw or heard from her again. Later, I learned she became pregnant and went to California.

My relationship with Pearl Johnson, a statuesque 17 year-old beauty who graduated from Cook with me, went slowly from platonic to passionate. Now, instead of just driving through Sweet Home, I spent considerable time getting to know Pearl's family. She lived with her family, just off the main highway at 919 Church Street, a dusty, narrow, unpaved, single-lane pathway that was more akin to a lane.

Her house was wood frame, pier and beam and nondescript, except for one distinctive feature, which literally shone at night – an outdoor gas lantern. Her family had the only gas lantern (often called gaslight) in the neighborhood. There were no streetlights so this gaslight commanded attention and initiated many conversations. It stood erect and tall in the front yard like a lighthouse to aid lost mariners, in this instance drivers and wayfarers.

Pearl was the second of five siblings; there were an older sister, a younger brother and two younger sisters. Her father, Reverend George Johnson, was a tall, well-built man who commanded respect on sight. Reverend Johnson drove a school bus and was a circuit preacher, who performed lay duties at two small churches in different small towns. Her mother, Carrie, was a slight, frail woman who was a homemaker and an accomplished cook, an ability that Pearl did not inherit. Her scrumptious apple pies made my gustatory organ stand at attention and salute. I felt she made them especially for me.

Pearl's family was typical in all aspects. However, one incident is seared in my memory. One night while I was visiting Pearl, the family cat kept crying outside the house for a long time, perhaps a half-hour or longer. The cat's cry was not just an ordinary meow; rather it was more like a vicious blood-curdling growl. Reverend Johnson acknowledged the cat's noises, stood up and said, "That's it," and walked into the back room and out the back door. Seconds later, we heard a single shot. The cat suddenly went silent. The reverend came back into the house and sat down. The room was completely silent and remained that way for several minutes until Pearl's mother offered everyone Kool-Aid. I thought, it would not be wise to wrong his daughter. In time, however, I learned he really was a gentle, God-fearing man.

By early winter, we both concluded that we were in love. On a cold Sunday night in early December, Pearl and I planned to attend a movie at the Gem Theater. After work, I drove down to pick up Pearl and went inside her house to talk to her family for a few minutes. Pearl was wearing a sexy gray wool suit, with a tight skirt and black patent leather high heels. After about ten minutes, we left, ostensibly for the theater. We had plenty of time, so we decided to visit one of the local lovers' lanes, then head for the movies.

We wound up at a site that we had reconnoitered in daylight and thought to be impossible to find at night. Just behind Sweet Home was an impossible

233

maze of dirt roads, trails and berms. The average person could not have found our position with GPS, or so we thought! We were there for about ten minutes when we saw the blinking emergency light on the State Police cruiser and the bright flashlight that the trooper shone inside the car. We were really distracted or his cruiser was in stealth mode. We heard nothing until he was upon us. "What do you two think you're doing back here?" the trooper asked.

"Sir, just talking, sir," I gently answered.

He said, "Do I look like a stalk of corn to you, boy? 'Cause you shucking my ass now. You two did not come all the way back up in here to talk. You came back here to get some nookie, didn't you, boy? Nigger gal took her shoes of to talk? She unbuttoned her top to talk? I should write you a ticket for fornicating in public. You go ahead and get your nookie, and I'm going to stand right here and watch two niggers get it on. You better make her feel good, or I'll screw her myself."

Pearl and I were really afraid. Throughout this entire ordeal, Pearl said nothing, petrified into silence. I thought there might be a statute against fornicating in public, but this was anything but public. Both of us instantly concluded the only way out of this was to comply with the trooper's lascivious, voyeuristic wishes. We hoped that he would receive an emergency radio call to immediately respond to a real crime or traffic situation, but that did not happen. So Pearl and I launched into an Academy Award performance of simulated sex. Fear kept me from any real performance. I climbed on top of her, made some snorting sounds like bulls after copulation, and Pearl some guttural moans that didn't sound very sexy to me. But it worked for the trooper. He said, "Good job! Now get the hell outta here before I change my mind. And don't let me ever catch you back here talking again. Go!" We still made the movie. He never caught us again.

On numerous occasions since that Sweet Home encounter with the state trooper, I cringed when I imagined what would have happened if that trooper or another more racist one, with the same perverted tendencies had caught me in a lovers' lane with Miss Fairlane. When I was with her, my greatest nightmare was being caught by a state or city law officer. Miss Fairlane always played it down. However, I knew she could exonerate herself just by crying rape.

32

Halls of Ivy – Philander Smith College

Student life at Philander Smith College was routine for me. There was my cute, young, rookie communications teacher, Miss Cook, who caused a minor stir with me. However, she was not a Professor Townsend and when the semester ended, so did the lust. I earned a "B" in the course. Numerous students, young guys and women who were away from the long arm of their parents, enjoyed the wine, sex and song of life and all the excesses – without limitations. It was typical college demeanor, even for a school related to the Ministry of the United Methodist Church.

I drove my Chevy convertible to and from class, usually with the top down. I thought I was cool and played at least a good (not a great) game of girls at college until I interfaced with four collegiate personalities, also students at Philander. The first was an African named Daniel Mboi from Ghana. He described himself as Black African and me as American Negro, a big difference by his standards. We were the same color but we did not look, dress or speak alike. I was eighteen. He said he did not know his true age, but that he was at least forty. He was smart beyond belief, but he explained why. His country sent only the smartest and most cultured to study abroad. Daniel's education, unlike mine, was completely paid for by his government, but he had to return to Ghana after earning his degree to teach there for five years. The most intriguing thing about Daniel was how, when he dressed up in his native attire, he repeatedly integrated, without incident, Frankie's Cafeteria, a bellwether for segregation. At the time, I could not have pulled off that feat.

The second was a cute young woman, Anne Pitts, who was a senior and two years older than I was. Anne recognized that my girl game was very weak and one day gave me what she characterized as good, sound advice. She told me in a very condescending, terse, but succinct advisory, "Eddie, son, you will never get the beautiful, bourgeois ladies, like me, here at school. You don't have the three L's: looks, lingo (game talk) and loot (adequate funding to play the game)." She was right. In an instant, she softened the lead in my pencil, taking it from a 4 to a 1.

The next two personalities to convince me that I did not have a game were a pair of identical twin quail (an attractive young woman) hunters named Minor and Finor Cunningham. They were Army veterans who did possess the three L's that Anne described. They even had some extra advantages; the twins had a well-appointed crib (apartment) close to campus and a well-appointed short (they often called it a chariot.), a 1958 black Ford four-door hardtop with all the goodies, including air conditioning. The brothers appeared to share everything, including the car, crib and the girls. They operated singularly and collectively, often passing girls off to each other like a baton in a relay race.

The Cunninghams had everything, it seemed, that the rest of us guys wanted: style, fashion, good hair, charm and clothes – all multiplied by two. They had identical class schedules and, of course, they dressed identically. I took two classes with these guys. They were suave and debonair, but I never fully understood their mystique, why so many girls were willing to be sucked into their love machine only to be ground up and spit out in painful pieces. These guys were players – identical twin players – long before the word player was coined. In short, the Cunninghams were philanderers at Philander.

Despite the lack of the three L's and competition from the Cunninghams, I had enough flash, splash and dash to date some of Philander's finest ladies, including a nude model, a minister's daughter and a former beauty queen from a small southern Arkansas town. These relationships were fun, fast and futile – merely topical social experiments with inconsequential results. Because of this, I turned my attention in earnest to my relationship with Pearl Ann Johnson.

33

From Grad to Groom

By the summer of 1960, Pearl and I were a romantic item that excluded all others. My visits to her home in Sweet Home became routine, expected, and daily. During one of those visits, I asked her father, Reverend George Johnson, for her hand in marriage. He said yes and offered his blessing. At that moment, we became verbally engaged, and the hunt was on for a set of rings. There were two choices, two jewelry stores, both located on downtown Main Street. Gordon's was the working man's jewelry store and two blocks south stood Stiff's, jewelers for the sophisticated elite. We chose Stiff's and I bought a white gold set for $125.00. Everyone asked the same question, "Girl, where did you get your ring?" Pearl always answered proudly, "Stiff's, of course!"

It was 1960. I watched the movie *Psycho*, Chubby Checker did *The Twist* and Fats Domino was *Walking to New Orleans*. The United States and the Soviet Union were in the middle of the Cold War. Words such as megatonnage, throw-weight, inter-continental ballistic missile, mutual destruction, and civil defense were added to our vocabulary. President Dwight Eisenhower and Premier Nikita Khrushchev appeared to be racing towards a nuclear Armageddon, which raised the angst, alarm and raw fear in Americans, including Pearl and me.

Nuclear war seemed imminent, and Americans sought ways to protect themselves from the annihilation that would result from it. Many who had the means built fallout shelters to protect themselves from the deadly radiation, not the direct blast. The basic units were usually built underground and provided space only for a two-week supply of necessities. Pearl and I did not have such a shelter and were prepared to perish in what was then called mutually assured total destruction of the United States and the Soviet Union in the event of nuclear war. Because of all this, we decided that we should marry as soon as possible, before the impending nuclear holocaust.

Pearl spent the summer of 1960 living in Little Rock with a relative. She worked various jobs, including babysitting, short order cook, waitress, and malt stand attendant before landing a job at a downtown department store in the custom drapery department. I spent the summer, as usual, working full-time at the filling station. However, the customers, opportunities and challenges were just normal; there were no eureka or renaissance moments, no more magical horizons. Increasingly, I knew it was time to play in a new sandbox. However, like always, I soldiered on.

The Executive Council convened less and less; we just went our separate ways. In every practical sense, the council had disbanded. All perceived threats were gone. The other members, like me, spent all their free time with their girlfriends.

Pearl expressed her feelings about our relationship by playing and singing the Etta James' hit song, *At Last*, but my feelings were better summarized by the Little Richard song, *Heebie Jeebies*. She was planning a wedding; I was running from one. Finally, I acquiesced, and we set a date, December 18, a week before Christmas. She planned a simple, small wedding at her church with my pastor officiating.

Seasons changed and time flew. Suddenly, it was December 18th. I worked a full day, went home, showered, put on my wedding costume. I picked up my best man, Wayman Barnes, and headed for the church, Allen Chapel, A.M.E. in Sweet Home.

The wedding began on time. Pearl's sisters were bridesmaids and my pastor, Reverend F.T. Evans, performed the ceremony, which was short and simple. We said I do to the traditional vows, performed the ceremonial kiss, and were showered with rice. Relatives, friends, and my bosses, Lester Price (the Old Man) and his son, Dariel Price (Bud) and their wives attended. After the wedding, we retreated a hundred yards up Church Street (Lane), past the gaslight to Pearl's parents' house, where they hosted the reception and took pictures. The Prices did not attend the reception.

By 10 p.m., we had cut the cake and taken our pictures, and I left for home at my aunt's place. I had not acquired an apartment or any furnishings. As a result, on our wedding night, I went home and she stayed home. There was no honeymoon. Alone, on the way home I thought, what have I done? Now what? I was 19 years old; my new wife was 18. The next day, Monday, I went to work.

Over the next two weeks, I diligently looked for an apartment. I thought I held enough sway over two longtime black lady customers who knew me well and happened to be owners of apartment houses, but I was wrong. I could not convince Miss Dilworth or Mrs. McDowell that I was married and needed an apartment to rent. At the pumps, Mrs. McDowell, an octogenarian, told me, "Eddie, you are just a boy, a smart boy, but you can't be married. You are too young. Wait until you grow up. Then come see me." She had no problem with me servicing her car, but she never took my marriage seriously.

Neither did Miss Dilworth.

The first person to take my quest for an apartment seriously was Mrs. Barnes, mother of the Best Man, Wayman Barnes. However, she only had one apartment that she rented, which was currently occupied. She offered me the first right of refusal when the current tenants vacated the quarters.

Finally, I found another black woman who rented me a tiny crawl space apartment that few others wanted. It was located at the corner of 18th and Pulaski Streets, within earshot of St. Peter's Rock Church and one block from the Dunbar Junior High School campus. I furnished it primarily with furniture and appliances from a Western Auto surplus store.

The property owner refused to let me park my Chevy convertible in her back yard, although there was no fence or any other valid reason to deny me access. I was relegated to parking on 18th Street, which was a major walk route for students traveling to and from Dunbar. No parking was allowed on Pulaski Street because it was a city truck route. Parking became a major issue for me, especially at night, when students walking past my car found it an inviting target for their malicious mischief. Youthful vandals cut and destroyed one tire, scratched the paint on the driver's side on two separate occasions and cut and destroyed two new vinyl convertible tops.

Pearl and I lived there for about a year before Mrs. Barnes' tenants moved and her apartment became available. We quickly moved in and found this second floor abode to be bigger, brighter, and overall just better. It had two private external entrances/exits and better yet, it had a safer place to park on the street and in the back yard. My convertible top was never cut again. This place, like the former one, was only four blocks from my job at the filling station. Likewise, two different routes of public transportation were within two blocks of our front door, which made Pearl's commute to her department store job a snap. One strange footnote: Wayman Barnes, the Best Man at my wedding, lived downstairs with his widowed mother, but I saw less of him than ever before. He was just never around.

On the surface, it appeared Pearl and I had it all, a wonderful marriage, a nice car, two good jobs, a great apartment in a nice location and a great landlady. However, at the subsurface, I asked myself, what is next. What options do we really have? Where are the real opportunities? I was looking for a roadmap to our future.

34

The Horse Morphs into a Tiger

By 1961, the demographics and competition in our market space had changed significantly. Daddy Parker's prophecy that Negroes would invade and overtake the community had come true. The neighborhood was virtually 100% black. Our market share of white customers faded rapidly. The colorful former white patrons had either moved away or simply taken their business elsewhere. Most Negro customers came in more often, but spent less on each visit. White customers, on the other hand, tended to come to us less often, but spent much more per visit. In other words, whites filled their tanks more often, followed the service schedule to the letter and bought more new tires and batteries per household than black families.

In addition, two new filling stations had entered the market as our direct competitors. One was a small mom and pop Conoco Filling Station directly across Wright Avenue from us, which was crewed by two men and offered most services expected at the time. The other was a full service Lion station just five blocks north at 14th and Chester Streets. Both were black proprietorships with all black service attendants. The Lion station was a very formidable competitor and attracted many of our customers.

My star power faded; I was no longer the cute skinny black teenager who serviced cars after school and during summers. I was no longer 13 years old; I was 20 now and had graduated from high school. I was no longer a novelty. I had served my purpose, and now blacks were free to service their

241

cars elsewhere and they exercised those options.

The Mobilgas district manager approached me one day, I'm sure with Bud and the Old Man's knowledge and permission, and asked me to be the new proprietor of our filling station. I immediately knew that Bud and his dad had other plans; I just did not know what they were. I asked the district manager to let me talk to my wife, mull it over for three days, and then I would call and give him an answer. I knew that I had one looming issue, which was my 1-A draft status.

I was flattered and honored by the offer to take over my beloved filling station, which I poured my soul into for more than one-third of my life. The next day I called and told him thanks for the consideration, but my draft status was too tenuous. I knew I would be drafted, probably within a year. He understood. Bud and the Old Man had fully engaged me in the business of running a filling station, so I knew the pros and cons. The hours were too long, the margins were too short, and labor was too intensive for me. I would have declined the offer regardless of draft status.

Finally, Bud and the Old Man discussed the filling station's status with me. I knew customers and profits had declined and began to think about my future. The Lion station's manager had offered me a job, which I declined. Bud told me they could no longer survive the status quo. They had discussions with local Esso officials and signed a lease for the Esso Service Center on Roosevelt Road. I was surprised and perplexed at the logic for this location. I did not research it; but this location, too, seemed to be in decline. In addition, the Esso Service Center had been closed for months – not a good sign. The good news was they wanted me to come with them. I told them I would follow.

35

The Esso Enigma

The Old Man, Bud, and I moved to the Esso Service Center on Roosevelt Road amid great fanfare, expectations and potential. Historically, this location had always been a great producer. This place had more of everything compared to the Mobilgas Filling Station – more service bays, two different types of hydraulic lifts, a service pit, and much more usable real estate. It had more gas pumps, a much higher traffic flow and ostensibly more customers and opportunities for higher profit.

This location had sentimental memories for me. Allan Jones' shack was located just next door to the west. I had walked directly past this place many times on my way to his shack. Two of the lawns Allan and I used to service were just minutes away. The bathrooms I cleaned now were the same ones Allan Jones had sneaked into years before. I took my driver's test and earned my driver's license just up the street. Mr. Lindsay Johnson, who allowed me to use his vehicle for my driver's test, lived close by. My close friends Terrence Roberts and Cleo Graggs had once lived a short distance away. The livestock grounds and rodeo arena were our next-door neighbors.

The Esso Center was in a straight line, in the middle, between Hot Springs and Pine Bluff. Travelers and tourists tended to fill their gas tanks and buy higher end items like tires and batteries, thus more profit. At least, that is what everyone thought.

Additionally, the new Dwight D. Eisenhower National Interstate Highway System was already under construction. When the Little Rock phase was completed, it would dramatically change the interstate traffic patterns across the city and the state of Arkansas. As a result, there would be even less traffic driving past the Esso Service Center. Less traffic translated to less gas being sold, which also meant fewer other goods and services sold.

To me, this place never lived up to its promise. It never had the charm of the old place. It seemed the previous proprietor had surreptitiously sucked all the life out of the place; just its ghost was left. There were no grocery stores nearby, no long johns to buy. There was no intimate neighborhood to wear like a vest. I missed the eclectic repeat walk-up and drive-up customers. Old Mobilgas customers who initially patronized this location ebbed. In short, the place was dying. It was time for me to review seriously my career options.

I often thought about the first filling station I ever saw – the Esso across the street from our shack at West 5th and Cross Streets. I mused about all the times I visited this station, as a five-year-old. I always got in the way and was sent back across the street. That was where I drank my very first Coca-Cola. Now I was working at the same brand filling station, but a much larger one. I was entranced with that first Esso Filling Station, captivated by the Mobilgas Filling Station and now disenchanted with this one. The filling station magic was gone; a new career loomed across the horizon.

During my final week at the station, I wired a small cross to the fence adjacent to where Allan Jones' shack once stood. It was a small memorial for a man who helped shape my character for the better. It was a silent goodbye, a substitute for the one I never said in person. Goodbye Allan, you taught me well.

36

The Military Option

After we graduated from high school, Larry Richardson, a fellow classmate, and I decided to take the written Armed Forces Qualification Test Battery (now called The Armed Services Vocational Aptitude Battery or ASVAB) just for the challenge. I was influenced mostly by the Navy sea stories of Harvey Ray, big brother to Gloria Ray of the Little Rock Nine. The tests were easy for me, and I scored well enough to qualify for all enlisted job options. To my surprise, Larry failed to qualify.

After my nineteenth birthday, I was summoned to the Armed Forces Induction Station in Little Rock for my pre-induction physical to determine my physical and mental fitness for service. After the physical, I received my draft card, which gave me my status and presented my level of availability to be drafted into the Army. I was determined to be 1-A, which was the highest priority and meant that I would probably be called near my twenty-first birthday.

The Esso Filling Station, while much bigger than the Mobilgas Filling Station, never lived up to its potential. It never had the cozy feel for me. Only a fraction of the old customers patronized the new location. New traffic patterns had changed the traffic density past the station, hence fewer customers. I was earning $65.00 a week, working six days a week and twelve hours a day with no chance for an increase. I had outgrown the business and was ready for a new challenge.

It was early 1962, and I was closing in on my twenty-first birthday and a draft date. I had no additional money for college. Therefore, I decided to enlist voluntarily, which gave me more options. I could choose among the military services – Army, Navy, Air Force, or Marine Corps. I could not swim, so I quickly ruled out the Navy and Marine Corps. The Army and Air Force presented equal opportunities, but I reasoned I knew more about automotive engines than jet engines, so I started negotiations with the Army recruiter. He stated the general options in simple terms: sign up for two years for combat arms; sign up for three years or more for anything else. I chose the anything else option. Based on my test scores, all enlisted military occupational specialties were open to me. Based on my experience during the Pegasus period, automotive or tracked vehicle mechanic was the right choice. All I had to do was sign up for three years.

I told the recruiter that I was definitely going to enlist but wanted a few weeks to think about it. I thought about it many times over and concluded automotive or tracked vehicle mechanic was the best choice. The recruiter, an older, white, affable staff sergeant thought otherwise. "Eddie, look, you can do much better for yourself. Think about these jobs where you don't get dirty. You know, white collar," he said.

"But I took a year of automotive mechanics in high school and have eight years of experience at the filling station and garage!" I reminded him.

"Let me make an appointment to talk to you at home. Is that possible? I have some things to show you. I do better away from the office."

"Of course!" I replied.

Over the next three weeks, the recruiter visited me weekly at my apartment after work. He introduced me to military intelligence, a term I had never heard of. He explained to me that my technical scores and penchant for electronic gadgets made me an ideal candidate for a little known branch of the Army – the Army Security Agency. He told me I would be granted a Top Secret security clearance, which sounded intriguing to me. After much friendly persuasion, at the last meeting, I enlisted for three years and the Army Security Agency option. I signed some papers that night and agreed on an induction date.

I had several weeks to give my resignation notice to Bud and the Old Man. They chafed at the fact that I was leaving them for the Army. Bud attempted to talk me out of leaving to no avail. Therefore, I prepared my wife, sold my car and furniture, and told my friends and customers goodbye.

At 10 a.m. July 18th, 1962, I reported alone to the recruiting office on downtown Main Street for induction into the Army and the Oath of Allegiance ceremony. Eighteen souls from all over Arkansas took the oath that day. I was the only black doing so. I proudly recited the following oath:

"I, Eddie Joe Washington, do solemnly swear that I will support and defend the Constitution of the United States against all enemies, foreign and domestic; and I will bear true faith and allegiance to the same; and that I will obey the orders of the President of the United States and the orders of the officers appointed over me, according to regulations and the Uniform Code of Military Justice. So help me God."

My recruiter attended the ceremony, shook my hand afterward and said, "Congratulations! You're in the Army now. Good luck." We exchanged Christmas cards and notes for about three years. I knew immediately after basic training that he had convinced me to make the right decision – being a mechanic was not the highest and best use for the Army or me. In every correspondence with him, I thanked him for his wisdom, diligence, and patience.

My bag was packed, and I was ready for the bus ride to basic training at Fort Leonard Wood, Missouri. Seven of us were travelling by bus, so we were given two chits each: one for the bus ride and another for a lunch meal at the restaurant across Main Street from the recruiting center. There was one last indignity before I left Little Rock – never to live there again. The six white recruits went in the front door and sat down to eat. I had to go to the back of the restaurant and stand in the alley, present my chit at a small walk-up, take-out window for my meal. After a rather long wait, I finally got my food and walked the two blocks to the bus station where I could sit down and eat. My six fellow recruits joined me there shortly.

We boarded a Trailways bus in the late afternoon. I instinctively headed to the back of the bus and took my seat. The bus was not crowded and about two hours into the trip; the other recruits joined me in the rear of the bus. We talked about our collective fears of the unknown and tried to get some sleep. We arrived at Fort Leonard Wood about midnight. A big gruff sergeant greeted us as we stepped off the bus, "All you despicable maggots here for basic training, fall in over here." I knew then I *was* in the Army. The Pegasus period was definitely over.

37

Epilogue

It has been almost 50 years since the end of the Pegasus Era. I did not realize until I wrote this book, how many significant events I witnessed during that period. In retrospect, the Pegasus Era gave birth to *Rock 'n' Roll*, fallout shelters, the Cold War, Korean and Vietnam military actions, Sputnik and Martin Luther King's Dream. It was the dawn of civil rights. We saw the rise and quick demise of Nat King Cole's TV Show. We experienced The Little Rock Central High School Crisis.

I was intrepid back then. Many activities that I participated in then, I would not do under any circumstances today. For instance, I would not take daily morning drives through the 16th and Park Streets intersection, crowded with white protesters, during the Central High Crisis. I certainly would not jump out of my car to challenge an angry mob burning a black-faced effigy hanging from a tree at that intersection. The Sammie Dean Parker rescue on West 6th Street? No way. The rendezvouses with Miss Fairlane? Never.

Pearl and I divorced in 1971 after ten years of marriage. Our union produced a son, Duane Eddy Washington, who was born in Eschwege, West Germany in 1964. In 1987, while playing for Middle Tennessee State University, Duane was the 13th pick of the second round of the 1987 National Basketball Association Draft by the Washington Bullets, now the Wizards. Duane's NBA career was very brief, just 19 games spanning two seasons: in 1987-88 with the New Jersey Nets and in 1992-93 with the Los

Angeles Clippers. He is the older brother of former NBA guard Derek Fisher.

Pearl later married Johnny Fisher and that union produced two children, Derek and Deandra Fisher. Derek earned five NBA championship rings while playing guard for the Los Angeles Lakers. Pearl is now divorced.

Herman Jones and Samuel Tenpenny, both members of the Executive Council, still live in Little Rock. I communicate with them sporadically. My long-time girlfriend, May Helen Coakley, died in Little Rock at the age of 61, in 2002.

My uncle, Brother Albert, died in 1977. My Aunt Babe moved to Cleveland, Ohio, to live with her daughter and grandchildren. She was 97 years-old when she died in 2009. Her daughter and oldest grandchild predeceased her. My sister, Alice Faye, married, had four kids, divorced and lived in Omaha, Nebraska, until she died at age 66 in 2012.

There are many people that I would love to meet again, perhaps on Oprah, and reminisce the bygone days of Pegasus. There are hundreds of people whose names and faces I have forgotten who had a great influence on me.

Without the experiences of the Pegasus Era, my foundation would be completely different and not necessarily better. Those experiences gave me a roadmap for life, which I still use.

I had so much fun and excitement writing this book, I am considering doing another: Post Pegasus – A New Beginning. There is so much more to tell.

Eddie J. Washington 2013

38

Postscript: Little Rock-Fifty Years Later

I returned to Little Rock during July 2009 for my first ever high school reunion. Horace Mann High School, Class of 1959, held its 50th Class Reunion. The theme was celebrating the legacy of "The Class That Should Have Been" alluding to the fact that our class was denied a yearbook, prom, or graduation because all high schools in little Rock were closed that school year.

My wife Mary and I arrived in the afternoon on Thursday, July 9, at Little Rock National Airport, which was called Adams Field the last time I was there. I expected to see major changes in the city after fifty years and saw many right away. The airport was still in the same place, just much bigger and served by more airlines. In our rental car on the way to the hotel, I drove on one of the new Interstate Highways that crisscrossed the city. I drove past the new William J. Clinton Presidential Library and Museum on the Arkansas River, which could be seen from our hotel. I noticed three prominent streets had been renamed after famous local and national black civil rights leaders: 14th Street was now Daisy L. Gatson Bates Drive, 20th Street was now Charles Bussey Avenue, and High Street was now Martin Luther King Drive.

We drove to West Capitol and Ringo Streets, the location of the apartment building where my mother and father once worked. The building had been replaced by a new multi-story AT&T Office Building. Every house that I occupied with my mother had been replaced by other structures. The detached house a half block from Dunbar on Wright Avenue where I lived with my aunt was also razed.

West Ninth Street, once pulsating with black commerce, was still, empty and void of life. Even my beloved Gem Theater was gone. One tiny white building, that once housed Bob and Orin's, a small two-man company that rebuilt generators, starters, voltage regulators, carburetors and fuel pumps, stood defiantly at the upper end of Ninth Street. The white name sign was faded and rusted, but still legible. I briefly recalled all the time I spent there picking up and dropping off electrical and fuel subsystems a half century ago. Other auto parts suppliers in the area, such as 555 Incorporated and Crow-Burlingame, had largely been replaced by newcomers Advanced Auto and Auto Zone.

First Baptist Church, my first church home, was still standing but showing its age. Philander Smith College had grown into a large modern campus, which included both the location of the first detached house that I lived in with my mother and our alley duplex that was directly behind it.

Friday, July 10, was the first formal day of the reunion. The 6 p.m. Meet and Greet, at the Holiday Inn Presidential Hotel, was the only event scheduled for the day. Therefore, Mary and I spent the day sightseeing, visiting my former haunts and historic landmarks. Our first stop was the Arkansas State Capitol that was the constant backdrop for my West Capitol Street shack. The new Little Rock Nine Civil Rights Memorial, which is actually nine sculptures of my friends who desegregated Central High School in 1957, stood nearby.

We then drove to Central High School via the intersection at 16th and Park Streets. That school year, I drove through here almost every day on my way to Horace Mann High. I witnessed the reporters, angry crowds, and the soldiers of the 101st Airborne.

In the middle of the summer, there were no students, but Central was just as I had remembered it: large and imposing. My wife, a longtime St. Mary's County, Maryland, Board of Education Member, was intrigued and said enthusiastically, "Let's go inside!" I took a couple of pictures of her in front of the famous school and we headed up the massive stairs to the entrance.

To our surprise, the doors were open, so we went inside. We met an African American security guard who allowed us to take an unescorted informal tour of the iconic school. Mary spent most of her time talking to people in the main office. I spent most of my time in the huge auditorium thinking about the school's history, especially during the most famous 1957/58 school year. This was the first time I was ever inside Central High School. It had taken me over 50 years to get there.

We went across the street to visit The Central High Museum and Visitor's Center to explore the events that surrounded the 1957 Integration Crisis. The exhibits were historic for Mary and nostalgic for me. We bought some memorabilia in the gift shop and walked to the Mobil Filling Station at 14th and Park Streets, which is restored to the way it was in 1957. It is now part of the Museum Campus. In 1957, it was one of the Mobil filling station triplets; the others, McGuire's, located in the East End of Little Rock and 922 Wright Avenue, which was where I worked.

We drove up Wright Avenue past Dunbar International Studies/Gifted & Talented Education Magnet Middle School (formerly Dunbar High School), past my old address, to the former location of Price Mobil Service, where I worked for seven years. My old house was gone and a new structure stood on its old lot. The landscape around the filling station intersection at Wright Avenue and Chester Streets was different, worn by 50 years. All the grocery stores and many of the houses had been leveled. Some houses were abandoned amid withering decay.

Amazingly, my filling station building was still standing, albeit a ghost of its former self. It was no longer a filling station; the gas pumps were long gone. The elevated pump islands stood there diligently like soldiers waiting for their next mission. The location had evolved into an auto service center with a car wash and beauty salon. This was in stark contrast sister station near Central High. I talked to some of the people I found there about the history of the building. I walked around the place a couple of times; reminiscing about the long days I spent pounding the concrete. I stared at the bathrooms I used to clean and thought about The Urinating Man; I stood at the exact spot where he relieved himself. I walked to the back lot where I used to talk to Sally Parker, Sammie Dean Parker's younger sister. Briefly, I longed for the good old days. Then I snapped back to reality, Pegasus was forever gone!

After taking some pictures, we drove to 21st, and Ringo Streets, to see the house where I first lived with my aunt and uncle when I was nine years old. It was in remarkably good shape compared to many I had seen. The siding, roof and chain link fence were recent. There were window air conditioners in the upstairs windows and a lone unit in one of the windows in the crawl space apartment where I once lived. A white Lexus LS400 was parked outside the apartment.

The next stop was the close-by Pulaski Street vicinity. Mrs. Davis's house, where I spent time in home daycare, looked unfit for habitation; the upstairs apartment that Pearl and I rented at 1915 Pulaski was abandoned and falling down, literally. The landlady, Mrs. Barnes and her son, Wayman Barnes, the best man at my wedding in 1960, are both deceased. Dr. Robinson's former house and the old and newer Powell's Grocery Store buildings were all abandoned, dilapidated and probably condemned. Dr. Robinson was my consulting M.D. at the gas pumps. The former St. Peters Rock Church building was erect but suffering old age. The building bore a sign that read: Greater Little Rock Quartet Union Convention Center.

After a day of exploring the city, my wife and I arrived back at the hotel. Everyone there recognized me, even after 50 years. Some of my classmates had been physically changed by age and illness. Most I recognized by sight and or by sound; other I needed strong hints to identify. Several members of my class I did not recognize at all.

The spontaneous socializing at this Mix and Mingle was the most fun. I was surprised the accomplishments, triumphs, and tragedies this group had experienced over the last half century. Many had retired after rewarding careers; some like me were still working full-time. I was inspired by the dignity and resignation with which each member approached the vagaries of life; there were no expressions of regret. I was surprised by the apparent memory lapse of two class member who were close to me. A female classmate who had a two-year tempestuous relationship with my best man, Wayman Barnes, said simply: "I don't remember him." Another female who was a one of the passengers I transported to J.C. Cook High School for an entire year did not remember the experience. She said, "I thought I rode with someone with a truck." I did not correct either person. A lot can be forgotten in 50 years.

The next day, Saturday, had events scheduled for the entire day. After breakfast, our class boarded a bus for a tour of Little Rock. The first stop was the Governor's Mansion. I knew, after a quick inspection, this was not the mansion that I walked and rode my bicycle past 60 years ago. The new one was at least twice as big as the old one and was better appointed inside and outside. We were welcomed by the governor's spokesperson and told to lineup at the bottom of the stairs for a photo shoot with the governor. Our visit was also covered by the local media.

Mike Beebe, the governor, walked down the stairs and spoke extemporaneously about our *Lost Class* 50 years ago. His tone was conciliatory and empathetic but not apologetic. After the governor's remarks, his photographer took our group picture, all of us wearing our class reunion t-shirts. The governor retreated up the stairs to his private office. The stairs were remarkable because each step had a governor's last name embroidered in the carpet going up the stairs in succession of office. I noticed the seven governors sandwiched between Orval Faubus (the Governor of Arkansas in 1957) and Mike Beebe: Rockefeller (Winthrop), Bumpers (Dale), Pryor (David), Clinton (Bill), White (Frank), Tucker (Jim Guy) and Huckabee (Mike).

The governor's staff presented our class with several briefings. Afterward, we were allowed to tour the mansion downstairs and its grounds until it was time to board the bus. For most of us, certainly Mary and me, this was the first time we had been inside a governor's mansion. It was a long 50 years between washing the then-Governor of Arkansas son's Corvette and visiting Governor Mike Beebe in the governor's mansion.

A short time later, the bus pulled up to the entranceway of the former Horace Mann High School (now an Arts and Science Magnet Middle School) at 24th and McAlmont Streets. The principal, Miss Pat Boykin, met the class there to open the school for our tour. The school had changed considerably in five decades; it had a different look and feel. It was more enclosed; the open-air breezeway design of my day was gone. It also had a new second level. For me, it had a foreign feel; all the rooms and corridors as I knew them were displaced.

Then I looked at some trophies and pictures in a display case in one of the main corridors and found a surprise: a class picture taken in 1956, which included several of us in the tour. Elizabeth Eckford, one of the Little Rock Nine, was sitting in the center of the frame. I was standing in the rear row, anchoring the left end. None of us recalled what class it was. It was the highlight of the school tour. For most of us, certainly me, it was the first time back in Mann since the school was closed in 1959.

The William J. Clinton Presidential Library, on the Arkansas River, was the final stop of this tour. Of all the activities here, the replica of President Clinton's Oval Office was the biggest attraction. Mary and I looked at all the exhibits at the library and walked to the River Market District for catfish dinners.

The dinner, banquet and dance Saturday night at the hotel was engaging, social fun. The only thing that resonated with me from the keynote speaker was "take time to write your own history, lest it be written incorrectly." That is one of the reasons I wrote this book.

The Sunday Memorial Breakfast Program was riveting and solemn. Prayers were said, names were read, and candles were lit for all known deceased Horace Mann High School Class of 1959 members. The list included 73 names; I personally knew almost all of them. Among the dearly departed were two of my best friends, Robert House, one of the Four Musketeers and Lavern Walker; a long-time on-and-off girl friend of five years, Mae Helen Coakley; and two of my adversaries, John Trammel, who sliced my seat covers in my 1950 Ford and Johnese Wright, who one night many years ago, ordered her gang to kick my butt and damage my 1939 Chevy.

In 50 years, Little Rock had undergone profound layout changes, defined primarily by Interstate Highways. The city had grown and spread far beyond the city limits known in the Pegasus Era. All the areas where I lived, worked, and worshiped had declined, been condemned or razed. The trends of white flight and urban blight that started 50 years ago were now complete. All three high schools I attended, Dunbar High School, Horace Mann High School, and J.C. Cook High School, will never again host a senior prom or a high school graduation. Dunbar was a high school from 1929 to 1955; Mann was a high school from 1956 to 1971, while Cook's timeline is less clear. Dunbar is now Dunbar Gifted and Talented International Studies Middle School and Mann is Horace Mann Arts and Science Magnet Middle School. J.C. Cook High burned down and was not rebuilt.

On our final day in Little Rock, Mary and I visited my mother's grave in Haven of Rest Cemetery on West 12th Street, which I had last seen in 1977 at my uncle's funeral. James Albert Flemons, Aunt Babe's husband, is buried right next to my mother, a fact I had forgotten. Just across the car pathway was the grave of Zeb Barnett, grandfather of my first best friend, Milton Barnett Smith. We departed the cemetery and drove directly to the airport. There we saw another departing class reunion member heading back to California. We talked to her for about an hour, and then boarded our plane for our non-stop flight back to Baltimore.

During my whirlwind return to Little Rock, I was reminded of the unique nature of our Horace Mann High School Class of 1959. It was an honor to be a member of *The Lost Class* and to celebrate the legacy of the class that should have been. I was also reminded that class members had lived more life than we have left to live; and that I should attend as many future class reunions as possible. I *will not* wait another 50 years.

Please continue your Pegasus reading experience by visiting readpegasus.com. There you will find pictures, interesting facts and the opportunity to be a Pegasus Person.

39

1950s Filling Station Facts

Filling stations like mine offered full service. Deluxe full service consisted included: filling the tank with gas, checking the air pressure in the four tires on the ground and the spare in the trunk, checking the hood , including checking the fluid level in the battery, radiator, and windshield washer; then checking the engine oil and automatic transmission fluid levels, master cylinder hydraulic fluid levels. Then I cleaned *all* the windows, including removing bugs, if the car had been driven on the highway.

- 10 gallons of regular gas cost less than $3.00; one gallon costs more in 2012

- Anti-freeze was either ethylene glycol or alcohol based

- Car automatic transmissions had unusual names like: Buick Dynaflow, FordaMatic, MercaMatic, Packard Ultramatic, GM Hydramatic, Chevy Powerglide, and Chrysler Fluid Drive

- Windshield wipers and trunk latches were vacuum powered

- Motor oil came in one and five-quart cans; bulk, rerefined oil sold for ten cents/quart; Mobil Oil sold for $0.30/quart

- Lubrication services were recommended every 1000 miles; filters were changed every 2000 miles

- Lubrication documentation was stuck on door jams instead of on the windshield

- Many car electrical systems were 6 volt. Cars had generators instead of alternators

- Tires were recapped, regrooved, and retreaded. New tires contained rayon or nylon cords. There were no radial or steel belted tires

- Carbs meant carburetor and had nothing to do with diet. Engines were aspirated and not fuel injected

- Exhaust systems had resonators instead of catalytic converters

- There were only two grades of leaded gasoline: regular and high octane, which could be 100+

- Stabl Flo, Bardahl and Motor Honey were three top selling crankcase additives

- Bygone Gas Station Brands: Peoples, Pan Am or Pan American, Lion, Esso (now Exxon Mobil) Sinclair, Phillips 66

- Naphtha (a solvent) and kerosene were sold in bulk at filling stations

- Bygone cars: Sears, Willis, Crosley, Hudson, Henry J, Kaiser, Frazier, Edsel, DeSoto, Packard, Nash (and Metropolitan) Studebaker and Corvair

- Used crankcase oil was sold to a recycler for $0.05/gal; later for $0.02/gal

- Some transmission buttons and levers were on the dash or in the middle of the steering wheel

- There were plenty of three-toned cars

- You still adjusted automobile brakes

- Automobile paints were acrylic lacquers

- There were wide-track Pontiacs

- There were wrap-around windshields

- Cars had lots of chrome and fins

- The Big Three automakers had their own parts houses: Guide and AC Delco (GM), FoMoCo (Ford) and MoPar (Chrysler)

- Spark plugs were cleaned periodically and wheel bearings were packed every 20,000 miles or sooner

- Some engines were slant fours (one-half of a V-8) with flexible drive shafts

- Headlight dimmer switches were located on the floorboard and operated by the left foot

- Chrysler Brands (Chrysler, DeSoto, Dodge, Plymouth) had torsion bars in the front suspension instead of springs

Please continue your Pegasus reading experience by visiting readpegasus.com. There you will find pictures, interesting facts and the opportunity to be a Pegasus Person.

Thank You

for reading my book. I hope you found it interesting.
If so, please tell your friends. Send your comments to me through
social media and readpegasus.com. Likewise, you can follow
releases of my new books, including children's books and engaging
short stories.

Eddie J. Washington

About the Author

The author, Eddie Joe Washington, was born 3 April 1941, in Little Rock, Arkansas, and enlisted in the United States Army 18 July 1962 and served his entire career in Military Intelligence. His life during this 21-year period is described in detail in this book.

The military training and assignments, formal college education, worldwide travel and other personal experiences, spanning military and civilian careers, helped the author present Pegasus in context. The author was especially enlightened by the opportunity to live outside the United States, in Germany and Turkey for over ten years, which gave him an objective look at his homeland.

Eddie experienced his first high readiness alert during the Cuban Missile Crisis of October 1962, considered by many to be most dangerous period of the Cold War.

Washington's first overseas assignment was a 51-month tour at Rothwesten, Germany. He lived in military housing in Kassel, Germany, and commuted to his duty station atop Mt. Meissner, near the town of Eschwege, Germany. During that tour, he and his wife, Pearl and their son Duane Eddy, vacationed in numerous European countries including Austria, France, Switzerland, Belgium, Netherlands, Luxembourg, Spain, Denmark and Italy. Eddie also enjoyed leisurely activities in the premier German cities of Berlin, Munich, Frankfurt and Cologne.

In the summer of 1970, Eddie was detached to serve a one year tour in Sinop, Turkey, along the Black Sea Coast. The author enjoyed the rich multi-cultural experiences he encountered while living in a third world Muslim country. He shopped in the Grand Bazaar in the ancient Turkish city of